SALTWATER FISHING GUIDE

SALTWATER FISHING GUIDE

CAPTAIN PETE BARRETT

THE FISHERMAN LIBRARY
1620 Beaver Dam Road
Point Pleasant, New Jersey 08742

PRINTED IN THE UNITED STATES OF AMERICA
Library of Congress Cataloging-in-Publication data
ISBN 0-923155-14-7

THE FISHERMAN LIBRARY CORP.
1620 Beaver Dam Road
Point Pleasant, New Jersey 08742

Publisher . . . . Richard S. Reina
Associate Publisher . . . . Pete Barrett
Editor . . . . Linda Barrett
Design . . . . Allison Eagle-Rudnick
Cover Design . . . . Steve Goione

INTRODUCTION:
Something old, something new.

This book began about twenty years ago as I met fishermen at boat and sport shows, on the docks at marinas, in tackle shops and at The Fisherman Workshops who asked for a guide about local fishing. There were plenty of books about far away places in Canada, Florida and distant lands; and there were books about trout fishing, largemouth bass and salmon. Few books, however, were devoted to the great salt water fishing in the Northeast and mid Atlantic part of the Atlantic Coast.

The first edition, published in 1983, was called the "New Jersey Salt Water Fishing Guide" but we discovered many fishermen outside the Garden State were reading it, too. Fish pay no attention to state borders and many of the fishing strategies and techniques that work well in my home waters off the Manasquan River applied equally well to other coastal fishing areas. Likewise, as I visited new places, I picked up new fishing ideas to take home and try. They usually worked just as well in New Jersey as they did in Connecticut, Maryland, Virginia and Long Island. It seemed appropriate, therefore, to not only update the book, but to expand its coverage.

I've been blessed with a career as a writer and charter captain that has taken me to many good fishing places from Massachusetts to North Carolina and this latest edition of the "Guide" tries to bring it all together. I'm grateful to the many surf fishermen, charter captains, and fellow fishermen who have given me tips and advice over the years. Whether fishing the surf at Chincoteague in my old beach buggy or running offshore of Cape May in the "Linda B", I've been impressed with the many fishermen who willingly gave of their time to help guide me, and others, along.

No book can tell it all, but I hope you find this one to be interesting reading and that it provides a few tips that will add to your fishing pleasure. If this book gives someone else a tip or two that makes their fishing more fun and more productive, then in some measure, it may help pay back the debt I owe others who showed me the way.

Good luck, good fishing and have a good day on the water; tag a few for tomorrow!

Pete Barrett

To my mom and dad, Nell and Harold,
who always encouraged and supported me.

TABLE OF CONTENTS

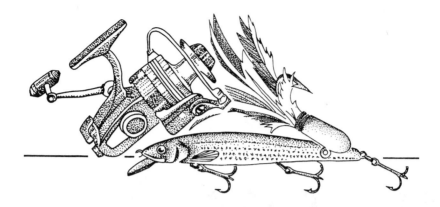

Chapter One

STRIPED BASS

Coastal fishermen from Massachusetts to Maryland have long regarded the striped bass, or rockfish, as the ultimate game fish. The species has all the qualifications of a champion; size, strength, wariness, aggressiveness and fighting spirit. While school-size fish have been abundant since the late 1980s, trophy bass of over 50 pounds are not that plentiful. Catching a bass that surpasses the magic 50 pound mark is an accomplishment many anglers dream of, yet few actually achieve. Anyone catching a big bass has a lifetime memory to tuck away and call upon on cold winter days.

Several fish over 70 pounds have been recorded in the last 20 years and the record has been broken twice. Once by Bob Rochetta while fishing off Montauk, with a 76 pound catch and again by Al McReynolds fishing off a jetty at Atlantic City, New Jersey. Al's 78 pound 8 ounce fish was a huge striped bass and may last for many years to come. You can bet that a lot of dedicated striped bass fishermen dream of busting that record.

The striped bass population is now experiencing a delightful upward trend after more than two decades of dwindling catches. A combination of natural forces and man-made pollution caused severe spawning problems for striped bass, but an intensive effort at managing this magnificent fish by the Atlantic States Marine Fisheries Commission (ASMFC) through restrictive regulations and protection of prime spawning year classes has resulted in a dramatic improvement of catches.

The striped bass is still not in the clear, however, and the ASMFC management plan will no doubt remain in effect for a number of years to come. Still, most fishermen are ever more optimistic that this great game fish will be providing sport fishing recreation long into the future.

So, the striped bass picture is improving. The Hudson River is contributing many stripers to Long Island Sound, Sandy Hook Bay and North Jersey waters, providing some very good summer and fall fishing. The Chesapeake stocks are on the rise and adding to the overall population of the coast from Massachusetts on to the south into North Carolina.

The Seasons

Each spring brings a migration of bass from their wintering grounds northward to Delaware, New Jersey, New York and New England. The smaller fish generally spend the winter in bays, such as the Chesapeake, while larger fish wintered in the security of deep waters off the Carolina Coast. Fishing for the smaller bass, called schoolies, starts in April, with the bigger bass coming along a month later. Many bass will concentrate their feeding and daily activities around the numerous jetties and inlets found along the coastal shoreline. Other fish choose the open waters of large bays, like the Chesapeake, Delaware and Sandy Hook Bays, Long Island Sound and back bays like Great Bay, Great South Bay and Pleasant Bay or rivers like the Mullica and Shrewsbury.

In the fall, the migration pattern is reversed as the fish head south for the winter. Some of the best fishing of the year occurs in the fall, with the action often lasting into December, or until it just gets too cold to fish. Many a die-hard bass fisherman will still be fishing, given a break in the weather, right up until Christmas.

I once spotted a carved wooden sign on a beach buggy that read, "The price of a striped bass is eternal vigilance!" Those are the words for a bassin' man to live by. Successful striper fishing demands a lot of time, plus a knowledge of the tides and bait migrations, the lay of the surf or jetty and what makes a striper tick.

Fishing Techniques

Fishermen in boats have an obvious advantage over shore bound anglers. Boaters usually employ three methods of bass fishing; drifting baits, trolling with wire line or casting with plugs, bucktails or spoons. The baits may be sand or blood worms, clams, shedder crabs, mackerel chunks, live eels, bunker or menhaden, (also called pogy), or herring. Favorite fishing areas will be off the ends of jetties, along sea walls, in rough water rips, or across rocky reefs and ledges. Many bait fishermen enjoy good bass fishing in the inlets along the coast. From the mouth of the Chesapeake Bay to the Cape May rips and on up to coastal harbors of New England, inlets attract striped bass like metal filings to a magnet.

Tackle for fishing sea worms, crabs or chunk baits can be on the light side, with a rod able to handle 15 to 20 pound test line certainly adequate. A conventional revolving spool reel holding 200 yards of 15 pound test line and mounted on a stout popping style rod is an ideal combination that I've used from Connecticut to Maryland and it is just fine for striped bass of schoolie size to bass over 20 pounds.

Fishermen using live baits, like bunker, eels or herring, use much heavier tackle, partly to be able to pull a fish away from the jetty rocks or rocky reefs where live baits are most commonly fished, but also because some really huge fish may be hooked on live bait. A conventional reel filled with at least 200 yards of 20 to 30 pound test line mounted on a seven to nine foot rod with plenty of backbone is preferred by striped bass sharpies. The longer rods can be helpful when baits must be steered towards the rocks. The rod length helps the angler guide the bait where he wants it to go.

Surfcasters will fish cut or whole dead baits, cast lures or use live eels, herring or bunkers. Either spinning or conventional tackle can be used for fishing bait. Rod lengths run nine to thirteen feet, depending on how much distance is needed to reach the fish; the longer rods having the edge. But, a longer rod is heavier and more tiring so the angler must decide where to compromise. I've used an 8½ jetty rod and a 10 foot surf rod for most of my beach angling and it was a rare day when either of these two rods couldn't do the job of catching bass in the suds.

Striper buffs doing a lot of continual casting will usually pick spinning outfits for versatility. By carrying an extra spool with lighter line, they can switch to smaller, lighter lures if conditions dictate. Rods generally run eight

Striped bass worm rig

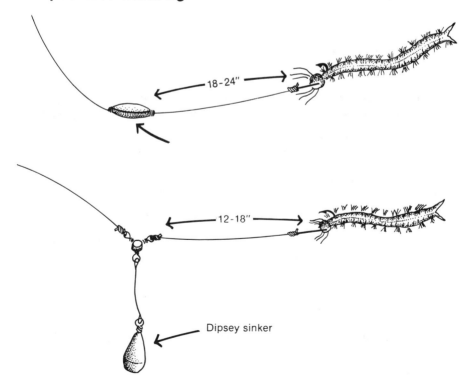

18-24"

12-18"

Dipsey sinker

to nine feet. These anglers will be casting metal squids, popping and swimming plugs, rigged eels, bucktails and a variety of other lures. Some casters are switching to some of the newer conventional reels that offer light weight, extra long casting distances and lots of pulling power. In any case, a light weight outfit is appreciated after long hours of casting. Jetty specialists often use shorter rods seven to eight feet long since they don't need to cast out so far. Much of the time the bass will be close to the rocks, not far out from the jetty rocks.

Striped bass found in the shallow coastal bays in the spring are great sport on light spinning tackle, freshwater bait-casting tackle or even a fly rod can be used for these schoolies. Small bucktails, swimming plugs, spoons and sand and blood worms take their share of bass in May and June. Tackle for this spring fishing can be on the light side and a freshwater rod and reel combo capable of handling 10 or 12 pound test line is about ideal. I've had some delightful action with school fish along the Connecticut shore at Norwalk, in the Hudson River at Croton Bay and in New Jersey's Mullica River with even lighter tackle. A six foot, fast taper rod with a spin reel filled with 6 pound line provided a lot of sport.

Thirty pound class trolling rods are good choices for trolling wire line. The roller guides won't wear out and make reeling in the line less fatiguing. Other trollers prefer rods with carboloy or Fuji style DHG guides. All other guides will wear out quickly so only choose a rod that has the types just mentioned.

Trolling Techniques

Among the most popular and productive trolling lures are umbrella rigs, single tubes, large swimming plugs and spoons. These are usually trolled on wire line, but many anglers are using downriggers for more sport, and to reach fish when they are too deep even for wire.

Umbrella rigs are still considered the deadliest of bass lures, but umbrellas rigged for bass differ from those meant for bluefish. Bass rigs utilize longer tubes, often hung on lengths of mono to give the tubes more freedom of movement. A slow, undulating motion gets more attention than a short fast spinning tube.

Stripers and blues have different color preferences. Whereas bluefish like the gaudy reds, oranges, lime greens and whites; bass are often fooled by darker colors, such as wine, purple, dull amber, black, dark green and deep blue. As a general rule, use dark tubes on overcast days and over dark-colored bottom, and lighter colored lures on bright days when trolling over a light, sandy bottom.

The center tube of the rig is the primary fish catching lure. It should be larger than the rest and dropped back from two to six feet on a 60 pound mono leader. Day in and day out, this tube running down the middle will catch the most fish. Jointed tubes with squid heads or with bead chain through the center to enhance the spinning action are also good choices.

Single tubes have always been favorite lures of striped bass fishermen. Trolled slowly over a rocky bottom, these simple lures have taken many big fish. The best colors are deep red, purple or amber. Rig a single tube on about 10 feet of mono and troll it behind a wire line. One type of tube has a stiff piece of wire inside so it can be bent to undulate and spin exactly as the angler chooses. Experimentation with different curves can pay off in a trophy fish.

Large swimming plugs are always productive on striped bass. Some of the old timers are no longer available, having been dropped from the manufacturers' product lines years ago, but there are still some around, such as the Danny Plug, M & M and Gibbs. The best colors are dark gold, yellow, blue back with white belly, black and rainbow.

Depending on its design, some of these plugs with large lips will run deep enough so that the wire line is not needed when trolling over fairly shallow areas such as in the rips at Cape May, the tip of Sandy Hook and Romer Shoal. There are also spots at Montauk, Rhode Island and Cuttyhunk where bass hang out on rocky reefs and can be fooled on plugs trolled on straight mono with no wire.

Special rod holders, made of aluminum or polished stainless steel, hold rods out at 90 degrees for greater spread of trolled lures.

These big swimmers work very well when trolled in combination with other lures. A good arrangement is to run two lines off the stern each with a plug at the terminal end and then place an umbrella rig or spoon down the center. "T" shaped rod holders help hold the side rods with their tips at right angles away from the boat and add some spread to the lines so they don't tangle.

Bunker spoons look awesome, even intimidating, to novice bass trollers, but they really work when used properly. White is the best color for bass. The silver bunker spoons usually draw bluefish only. The big spoons are fished on 10 to 15 foot heavy mono leaders off of the main wire line, with the trolling speed just fast enough so the spoons pulsate and dart through the water. Two other excellent bass spoons are the Crippled Alewife and the Acetta Pet spoon.

Many charter skippers who fish spoons have developed special, long rods positioned like outriggers at 90 degrees to the sides of the boat. The lures are kept apart for easier maneuvering and turning, something especially handy when the bass grounds get crowded on the weekends. The rods are cut down surf rods, shortened from 11½ feet down to nine or ten feet. They may seem ungainly but the added length really does make maneuvering much easier. The longer rods also help amplify the pulsating action of the spoon.

Jointed tubes trailed behind an umbrella rig are proven striped bass lures favored by charter captains.

Wire Line Trolling

For every fish you find up on top, ten more of his brothers and sisters are in the deeper water below. Like every "rule" there are exceptions, but a check of a graph recorder or color scope while trolling will usually show more fish below the surface than on top.

There are several methods to get down deep while trolling including the use of planers and downriggers, but wire line trolling is preferred by many fishermen. It is used from Florida to the Carolina Outer Banks for king mackerel, in the Chesapeake for striped bass and from New Jersey to New England for blues and bass.

Some anglers feel wire line fishing is unsporting. How wrong they are! Unlike monofilament that stretches, wire has virtually no stretch. Set the hook on a trophy-sized striped bass and the fight is amazing as every head shake, every lunge and every vibration is transmitted up the line to the angler. There's no rubber band effect to cushion the fight as with monofilament.

There are two kinds of wire to use; stainless steel and Monel. Both are single strand and of approximately the same pound test for equal diameters of line. Monel is a softer line, more easily spooled and is recognized by its dull gray color. It does fatigue after repeated bending and flexing, and will eventually break, even from normal use. Stainless wire is shiny silver, a little springier than Monel, and less expensive. It will last virtually forever but when kinked will break more readily than Monel.

Because of the abrasiveness of wire, rods must be equipped with tungsten carbide (carboloy) guides or heavily braced Fuji aluminum oxide guides. Standard hard chromed guides will wear out in a single day's fishing. Roller guides are another alternative, and work well but some of the wire to leader connections will not fit through the rollers.

Rod actions vary. Many anglers like stiff rods when trolling wire especially when they are looking for big fish, yet the best rods are those with a medium action that allows some bending and flexing of the rod while trolling. Six to seven foot rods are best with a medium action to give more action to lures like swimming plugs, jointed tube lures and even umbrella rigs and spoons. The large bunker spoons, so popular off New Jersey and the south shore of Long Island, and the large Crippled Alewife spoons of Chesapeake Bay, work best with long, soft rods of about eight to ten feet in length.

Medium and soft action rods have another advantage that helps maintain the action of the lure. As the boat enters a swell or wave while trolling, the boat will tend to slow down momentarily then pick up speed slightly as it leaves the wave, sliding into the next one. This speed up, then slow down of the lures can ruin the action of some lures, especially bunker spoons. The soft rods which are bent way back while trolling, sweep forward as the boat slows down, keeping the lure working, and then bend back again as the boat speeds up. The lures work more consistently.

The rods should be equipped with a gimbal at the butt and have heavy duty, hard chromed reel seats for strength and durability. Aluminum Uni-butts offer a slick surface that will not get hung up in rod holders at the strike of a big fish.

The Penn 112H and 113H are THE wire line reels. They have heavy duty, chrome plated brass spools, fast gear ratios and are famous for their durability and ease of operation. Avoid plastic spools that will break or aluminum spools that will corrode.

Use 100 yards of backing on the 112H, 200 yards on the 113H. The backing should be of at least 40 pound test monofilament or 50 pound dacron. Some wire line fishermen like the dacron because it has no stretch, an important factor when using wire for jigging bucktails or when fishing for the largest kind of striped bass.

The backing is connected to the wire in either of two ways. If you are proficient with knots, use an Albright to join the two lines. "PRACTICAL FISHING KNOTS" by Mark Sosin and Lefty Kreh will detail this knot. There is a problem with the knot if the line ever breaks. It is nearly impossible to tie another good albright in a bouncing, rocking boat with watery fingers and perhaps a chilling day.

An easier connection utilizes small barrel swivels of #1 or #3 size, which will pass through the carboloy or aluminum oxide guides. A simple clinch knot attaches the mono or dacron, while a haywire twist connects the wire to the swivel. After reeling the wire on to the reel, connect the leader with the same clinch knot-swivel-haywire twist sequence. A large snap swivel is added at the end of the leader with a clinch knot. A 15 foot leader of 60 to 80 pound test is standard to withstand scrapes against the side of a boat, the scales of a fish or abrasive bottom structure.

Every boat, every tide, every lure will fish differently while trolling wire, but as a general rule of thumb you can figure that for every fifty feet of wire you have IN THE WATER, the lure will run five feet down. If you put out one hundred fifty feet of wire, your lure will run about fifteen feet down. Naturally, the action of the lure itself, the speed of the boat, the rate of water current and surface water chop or swells will have an effect on how deep the lures will go.

Mark the wire at one hundred feet and then at every fifty feet thereafter. It is unusual to troll with only fifty feet in the water, so there's no need to mark the first fifty feet. There are two methods to mark wire.

TAPE: 3M elastic tape is easy to use and inexpensive. It has one major pitfall. If you don't wrap enough tape on the wire, the mark may slide up or down the wire. A moving mark does little to tell you how deep your lines are. Lay a ten inch strip of one inch wide tape on a clean cutting board and slit the tape into thin slivers about a quarter-inch wide. Wrap the tape along the wire in a spiral wrap for about four inches, then start wrapping it back over itself. When finished, the wrap should be neat and small in profile to slip through the guides and it should be immovable. I've used tape wraps for years with no trouble at all, and no slippage. The marks are easy to feel while fishing at night and are clearly visible during daylight hours.

RUBBER BAND/DENTAL FLOSS: Stretch a rubber band along the wire line and then wrap a length of dental floss over the stretched rubber band. After wrapping for about an inch to two inches, a pair of half hitches holds the floss in place. Trim the ends of the floss and the rubber band. When the tension on the band is released, the swelling of the rubber as it returns to its normal unstretched diameter holds the entire mark tightly in place. A quick spray with paint or a touch or two with permanent magic marker and you are ready to fish.

Wire is sold most often in one hundred yard lengths and so most fishermen put this amount on their reels. If you need to get even deeper, you can add trolling drails. For every four ounce drail you will add another five feet of depth. If you want to reach the forty foot level, let out three hundred feet of wire which will get you down thirty feet (six lengths of fifty feet), then add eight ounces of drail for the next ten feet for a total of forty feet of depth.

Wire line trolling depth

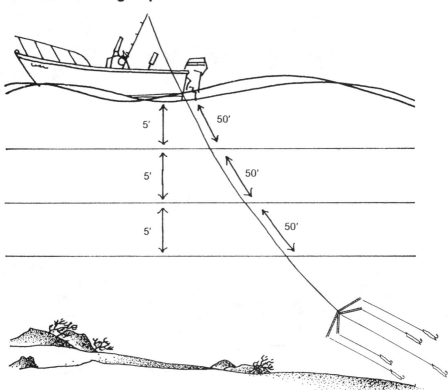

Depth Finder

A good quality graph recorder or color scope is essential to fish with wire line. The recorder will tell you at what depth the fish are feeding and the structure over which they are holding. Then you can match the same depth by letting out the appropriate amount of wire. Without the recorder you are fishing blind.

Even with the recorder to tell you the exact depth, it still pays to try three or more different levels of trolling. If the fish are marked at 15 feet from the surface in 30 feet of water you should try trolling one line at ten feet down (100 feet of wire out) another at 15 feet (150 feet of wire out) and a third at 20 feet (200 feet of wire out). Despite the fact that you should get all the strikes on the rod at 15 feet, fish are unpredictable and you may have all the hits coming on either of the other two rods.

Trolling Speed

Every boat is different in the way it handles in the water, the way it is powered, the depth of the vee, the weight of the hull and how it handles a sea; so there can be no hard and fast rule for determining trolling speeds. The speed must be varied until you find the correct speed for your boat on

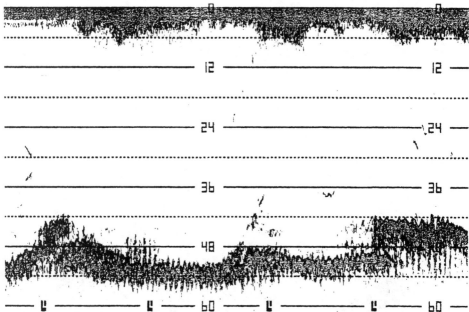

A graph recorder, color scope or LCD will show bottom contours, bait and the feeding depth of game fish, like striped bass.

that given day. As a guide line it is safe to say that striped bass and weakfish usually prefer a slower moving lure, while bluefish will strike at a faster lure. However, this rule was made to be broken!

Bass will often hit tubes trolled at 1200 RPMs, a speed usually thought of as a bluefish speed, while there are days when blues will only look at a slow trolled spoon with your engine at 800 RPMs. Start at a known speed and troll over the area you are fishing. With no results at that speed, add 50 RPMs and continue to experiment until the best speed is found. For outboard engines the speed will most often be within the range of 800 to 1200 RPMs.

Trolling Patterns

A beamy inboard 36 footer can troll more rods than an eight foot wide center console boat. Larger craft can handle up to six rods, while smaller outboard boats can manage two rods, perhaps three. Usually the lures closest to the boat are fished with drails to run the lures deeper so the lines won't criss-cross and tangle on a turn.

Fish are usually found schooling in, around or on structure like ridges, lumps, drop offs, or other bottom with an irregular shape or contour. Once the structure is located, you must next pinpoint the exact location of the fish. Use a grid pattern of north to south, south to north, east to west, west to east passes to thoroughly criss-cross the structure to locate the fish. When trolling parallel to a beach, a zig-zag pattern that takes the lures into the shallow water then back to the deep seems to work very well.

When working an offshore lump or ridge try several approaches. Run east to west sets (trolls) and then a few north/south sets. You may find the fish are all on one side of the ridge, or that they prefer the lures moving only in one direction.

When trolling along the edge of a drop-off into deep water, try a zig-zag course that brings the lures up onto the high part and then down into the depths again. The fish may be holding high or low along that edge. The chart recorder will be very helpful in pinpointing the fish and the profile of the structure.

Both the grid and the zig-zag pattern cause the lures to speed up and rise or slow down and fall every time the boat turns. On a right turn, the inboard or right line will slow down slightly, causing that lure to travel lower in the water. Likewise, the outboard line on the left will speed up slightly and ride at a slightly higher position. If the fish hit only on a turn on the outboard line, it shows they want a higher lure, more speed, or both. Or if they are only hitting on the slower inboard line, it shows that they may want a slightly slower trolling speed, a lower depth, or both.

Fish do show preferences for color. The angler can set out several lures and color combinations to increase the chances of placing the "right" lure under a fish's nose so it will strike it. Once a particular lure is found to be successful, troll two, three, four or more of these lures to greatly increase the catch of fish.

Trolling with wire line is a science that has intrigued fishermen for at least 60 years and during that time has also accounted for some truly outstanding catches. From Massachusetts to Florida, from striped bass to king mackerel, in large boats or small; wire line trolling is a proven trolling method.

Successful trolling requires much more than simply dragging lures behind the boat. Essential factors to consider are: speed, lure depth, trolling pattern and lure selection. If you keep these factors in mind, you should be able to score a good catch of striped bass.

Live Baits For Striped Bass

Lures are convenient and fun to use, but old-timers advise that to catch bass consistently, it's hard to top live bait. Nothing else has the appearance, action and smell of the real thing.

Live herring, live mossbunkers and live eels are the three most popular live baits for stripers. Herring are available in the spring and are favored

Striped bass eel rig

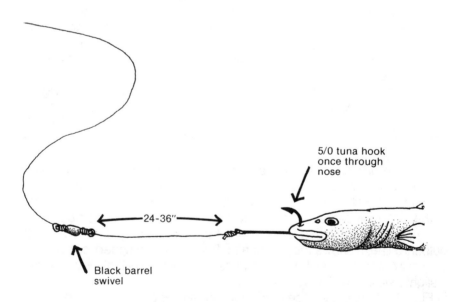

5/0 tuna hook
once through
nose

24-36"

Black barrel
swivel

Jetty fishermen usually hook bunker ahead of the dorsal fin using a 5/0 short shank tuna style hook. Boaters often use a treble, hooked through the upper jaw and nose.

during April, May and June. Mossbunkers show up from May throughout the summer and into the fall. Some bass fishermen prefer bunker over all other baits. Live eels are good all season long, especially after dark. They are very popular baits at Montauk, along the Long Island South Shore and in South Jersey. Good catches of jumbo bass are made at the Montauk and Cape May rips on eels.

To keep bait alive, you'll need a holding tank and an aerating pump. Some are sophisticated systems built into the boat's hull, while others are portable. Small boat fishermen carry a big cooler and battery-operated pump if the boat is not equipped with a live well.

The two most frequently seen systems for keeping bunkers and herring alive are the round tank with an aerating pump, or a modified cooler hooked up to a converted bilge pump. Both methods work. The pump provides the necessary oxygen but creates no water current to keep bunker and herring swimming and breathing easier. The most efficient aeration system incorporates a bilge pump and a long hose with holes in it. Water squirts through the holes for aeration and the flow of water out the end of the hose sets up a current.

Beside a tank and pump you'll also need a small net to pick out a bait and rough a cloth to handle eels. All this equipment can be found at most well-stocked tackle shops along the coast or from several mail order catalog firms that specialize in salt water tackle. Marine supply stores that cater to fishermen will also handle the needed parts and pumps.

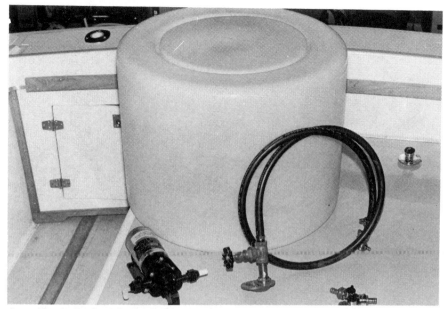

A good bunker tank can be made from a Caddy Company tank, Water Puppy washdown pump, thru-hull strainer and some washing machine hoses.

Fishing with live bait requires a lot of attention to the bait, such as frequent changes of water in hot weather, but it's worth it when a big bass gulps down the offering and peels line from the reel.

In addition to live baits, other good striper baits include clams, crabs (especially shedder crabs) and grass shrimp. A chum line of these small shrimp is deadly in some bays, like Barnegat in New Jersey and Great South Bay in Long Island.

Plugging

Casting lures to bass is commonly called plugging. You can do it from shore in the surf or from a jetty, you can wade shallow bays, or you can drift in a boat. Favorite lures include popping plugs, metal squids, swimming plugs, bucktails and spoons. The trick is to use a lure that closely resembles the prevalent bait.

Loud splashing surface poppers are perhaps the most fun to use because you can see the strike of the fish. Bucktails are the most versatile because the retrieve can be varied infinitely to imitate the swimming action of nearly anything that a bass might feed on. Swimming plugs with their wobbling swimming action, are the easiest to fish. Spoons are often overlooked but they can dance a very seductive motion that fools many striped bass.

Often the plugging is blind; that is the fish can't be seen, we just cast to likely looking places that usually hold fish. Tie rips, the edges of channels and sloughs, the edges of marsh banks, the mouths of tidal creeks and the surging water that surrounds a jetty are all likely places to plug cast.

Boaters may find striped bass breaking water as they chase bait fish. Approach the school carefully and with a minimum of noise so they don't get spooked. The trick is get close enough to fire off a cast without making the fish sound at the approach of the boat. Shut the motor off while still a short ways from the fish, then let the boat coast into casting range.

Usually a slow retrieve works best with striped bass. The fish attack lures in a short burst of speed and will seldom follow a lure for long distances if it is moving too quickly. At night, swimming plugs, bucktails and rigged eels are retrieved in a dream-like speed for best results. Bucktails work best with short, easy hopping action, although while jetty fishing I use a straight retrieve with no added rod action. The tumbling action of the water seems to provide action enough.

No matter what size you catch, the striped bass is a worthy opponent, fun to catch and a true challenge for every angler.

Casting from jetties

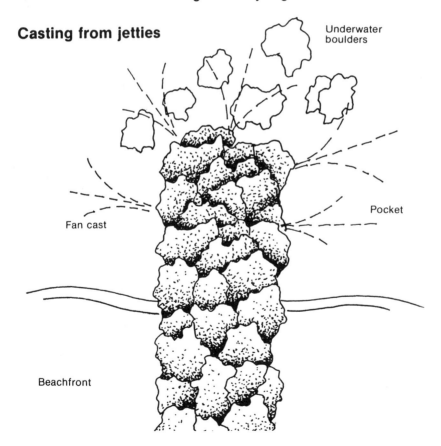

23

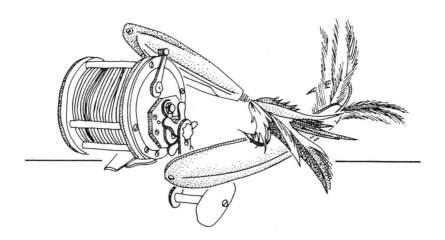

Chapter Two

BLUEFISH

The bluefish is the buccaneer of the Atlantic Coast. Large schools of these marauders roam inshore as well as offshore, ripping into bait fish and providing some of the most exciting fishing anywhere in the world. When they're feeding on the surface, the scene is chaotic with bait jumping out of the water to escape, and terns and gulls whirling and diving overhead.

Blues come in many sizes, from bay snappers of a few ounces to giant 'gator blues close to 20 pounds. All have razor-sharp teeth and don't hesitate to use them on anything that moves, even fingers, so be careful when unhooking blues of any size.

The largest documented bluefish ever taken on rod and reel is the International Game Fish Association record caught in 1972 by Jim Hussey off Cape Hatteras. The 31 pound 12 ounce blue was so big, that at first, Hussey thought he might have hooked a big channel bass. Upon closer view as the fish came within gaffing range, he realized what a remarkable catch he had made.

One of the greatest things about the species is that they can be caught by fishermen of all ages in a wide spectrum of fishing situations. Young children can catch snapper blues off the backyard dock using tackle as simple as a cane pole; while their fathers grandfathers troll 15 pound slammer blues from fancy sport fishing boats further offshore. Wherever you find them, bluefish can be depended on for fun, excitement and delicious eating. Blues are the mainstay of the party boat fleet that fishes for them night and day. No one knows how much money is generated directly, or indirectly, by bluefishing, but the total monetary value of the precious natural resource must be tremendous.

Although biologists do not have all the facts about bluefish migrations, there is a trend to offshore and southern waters when northern waters cool off in the late fall. Around the beginning of April the first blues appear in North Carolina and Virginia waters. By early May they invade New Jersey and by June they are terrorizing Montauk and New England bait fish. These early fish are spawners and are not always easy to catch. Once having spawned, however, they develop a voracious appetite and go on a feeding spree.

Because blues are cannibalistic, considering a smaller member of the species just another snack, all the fish in any one school will be roughly the same size. As the main schools move northward, groups break off and set up "resident populations" of the same age class. They settle in at familiar places such as Fenwick Shoals, Barnegat Ridge, the Klondike, Montauk, the Race and the islands off Massachusetts. The larger fish stay offshore, usually, while smaller blues work up into the bays and rivers, and sometimes right into the surf.

Surf Fishing For Bluefish

Surf fishermen catch blues on all sorts of lures resembling bait fish. Yet, sometimes the fish are finicky, so a good selection of lures should be in the tackle bag. If you see terns diving into the breakers, get over there quickly. Birds will often tip you off to fish activity. Even one tern, hovering for a few seconds, should be noted. If that bird has spotted bait being chased by blues it will dive to pick off a tidbit at the surface. The message is somehow transmitted to other birds and within moments dozens of terns will appear as if by magic. It's quite a spectacle.

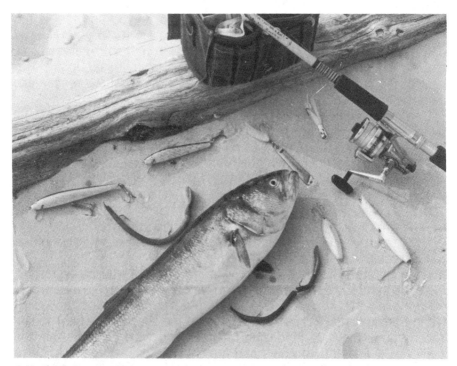

Surf anglers use swimming plugs, metal squids, poppers, jointed tubes and bucktails to fool hard-fighting bluefish.

When casting blind into the surf, the fisherman should vary the angle of his casts like the spokes in a fan. The fish could be in surprisingly close and at least one cast should be made nearly parallel with the wash, particularly if the tide is high.

One problem frequently faced by fishermen, is having a strong onshore wind blowing directly into their faces while a school of small blues feed just beyond the breakers at maximum casting range. A dense, heavy lure, such as a 3 ounce Hopkins or Kastmaster, is needed for distance but the lure is too big to attract the small blues. Even bluefish have their limitations. The answer is to use a small dropper fly tied in on six inches of mono to a three-way swivel two feet ahead of the main lure. The fly can be a simple tuft of white bucktail tied on a 1/0 hook. The heavy lure will take the fly out where the fish are, then the fly becomes the prime attractor. Even double-headers can happen.

Under more normal circumstances, with a quartering wind and blues of two pounds and up stalking the surf, a variety of metal lures and plastic plugs will all take fish. Favorites include RedFin, Rebel, Windcheater Rebel, Danny, Atom Junior and the Atom 40.

Whatever the lure, try different retrieve speeds. The addition of a strip of squid or pork rind to metal lures such as Kastmaster, Hopkins and Ultimus sometimes brings more strikes, although the extra wind resistance will shorten casting distance. Blues will hit at all levels and speeds, depending on how they feel that day. It pays to experiment if the normal routine draws a blank.

Surfmen also fish whole or cut baits for blues, and this is a good way to fish after dark. Chunks or strips of butterfish, bunker fillets or mackerel are commonly used. A sinker keeps the rig on the bottom but a small cork is often attached near the bait to raise it a few inches. The crabs are less likely to bother it and the blues find the bait quicker when it's off the bottom and moves with the water.

Whole finger mullet, about the size of a cigar, are prime surf baits, but are not always available fresh. Special float rigs have been devised for using mullet baits. Usually referred to as a doodle-bug rig, it consists of a float painted white, red or yellow attached to a length of wire and a removable double hook. To rig the bait, remove the hook, insert the wire into the mullet's mouth and out the vent. Re-attach the hook and pull on the wire so the hook shank goes into the bait, leaving the hook points exposed. These doodle-bug rigs are well worth the cost and effort. They will often out-fish other rigs three to one.

In the fall, when mullet schools are hugging the beach on their southward migration, anglers skilled in the use of cast nets can catch their own bait, which in itself is a lot of fun. Others buy fresh mullet at local bait shops.

Bait fishermen will often use two rods. One rig is cast out far, and the other in close, to greet any fish that move close to the wash or through a slough parallel to the beach. Sand spikes are used to hold one or both

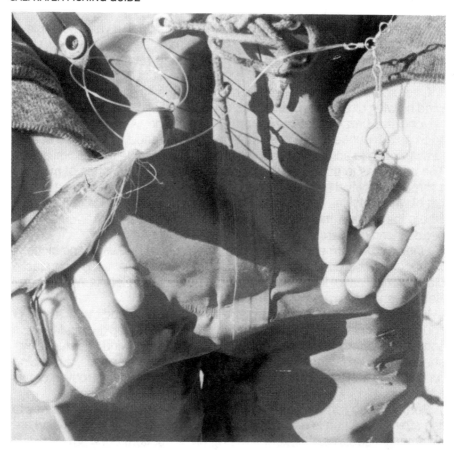

Balsa float known as a "doodlebug rig" is favored for fishing fresh mullet in the surf.

rods. These handy devices are essential for any kind of bait fishing in the surf. They keep the tackle up out of the sand and leave both of the angler's hands free to tie on rigs and hook baits.

Whether you're holding the rod or using a spike, when a blue hits the bait, you'll know it. The rod tip will jerk violently and the rod will settle into that wonderful curve that spells "fish on!"

The surf fisherman with a beach buggy has a big advantage in being able to investigate a long stretch of beach, or follow a school of blues. Unless the bait is trapped against a jetty they can race right down the beach and out of the range in a few minutes. The anglers must keep pace or get passed by. Sometimes there is an isolated small school of blues moving right along, mobility becomes important. Anglers on foot will have to trot to try to keep up, or go back to their cars and drive a half-mile or so to another access point where the fish can be intercepted again. Not all beaches are open to beach vehicles. Productive stretches of beach can be found in every state. For info on beach access, write to the Beach Buggy Association in your state.

Boat Fishing For Bluefish

Several hundred party boats and charter boats sail daily during the late spring, summer and fall months exclusively for blues. The surest way to fill your cooler with bluefish fillets is to be on board one of these crafts during the height of the season. Party boat captains are out every day, many making two trips daily, and keep close track of the blues' whereabouts. Unless a severe storm churns the ocean, upsetting the daily patterns of fish behavior, these skippers leave the dock knowing approximately where they'll find fish that day. The same applies to charter boat captains who fish the same waters.

Because of the many anglers aboard, party boats almost always chum to attract blues. The boat will drift or anchor over preferred areas. The chum is ground fish, usually mossbunker mixed with sea water to make a soupy mixture. This is ladled over the side to drift away with the current. The process is repeated every few minutes so that a constant flow goes out.

Bluefish chumming

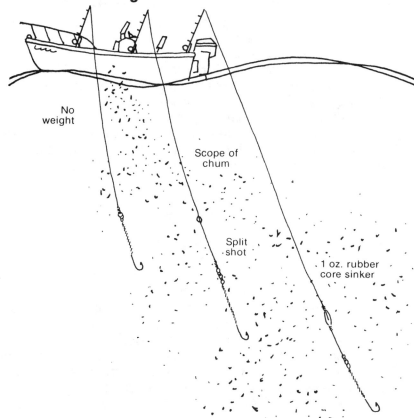

No weight

Scope of chum

Split shot

1 oz. rubber core sinker

Fishermen on their own in small boats may choose to use a frozen chum bucket hung overboard in a net or plastic bucket with holes for the water and chum to pass through. The rocking of the boat agitates the chum so that pieces break off constantly. It's not as efficient as having a deckhand on duty, but it works.

Once the chum slick is established, it's a matter of waiting for the blues to discover it and begin picking up passing pieces. The fisherman baits up with a chunk of bunker back, butterfish, mackerel, or whole smelt or sand eel. The bait is dropped into the slick and allowed to drift back in a natural manner. The line should pay out freely from the reel without interruption.

After the bait has drifted off 50 yards or so without a strike, reel it back in quickly and send it out again. Some additional weight may be needed by way of rubber-core sinkers of various sizes. Bluefish can be particular. Some days they'll take right on top, on others they'll hold several feet down and will only take baits coming by at that level. Therefore, if the strikes are slow in the slick, add a little weight about three feet above the bait. Start with a splitshot. Have your partner put on a quarter-ounce rubber-core sinker, and have a third party, if possible, try a half-ounce weight. Also, try different baits in combination with weights. Despite their voraciousness, bluefish can be very selective, so go prepared to experiment.

Party boat anglers will be fishing side by side, which makes light tackle impractical. You have to be able to snub a rampaging blue before it tangles other lines. Medium-weight boat rods seven or eight feet long matched with surf-type conventional reels filled with 30 pound monofilament are good choices. Blues up to five pounds can usually be lifted aboard. Bigger fish call for a long-handled gaff wielded by one of the mates.

One thing not to do when chumming, and you'll see it done all the time, is to let the bait hang in the current on a tight line. It looks completely unnatural and rarely will a fish hit it. You want your bait to look like another, but larger, piece of chum flowing with the current, seemingly unattached to anything.

Don't hesitate to change baits frequently. After several drifts and reel-backs a bait gets washed out. The oils are gone and it's much less appealing. Keep the baits fresh.

Some fishermen use a short length of wire leader to prevent bite-offs. It works but interferes with the naturalness of the drifting bait. We've found that tying the hook directly to a short length of 80 pound mono and setting the hook quickly before the fish has a chance to run and swallow the bait is a good alternative, especially when other fish, like bonito, kingfish or little tunny are nearby. These fish are usually leader shy, as bluefish can be at times, and the bulky wire will ruin chances at these other fish. Sometimes a fish will be hooked and the bait will slide up the line where another blue will hit it and cut the line. There's no way to avoid that happening. It's part of the game and hooks must be considered expendable.

Anglers chumming from private or charter boats will use the same techniques but have the luxury of using lighter tackle if agreed upon beforehand. A five pound blue will keep you very busy for a few minutes on a freshwater bass rod. And, you may have to follow the fish around the boat a couple of times. With four anglers hooked up simultaneously on light gear, the results can be hilarious.

Chumming for blues is very productive - it's also very messy. Some anglers prefer trolling, or drifting and deep jigging. The same lures that catch striped bass will take bluefish, which means the umbrella rig tops the list for trolling. Fished on wire, these rigs produce when the blues are holding deep over structures such as a ridge or lump.

Blues are often active near the surface and will hit spoons, tubes, strip baits, plugs, Hoochie Trolls, and eel lures trolled without extra added weight of trolling sinkers or wire line. That's the most fun way to catch them while trolling.

Go Deep For Blues

The early season is often the best time to troll because the fish are scattered and not yet tightly schooled as in the late summer and early fall. Sometimes they are so scattered that chumming won't bring them to the boat and the only alternative is to troll. There are times when the bluefish will be located in the top ten to twenty feet of water, but more often than not, you will find most of the fish holding in deeper water. Wire line works well for blues, and is fished just about the same as described in the previous chapter on striped bass. Planers and downriggers are two other deep trolling methods that work very well on bluefish.

I usually fish the planers off a stiff rod with just a little tip action, and with a reel filled with 25 pound test mono. The planers put a lot of pressure on the tackle and too light a rod just won't stand up to the stress. Heavy in action, the tackle is light in weight so the tackle is pleasant to use. A 2/0 or 3/0 reel is just fine, fast retrieve helps.

The only way to tell how deep your planers are running is take the time to experiment with them and run along a clear, sandy beach at different depths waiting for the sleds to hit bottom. Watch your recorder and watch the rod tips. When the planers hit bottom the rods will dip hard for a moment. Check the recorder and remember the depth at which the planers bottomed out. This is the depth they will run while trolling offshore.

I troll slow at 1000 RPMs with an outboard to 900 to 1100 RPMs with an inboard and have checked my planers at 20 to 25 feet of depth at those speeds. Going slightly faster will run the planers deeper; too fast and they will start to slide sideways and actually come up out of the water. Slower speeds will have them running slightly shallower.

Planers are simple to use and one advantage to them is the ability to quickly attach a planer to the end of most any kind of tackle, other than real

Trolling with downriggers

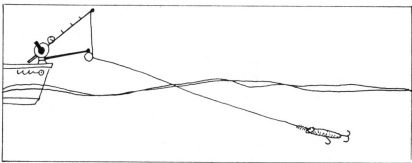

1 — Attach the lure

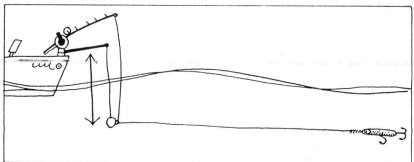

2 — Lower trolling weight

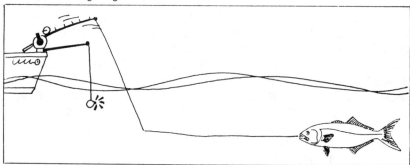

3 — Fish strikes, releases line from clip

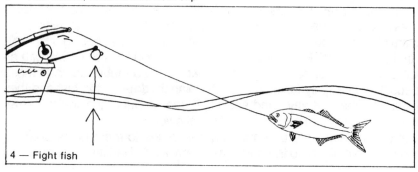

4 — Fight fish

light gear. You can stow planers in a small drawer or box and only bring them out when the fishing requires them. The rest of the time they are neatly stowed.

The disadvantage is the long 30 to 50 feet leaders needed to separate the lure from planer. The long leaders mean you will have to hand line the fish in for the final few yards. If you are a first time user of planers, this takes a little getting used to. I pull the leader onto the deck and let it lie at my feet, finally swinging the fish over the gun'l and off to the side so it doesn't fall to the deck into the coiled leader. What a mess it makes if you don't keep the fish clear.

Ideally the fish box will be open and the blue gets swung directly into the box, never even touching the deck or messing up the leader coils. I prefer not to gaff the fish so the decks stay clean.

The leader can take a lot of abuse from fish, or as you step on it on the deck and possibly as a fish rubs against the boat before you can swing him aboard. I've found 60, 80 or 100 pound test Ande mono to be perfect for leaders. I use the 60 pound on very small planers, like the #OO size and use 100 pound test on the size #1 or larger.

The pattern places a pair of planers off each transom corner to get two lures running down deep. A third rod rigged only with mono runs directly down the center and the lure rides just below the surface rigged with a four ounce trolling drail.

It is very common for a bluefish hooked on a deep lure, to bring other fish with him up to the surface. Maybe they are just curious, I don't know, but if you keep the trolling speed up for an extra 30 seconds you may get a second bluefish on the top running lure.

Downriggers are gaining in popularity each season and they can be deadly on bluefish. They are a little more complicated than planers because of the extra mounting of equipment and they require more attention from your crew to haul up and lower down the trolling weights, but they also have several advantages. You can troll with lighter tackle, you can do away with the long leaders and reel the fish right to the rod tip and you can fish the depths more precisely. For these reasons many anglers are switching to downriggers.

With a planer you have little room to change depths other than trolling a shorter line, but this may get you fewer strikes if the lures are moved too close to the boat. With downriggers you can pin point any depth from only a few feet to well over a hundred feet with repeatable accuracy.

The most critical thing about fishing with downriggers is the distance the lure or bait is dropped back from the trolling weight. Keep the lure too close to the ball, and you will go fishless. Place it too far back, and you may miss strikes because of the stretch in the mono line.

I usually use a drop back of from 30 to 70 feet, and try different distances if the fishing is slow to find which drop back is best for any given day.

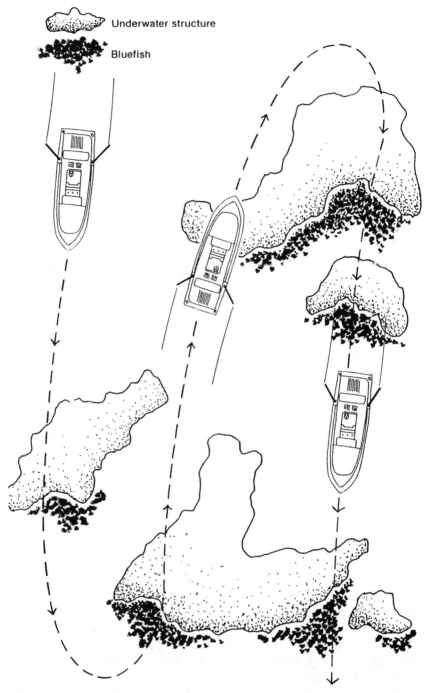

Underwater structure

Bluefish

Search pattern — Trolling with a zig-zag or grid pattern helps locate schools of bluefish. Use a graph recorder to "see" into the water around the structure.

Monday's 50 foot drop back may not work on Wednesday when you need a 70 foot drop back.

Tackle can be lighter than when fishing planers, but if you go too light it becomes difficult to set the hook. You will get strikes, but boat few fish. Most of the time I use 15 pound test line, switching to 20 pound if there are blues of over 10 pounds in the area. It takes a lot of force to sink a hook in the mouth of a big blue so the 20 pound line is more productive. If you don't mind losing a few fish, stick with the 15 pound.

Favorite lures for June and July bluefish trolling include nylons in green/yellow and red/white, spoons, single tubes also in green, yellow or red, and swimming plugs like the Bomber and Whopper Stopper.

My preference would always be to diamond jig bluefish. I get a big kick out of the jolting strikes and the fast action, but in the real world of fishing the bluefish just aren't always schooled up tight enough to have good action with jigs. When the fish are scattered and not holding in concentrated schools there is no other choice; if you want some fish in the box, you have to troll.

Many anglers are going to downriggers, which allows them to use lighter tackle yet reach the same depths as when using wire. This involves using a heavy trolling weight attached to a separate reel of braided wire run off a short outrigger device. The fishing line is attached to the weight at a break-away clip. The weight is lowered to the desired depth indicated on the counter readout. The fishing lure streams out behind the trolling weight.

When a fish hits, the line pulls free from the clip and the angler fights the fish off the rod. Someone else then reels up the trolling weight to avoid tangling. It takes a little practice, and downriggers are a bit expensive, but trolling deep this way does provide maximum sport. Also, much less line is out behind the boat, making close maneuvering that much easier, important on crowded waters.

Nylons

Many lures will catch bluefish, but the basic nylon trolling lure is simple, proven and effective. A lead head, much like a bucktail head, has a trolling eye located at the forward center or slightly above center of the lead casting. The head can be bullet, ball, torpedo or cut mouth Smilin' Bill style. At the rear of the head is another eye to which a length of brass chain is attached. The hook, usually a 5/0 to 8/0 size, is attached at the end of the chain. Long strands of nylon Fish Hair are attached to the lead head, wrapped in place just like a bucktail lure. The nylon strands are long enough to cover the hook and chain.

Nylons come in a wide variety of colors. Favorites include the green and yellow combination, red and white, blue and white, purple and white, all white and a new blaze orange offered by Andrus Lures. I've caught them on many colors, but the brighter colors seem to get more attention from the blues. I like the green and yellow, red and white, and blaze orange the best.

Other versions of nylons are available too. The plastic skirted Hoochies that are used so much off Delaware can be good alternatives and Seven-strand now offers a bluefish sized clone lure, appropriately called the Bluefish Clone, that is another sure winner. Although not actually nylons, in the manufacturing sense, charter skippers would lump these plastic skirted lures in the same category, so we will too. They are trolled exactly the same way.

A distinct advantage of nylons is their durability. The lures usually cost somewhere around $4 to $7, depending on the size of the lure, yet they'll last a long time. One year from May through June with nine bluefish charters I used a selection of six nylon lures to catch nearly all the fish for an average catch of 75 fish per lure. If you want to calculate economics that's only $.07 per fish! We replaced straightened hooks and the lure heads were chipped, but the nylon hair was still virtually like new. Nylons are nearly indestructible.

Nylons can be fished on monofilament, on planers, on wire line and with downriggers. Which method you choose is decided by the graph recorder. In mid-May to late June it is not uncommon to find bluefish holding on the

Bluefish of all sizes will hit trolled lures like spoons, jointed tubes, swimming plugs and lead-headed nylons.

top layers of water never more than a few feet below the surface. A set of four nylons run with two off the outriggers and two off the transom will usually yield a good catch of fish.

When the bluefish go to deeper water, then it's time to go deeper with wire line, planers or downriggers. Even when using wire or planers I still may run a nylon off each outrigger. Blues hooked on deep line will sometimes be followed by their brothers and sisters as they are played to the surface. On many occasions another fish can be hooked on a top water lure dragged off the outrigger. As the boat is slowed to play the fish, the nylon will sink slightly because of the slower boat speed so it is right in front of the rising blues.

No matter how they are fished, they don't require wire leaders. The lures have their own built in leader provided by the brass chain running under the skirt. At a typical length of nine to fifteen inches in length, and since blues always hit the tail of the lure, there's no need to run an extra length of wire ahead of the lure. In fact, that extra wire may inhibit the action or fish appeal of the lure.

When replacing hooks, purchase open eye hooks that can then be crimped onto the brass chain. A long shanked hook offers a little extra leverage when unhooking a bluefish and can speed up the unhooking time as compared to a short shank hook that almost always require pliers a hook disgorger to remove the hook.

Jigging Leader

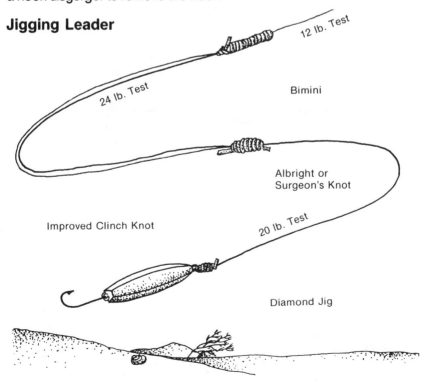

12 lb. Test

24 lb. Test

Bimini

Albright or Surgeon's Knot

Improved Clinch Knot

20 lb. Test

Diamond Jig

Diamond jigging technique

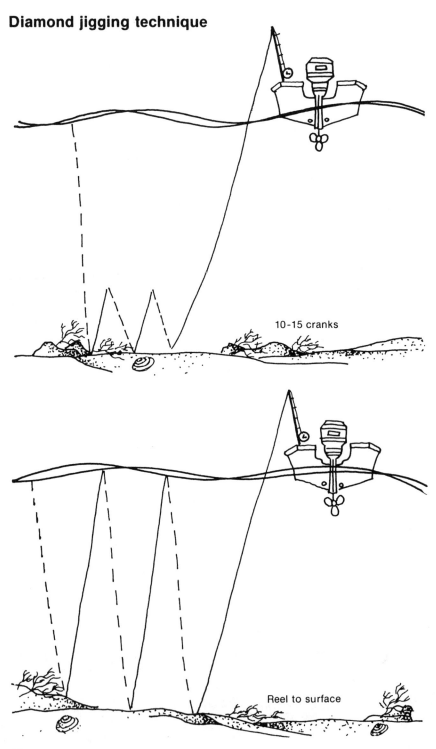

10-15 cranks

Reel to surface

Deep Jigging

Another method of fishing for bluefish, which will also catch weakfish and stripers as well, is deep-jigging. The enormous influx of sand eels in past years along the Atlantic Coast has rekindled an interest in this specialized fishing. A sand eel is not really an eel but the American sand lance, a small, slender fish growing to a length of about eight inches.

Deep jigging is most effective when blues are concentrated over a relatively small area. Chart recorders are invaluable in finding choice locations. Jigging can't produce if the fish aren't there. Assuming the readings indicate fish below, the lure is lowered to the bottom with the reel in free spool, or the bail on a spinning reel open, and then the reel is engaged and the lure is jigged with quick upward sweeps of the rod tip, or retrieved in jerks followed by fast reeling until the lure reaches the surface. Then the process is repeated.

It can pay in better catches if the fish finder (color scope, graph recorder or LCD unit) and the loran are watched carefully. When the fish finder shows schools of blues, jot down the loran TDs in a daily notebook so you can return to that exact spot time after time. I often find it much more productive to drift over schools of blues while diamond jigging. Writing the numbers in a log book gets me back on the fish quickly, after each drift.

The fish finder will tell you how to fine tune the jigging method. When the fish are located randomly in the water column, scattered from top water down to the bottom, a simple fast retrieve will catch a lot of fish. However, when the fish are schooled nearer to the bottom, as often occurs in the fall season, it makes no sense to reel the diamond jig all the way back to the surface on each retrieve. After the lure is dropped to the bottom, I click the reel into gear and reel about 10 to 15 cranks of the handle, then put the reel back into free spool to again drop the lure to the bottom. Re-engage the reel and crank another 10 to 15 turns of the reel handle, free spool and drop back down. Repeat this reel and drop, reel and drop, until you hook a fish.

A heavy tube lure such as the banana jig gets down rapidly and has the right action on the sweep. Green is the favorite color, but some days red, blue, white or yellow works best. The ancient diamond jig lure has more supporters among deep jiggers. Few lures look more inanimate in the hand but in the water the diamond jig appears alive. Most come with a single hook and some fishermen add a tail of surgical tubing for color and a longer profile. These are fished just like the banana lures.

Lead head jigs, or bucktails, can be fished this way, too, but they are usually retrieved slower and bounced along the bottom. Strips of pork rind, squid or the plastic Twister-type tails increase their appeal. Bucktails are extremely versatile and can be fished in many ways. They will catch nearly anything that swims in salt water along our inshore coastline.

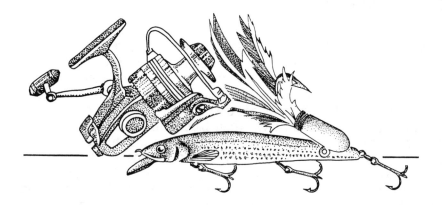

Chapter Three

WEAKFISH AND SEATROUT

Sleek and beautiful, the weakfish and seatrout are the glamour girls among coastal sport fish. These pretty fish are reasonably abundant although there was nearly a total disappearance of the weakfish during the 50s and 60s. These close cousins are similar in shape, feeding habits and life styles so most of the methods that take one, will also take the other.

There's no mistaking a weakfish with its purple-hued back, bronze and deep green coloring around the head, silvery sides and bright yellow fins. They also have sharp teeth so take care when unhooking one. Weakfish are found in more northern waters than the seatrout. Weakies can be caught from Massachusetts to north Florida with most of the catch coming from Long Island to Chesapeake Bay. The all-tackle record listed by the International Game Fish Association is a 19 pound, 2 ounce heavy weight that came from the surf at Jones Beach, New York. Dennis Rooney caught the trophy fish back in 1984, not too long ago.

Weakfish have many common names: weakie, trout, seatrout, tide runner and squeteague, depending on where you fish. Weaks average five to twelve pounds along the coast and open bays, but run smaller in the back bays such as Barnegat and Great South Bay. The IGFA 20 pound line class record is a 17 pound, 4 ounce fish taken off Brigantine Beach, New Jersey.

The seatrout is not as common in the northeast but the further south you travel into the mid Atlantic region, the more you will find seatrout. Below Delaware, they become just as numerous as the northern weakfish and in Chesapeake Bay you are likely to catch more seatrout than weakfish. The IGFA all-tackle record is 16 pounds on the nose caught by Bill Katko off Mason's Beach, Virginia.

The methods, tackle, baits and rigs used for weakfish are virtually the same for seatrout, so in this book we'll discuss the weakfish and leave the reader to decide where to fish, north or south, for weaks or trout. Either way, these fish are great sport and a lot of fun to catch.

The weakfish gets its name from the thin tissue on the sides of its mouth. But there's nothing fragile about its jaws and the way it fights to get away. Don't let the misnomer distract you. Most of the time the fish will be hooked around the lower jawbone or up in the roof of the mouth. Years ago it was thought that a soft action rod was the only kind to use on weaks. This may hold true when the fish are barely nipping the baits in very cold water and are lightly hooked. But for average fishing conditions a stiffer rod action is preferred. Many party boat anglers are scoring big with weaks by jigging diamond jigs or bucktails. A fish hooked solidly in the mouth will rarely get off because of the tackle used.

Each spring weakfish migrate into our waters from two directions. Some fish winter off the coast in deep water. These move inshore, to be joined by weaks coming up from southern waters. A few fisheries biologists believe that this burgeoning weakfish population in the Northeast is a result of surplus mid Atlantic fish expanding their range. Whatever the reason, it makes for terrific fishing.

Depending on water temperature, the fishing starts in late April or early May. The shoal areas warm up first, attracting fish and fishermen. Mid-May

Below Chesapeake Bay, the seatrout is more common than the weakfish or gray trout. It is distinguished by its vivid black spots along its sides.

to early June usually finds the fish moving into deeper water as shallow waters get too warm for comfort. Look for weakies in deep pockets, channels and sloughs in the summer months.

From June through late October weaks can be found scattered all along the shore. Summer fishing can be good in the bays and rivers, especially at night as the weakfish move into these areas to feed on worms, crabs and bait fish. Peconic Bay out on Long Island is a famous fishing ground for weaks. Great South Bay attracts its share, along with most inlets along the Long Island, New Jersey and Delaware Coast.

By late summer weaks have established themselves over inshore structure (bottom irregularities) along the beach fronts and can be found in good numbers from Maryland to Long Island in New York. Look for deep sloughs, sloping beaches, shoals and bars, small humps and ridges to hold these fish in small schools.

When striped bass populations were on the low side, weakfish filled in for surf and jetty fishermen. Weaks will hit live or cut bait as well as the same lures used for blues and stripers. Many anglers use the same tackle and techniques for stripers and weakies and can score on both fish on the same tide, from the same jetty.

The same applies to boat fishing for weaks through the summer and early fall. It is not uncommon to catch both striped bass and weakfish on the same drift while casting bucktails or jigging small diamond jigs. On a party boat a medium action rod of about seven feet is recommended for jigging. Anglers on private boats can choose lighter tackle, just as in bluefishing.

Many bay fishermen use one-handed baitcasting rods or light spinning outfits which allows them to use smaller lures with lighter lines in the shallower waters. Bay weaks can be spooky and the lighter gear makes less commotion. It's also a lot more fun to use, while providing maximum sport for these great fish.

In deeper, more open water, weaks often inhabit the same areas as blues, though usually closer to the bottom. They will take tubes trolled for bass or blues, but most fishermen do not like to use wire for weaks. But sometimes a single tube running way down is the only thing that will produce, like it or not.

Best Baits

A preferred method is to drift worms along the bottom, using just enough sinker weight to make contact. A three-way swivel is used: one ring for the line, one for a two-foot leader and hook and the last for a short line for the sinker. A single sandworm, hooked once near the head, is the natural bait of choice of regulars.

Hi-lo bait rig

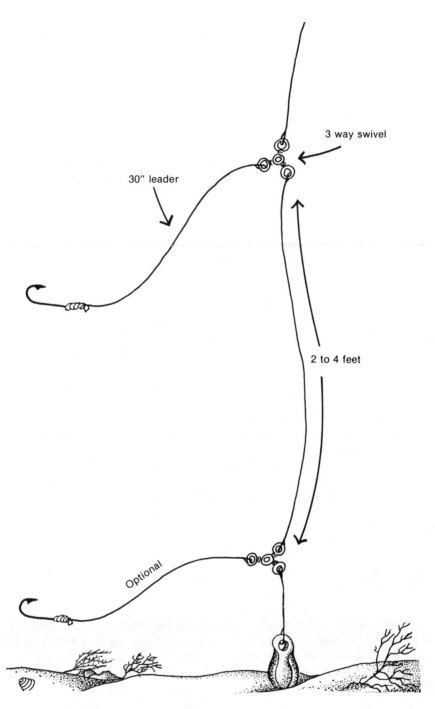

3 way swivel

30″ leader

2 to 4 feet

Optional

Weakfish also have a fondness for strips of squid, squid heads or even a whole squid if not too big. Squid is much cheaper than sandworms and although not as good a bait, still quite effective. A strip about five inches long and one half inch wide, with a slight taper, is generally used. A two-hook high/low rig drifted through a concentration of weaks is sure to bring results. If there are fluke around, one is liable to grab the low bait. Mixed doubles are not that uncommon.

From south Jersey to Maryland, shedder crab is a primary bait for seatrout. Although peelers can be expensive at times, they are deadly baits and catching a few fish is almost a guarantee with the crab baits.

Shrimp is a top bait in Florida and many mid Atlantic to northeast anglers never give shrimp a try. A pound of small size shrimp from a fish market will get you 30 to 40 shrimp that when cut into pieces will supply you with 60 to 100 baits. Shrimp are, therefore, surprisingly inexpensive bait and they catch weakfish like gangbusters.

Live bait can be deadly for tide runner sized weakfish. Small spot, snapper blues and even sand fleas catch very well. Boaters have it easy since most small boats today have live wells built right into the decks so keeping a supply of up to a dozen baits is no problem. Beach-bound fishermen convert 48 to 84 quart size coolers into live wells by installing a bilge pump in the bottom of the cooler and then running a short, 12 to 16 inch hose up to the top edge of the cooler. The hose is drilled with many small holes to make small jet streams of water that aerate the baits and keep the water well oxygenated. Hook the baits just ahead of the dorsal fin and cast them into the surf or drift them from a boat over shoals and bars.

Live spot rig

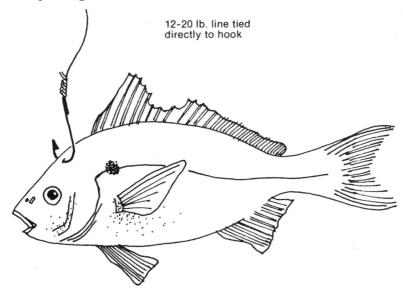

12-20 lb. line tied
directly to hook

Jigging while drifting

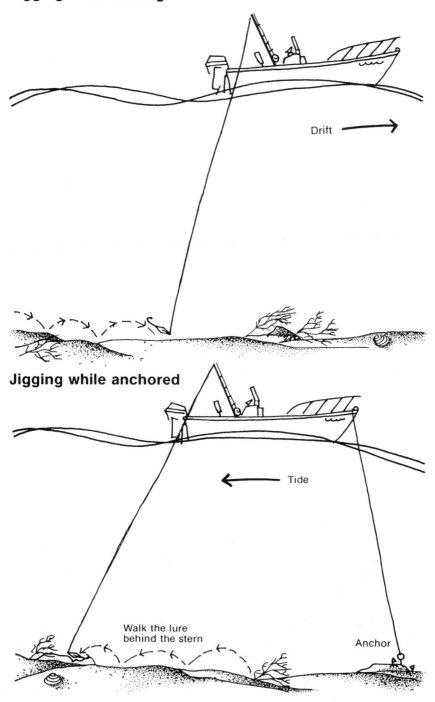

Drift ⟶

Jigging while anchored

⟵ Tide

Walk the lure
behind the stern

Anchor

Bucktailing Tips

Give me a handful of bucktails for spring fishing and I'd be real happy. They work great from Florida to Maine, catch all kinds of inshore fish, especially weakfish and seatrout, and they offer an infinite variety of shapes, sizes, weights and actions to suit most any fishing situation. I can vary the speed of retrieve, the hopping and bouncing action of the retrieve, or the size and shape of the bucktail to match most any water condition, water depth or bait preference.

The speed of retrieve can be critical, especially in the early season when waters are cool. Early trout in Chesapeake, Delaware or Peconic Bay are lethargic and slow moving due to the cool water. A fast retrieve will scoot right past the nose of these fish and get absolutely no response. Slow that retrieve down to a crawl and maybe a weakfish will jump right on the bucktail. One way to slow the retrieve speed down is to use conventional level wind reels that have slower speeds. Many of today's reels boast high speed ratios but several have slower speeds that are prefect for bucktailing.

One easy, effective way to slow the retrieve down, is to cast the bucktail in the same direction as the boat is drifting. At the end of the cast, let the bug settle to deep water, then begin the retrieve with short flicks of the wrist to get the bucktail dancing and doing its fish catching thing. Since the boat is moving towards the lure, the drift speed of the boat is subtracted from the retrieve speed of the lure. If you were to cast on the back side of the drift, the speed of the retrieve could be doubled since the boat's drift speed would be added to the reel's retrieve speed.

You can slow down the retrieve, from a boat or the beach, when casting up current to the mouth of a tidal creek that may hold striped bass, trout or summer flounder. The current of the creek moves the bucktail towards the boat or the casting position, again effectively reducing the overall speed of the lure.

If you cast at a slight angle to the boat drift or the creek current, the bucktail will move towards you at an angle, then swing in an arc about halfway through the retrieve as the lure gets 90 degrees to the angler's casting position. This change in retrieve angle, action and speed is often the moment when fish will hit the doodlebug. They probably have been following the lure with some curiosity and when they see it speed up and begin to rise off the bottom as retrieve arc changes, they may think the "meal" is trying to escape, which triggers a reaction from the fish that results in the strike. No one really knows what a fish thinks, nor does it matter. We do know for sure that a lot of strikes occur when the bucktail swings in the arc and begins to change its direction and speed.

Working the rod tip can change the action of the bucktail. Keeping the rod tip high and vertical makes the bucktail bounce and hop with an up and down motion on the retrieve. This is an action that frequently drives many fish right up the wall and they hit the lure either out of anger or from their inability to pass up what looks like an easy meal.

Working the rod tip down low and to the side diminishes the hopping action and the rod tip needs to be worked with a bit more sweeping action to get the lure dancing. This retrieve looks more like a darting bait fish.

I use both actions in the same retrieve. After making my cast into the direction of the drift, but at a slight angle to the drift, I work the bucktail with the rod tip held high to make the lure work in short hops and skips. As the angle of the retrieve changes and the bucktail begins to work at 90 degrees to the drift, I lower the rod tip and use more of a sweeping action.

Spinning tackle works fine for many fishermen, but many bucktail artists, prefer small level wind, conventional reels to do the job. Not only are the slower retrieve speeds helpful, but the way a conventional reel nestles in the palm of the left hand so the rod and reel can be worked with wrist action is just about perfect. A good bucktailer can make a doodlebug "dance all over the floor" and catch plenty of fish with a conventional reel.

Spinning tackle also has its place and I use spinning tackle for bucktails when the retrieve needs to be speeded up to a faster tempo, and especially when casting to fish that are out and away from the boat; like breaking blues, Spanish mackerel, shallow water striped bass or fish blitzing a chum slick. The long sweeps of the rod tip needed to get the

Bucktails for seatrout and weakfish are often tipped with a strip of fresh squid, a rubber worm or twister-style plastic tail.

bucktail working properly in these situations are best handled by spinning tackle. The way the spinning rod and reel fit into the angler's hands, cradled by the right hand, just makes the long, sweeping arcs of the rod tip easier to accomplish than trying this same retrieve with conventional gear.

Where To Find Them

Like most fish, weaks are affected by tidal movements and feed accordingly. The graph recorder may show fish below but they may not be hungry. Then, suddenly, something will trigger the fish into action, as if someone threw a switch. All rods will go down with fish on. So, if you locate fish and they're not biting, stick around or come back at the beginning of a tide change.

Fishing for weaks in shallow, busy bays poses special problems. Most of our inshore waters see heavy multi-recreational use. Powerboats race back and forth pulling water-skiers. Sailboats tack in all directions. Clam diggers tread or tong the flats. On a summer weekend the boat traffic can rival an expressway. None of this is conducive to good fishing. The secret is to fish after dark or just before dawn.

Local sharpies have favorite spots that they ease into after things quiet down. This may be a hole or depression in an otherwise grassy flat, or a channel between two marsh islands. Some spots are best on an incoming tide; others on the outgoing.

Bait can be a piece of shedder crab fished on the bottom or drifted down-tide with a small float. If you can get them, grass shrimp are like popcorn to weakies. A steady chum line is deadly. Hook two or three of these small shrimp on a light wire hook and toss them into the chum line to drift naturally with no added weight. Bait fishing is generally done from an anchored boat.

Other anglers prefer to drift past hotspots and cast lures. Sub-surface swimming plugs and bucktails are favorites. Even fly casters can get in on the action. Wind is the great enemy of saltwater fly fishermen but in the calm of sundown and pre-dawn hours the long-wand users can cast streamer flies and popping bugs.

Bay fishermen who specialize on weakies are close-mouthed about sharing secrets. Ask around at bait and tackle shops and boat liveries. Buy a chart of the bay and check for potential fishing areas: where a creek enters the bay proper; major channels that have minor ones intersecting them; sharp drop-offs along a marsh, or a deep slot around an obstruction such as a breakwater or bridge. Any place where the current and tidal flow carry bait past feeding weaks is worth a try.

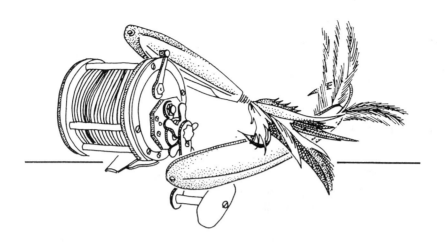

Chapter Four

SUMMER AND WINTER FLOUNDER

The tasty duo of winter and summer flounder delights coastal anglers from Florida to New England, and with good reason. Abundant, easy-to-catch and delicious to eat, flounder are the mainstays of bottom fishermen. You don't need a lot of fancy, expensive equipment and you have a choice of fishing areas: bays, rivers, inlets, the surf or offshore so they are within reach of every fisherman, young or old.

The winter flounder is the smaller of the two species. It is a right-sided fish, with its small fleshy mouth located on the right side, or the dark side, of the body. In contrast, summer flounder, or summer flounder, have large, toothed jaws located on the left. Once you see the two together there's no mistaking which is which.

Because they like cooler water, the winter flounder is usually caught in the fall, winter and spring. The summer flounder is available from the spring through the fall.

Winter Flounder

Winter flounder spend most of their time half-buried in soft, dark mud waiting in ambush for a small meal to come by. They like worms, tiny clams, shrimp and small crustaceans. They will also take a baitfish if small enough. Flounder have a good sense of smell and will be attracted to a chum line from a considerable distance. Flounder have been known to move long distances to adapt to changes in water temperature, winds, tidal currents and the season.

"Doc" Einer Grell of Long Island caught the world record all-tackle winter flounder in May of 1986. The plump flounder weighed a whopping seven pounds and was caught near Fire Island, New York.

Unlike some other bottom fish, flounder prefer cooler water. Spring and fall are the best times for flounder fishing. During the warm summer months they move to deeper, cooler water offshore. As fall approaches and bay waters cool, flounders move inshore and feed in the bays until the water gets too cold. Then they will bury themselves in the mud to snooze through the winter. Usually, the year's flounder season is over by the end of November. Mid-March is when anglers start looking for them again. The action will improve through April and taper off in early May.

Two Hook Rig

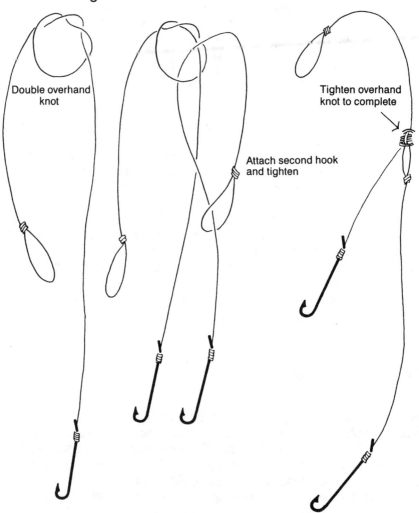

Double overhand knot

Tighten overhand knot to complete

Attach second hook and tighten

In northern waters around Rhode Island and Massachusetts the bays may remain cool enough to hold flounders all summer long, with good fishing under a warm sun instead of bone-chilling March winds. The winter flounder is not usually found below the coast of Delaware, although there is some limited winter flounder fishing in Chesapeake Bay.

Flattie experts have their own secret spots, depending on the tide and wind, but good places to check are the edges of channels and holes or depressions in a flat, muddy or silty bottom. The fish are most likely to be active during a moving tide when bait is carried along by the current.

Flounder are easy to catch but, as in anything, there are tricks of the trade. Some anglers consistently do better thank others. Aside from being at the right spot, the best advice is to use a chum pot, or two. The odor and juices of freshly-crushed clams or mussels will draw fish to your boat while others close by may get skunked without chum.

Kernels of canned corn have been used as chum and bait. Biologists tell us that the corn does not harm the fish, as thought at one time. Other chum ingredients may include canned pet foods, cooked rice and sand balls made up of compressed chum parts and dropped to the bottom.

Two Hook Rig

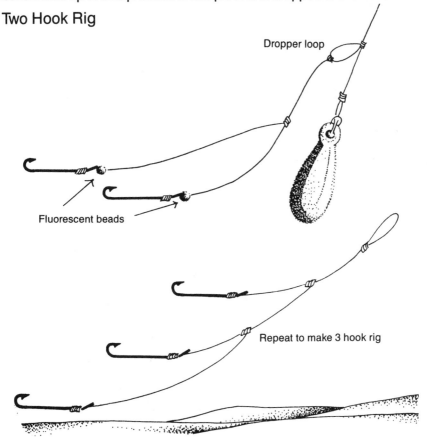

Dropper loop

Fluorescent beads

Repeat to make 3 hook rig

Stern Side View

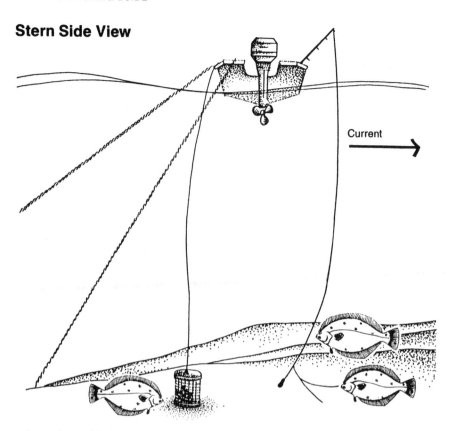

Current →

Overhead View

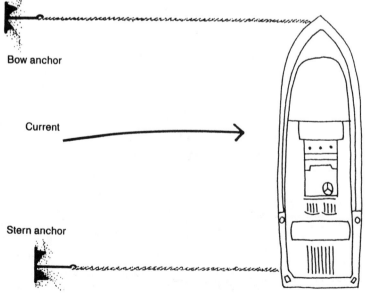

Bow anchor

Current →

Stern anchor

If anchored with one line at the bow, lower the chum pot forward and tie it to a bow cleat so the juices move with the boat. If tide and wind permit, position the boat across the current using two anchors and two pots to cover more bottom. You'll then have two chum slicks working for you. It is essential that the pots be smack on the bottom for success. Give the holding ropes a tug once in a while to stir up the chum and shake some bits loose.

Best baits for flounders are short lengths of blood and sand worms, tapeworms and strips of mussels and clams. Corn kernels and night crawlers also work. Remember that flounders have small mouths, so cut the bait accordingly.

Use only enough weight to hold bottom. This may be one ounce in six feet of bay water, or three ounces in a 20 foot channel with a good tide running. The fishing conditions will determine the most efficient tackle. Of course, you can't fish a 3 ounce sinker very well on a light spinning rod. Conversely, you'll be over gunned with a stiff boat rod in shallow situations. Pick something in between if you're limited to only one outfit. Spinning and conventional revolving spool reels are both used, with latter getting the nod for heavier sinkers. Whatever the rod, there should be some sensitivity in the tip to feel the peck of a flounder.

The fish will often nip at the bait or suck it in like spaghetti. When you feel a take, wait a second or two then lift the rod tip deliberately and the fish will usually be on. There's no need for a hard, fast strike. With one fish hooked, you may want to leave the bait down for another few seconds in hopes of a double-header. Once the barb is into the soft flounder mouth it seldom comes out until you take it out.

The favorite flounder hook design has always been the Chestertown, in sizes 10 to 6. Actually, any small hook will do, but the offset point of the Eagle Claw style seem more efficient.

Flounder regulars keep their rigs simple, scorning spreaders and un-necessary hardware. They'll tie the second dropper hook midway along the first leader. Some don't even bother with a three-way swivel, but we use one to help keep the hook leader from tangling with the line.

While anchoring and chumming are the most common flounder tech-niques, there are times when drifting will produce good catches. The drift should be slow and parallel to the edge of the channel or long depression. Raise the sinker occasionally a couple of inches and bounce it along the bottom. The moving bait will be spotted by hungry flounders and they'll come over to investigate - if it's not moving by too rapidly.

A great many flounder are caught by fishermen casting from shore. Piers, bulkheads and bridges all get a big play in good flounder water. Generally, they won't catch as many as the boat fishermen, but shoreline casters get by with a minimum of expense, sometimes a consideration these days.

Most flounder will run from one pound to two pounds, but an exceptional fish of three or four pounds is possible in deeper water of large bays especially the waters off Block Island and Montauk. Very small flounders are called "postage stamps" and should be unhooked carefully and tossed back. They'll be bigger next year.

Summer Flounder

As the winter flounders are vacating the inshore waters, their larger cousins, the summer flounder, are moving in. Whereas flounder provide "comfortable" fishing for delicious table fare, summer flounder can be downright exciting, plus being just as good to eat. Size, appetite and fighting ability make the difference.

Captain Charlie Nappi of Montauk, New York caught the all-tackle I.G.F.A. summer flounder back in 1975. The 22 pound 7 ouncer was a big fish, and one that many anglers hope to break some day. The all-tackle record for southern flounder, a very close cousin to the summer flounder, was taken by Larenza Mungin in Nassau Sound, Florida. The fish weighed 20 pounds 9 ounces and was taken in 1983. The differences in the southern and summer flounder are so slight that most fishermen would never be able to tell them apart. I've caught both and they look like twin brothers to me. For purposes of this book, we'll call them both flounder, even though some northern fishermen use the name fluke from Sandy Hook north to New England.

The summer flounder is a predator, equipped with a mouthful of sharp teeth and capable of bursts of surprising speed. They will watch the current for food to come past as they rest camouflaged on the bottom, but summer flounder won't hesitate to charge after any bait fish in the vicinity. This is the clue to successful flounder fishing - keep the bait moving.

Anglers casting lures for blues or bass are sometimes surprised to catch summer flounder instead. We've even caught them in bays while chumming for snapper blues; the summer flounder coming near the surface to take the baits. However, most of the time the summer flounder will be deep and your bait should be within inches of the bottom to connect.

Like winter flounders, summer flounder like to hold along the edges of channels, in inlets, deeper holes and at the mouths of major tidal creeks. Each area has its own well-known fluking grounds, and the best results are obtained by fishing carefully and paying attention to details.

A three-way swivel is the heart of the summer flounder rig. This fishing line is tied to one ring. A dropper line about six inches long for the sinker comes next. The leader is usually about 24 to 30 inches long and attached to the third ring. Generally, only one hook per rig is used for a more natural bait presentation. Hook sizes depend on the average size of the fish being caught; from 1/0 up to 6/0 for big doormats offshore. The Eagle Claw style with its offset point is preferred. Some specialized summer flounder hooks

One-hook rig

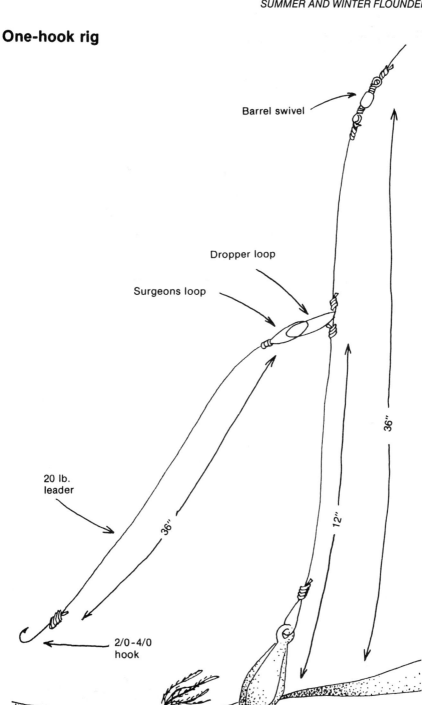

Barrel swivel

Dropper loop

Surgeons loop

20 lb. leader

36″

36″

12″

36″

2/0 - 4/0 hook

Fish-finder rig

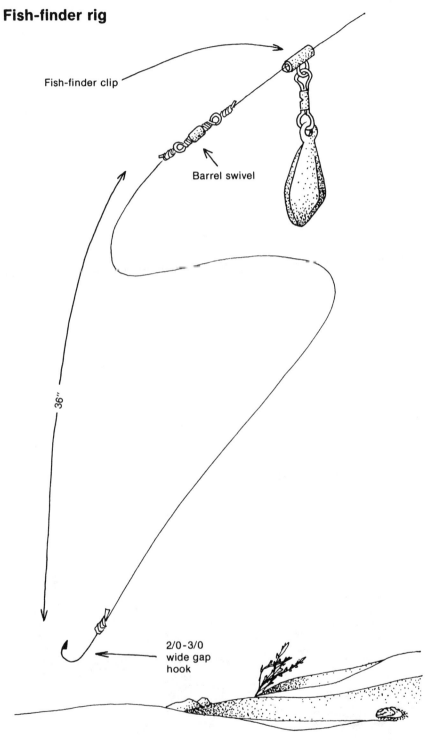

Fish-finder clip

Barrel swivel

36"

2/0-3/0
wide gap
hook

employing a small hook up at the eye of the main hook to hold the tip of a strip bait are used at times when large fish are expected. However, most of the time a single, simple hook will surface.

Some flounder fishermen swear by the use of spinners and/or beads in combination with the hook for added attraction. Personally, we like the unadorned rig. It picks up less weeds and works just as well for us. You may want to try the flashier rigs and make your own decision. Whatever the rig, use a dipsey, bank or round sinker that doesn't dig in. You want it to slide freely along the bottom.

Flounder tackle, like any kind of fishing, depends on circumstances. Light tackle and light sinkers in shallow water may suit your needs, or you may need heavier gear. An important factor is rod action. The 6 and 7 foot stick should have some backbone in the butt and mid-section and the tip should be sensitive enough to feel the sinker sliding over the bottom. Some of the best flounder fishermen have switched to graphite rods because of their extra sensitivity. These are more expensive than regular fiberglass rods, but some anglers feel they are worth it.

Spinning tackle can be used, but veterans prefer conventional reels. They'll hold the rod ahead of the reel and have the line pass through their fingers for a better feel of what's going on as the sinker moves along. Summer flounder will often mouth the tail end of the bait. When this slight resistance is felt, the fisherman should give slack by lowering the rod tip or allowing line to pay off with the reel in free spool. This gives the fish time to move up on the bait. When the line comes tight, lift the rod with a smooth motion to set the hook. At times it's best for the novice fisherman to leave the rod unattended in a holder and the summer flounder will hook itself.

If the tide and current are so that a good drift is not possible, try slow tolling for summer flounder. Call it power drifting. Some summer flounder experts fish no other way, and their catches are quite impressive.

One essential piece of flounder equipment is a good-sized landing net. Summer flounder shake violently when lifted out of the water and many will be lost at the boat without a net.

Summer flounder can also be caught by casting from the beach or jetties. A rod of about eight or nine feet long designed to cast one to four ounces is ideal. The same outfit can be used to fish from piers and bulkheads, and will do nicely for drifting along the beach or offshore on a party boat.

Summer flounder will hit a variety of baits and lures. Favorites include live killies, snapper blues, spearing, smelt, sand eels, baby bunkers, squid (small, whole squid for big summer flounder, squid strips for average fish), sea worms and live shrimp. Most of these baits are available live or freshly frozen at tackle shops along the coast. One of the very best baits for summer flounder is a strip of summer flounder belly or back about an inch wide and five inches long, tapered to a pointed tail to flutter in the current. A strip of sea robin belly will also work well. Trim the strip baits neatly and

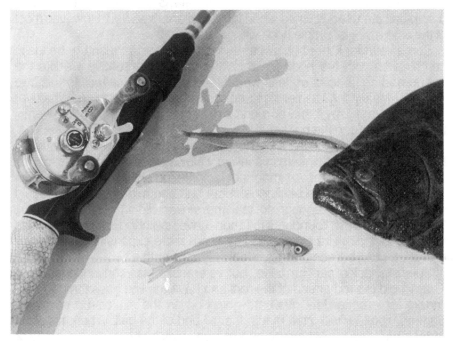

Summer flounder are caught on strip baits like squid, or small fresh baits like sand eels or spearing.

hook them once at the head.

The best summer flounder fishermen check their baits regularly for weed and mud. Clean, fresh baits catch the most fish. If your bait is continually fouled, increase the sinker length so the bait rides a little higher. There's no firm rule concerning the distance of the sinker from the swivel. Experiment to find the most productive combination for your particular situation.

Live baits are generally fished by hooking the bait through the lips so the bait swims naturally. On occasion a combination of live killie and squid strip brings the most strikes.

Live snapper blues or small bunkers hooked ahead of the dorsal fin and drifted through inlets, boat traffic permitting, account for some very large summer flounder each summer.

On party boats that regularly specialize in fluking, the usual bait provided is strips of squid. It works, but sharpies bring their own baits because it gives them an edge towards taking the pool-winning fish. Many use large, carefully-trimmed strip baits on tandem hooks. Others use smelt or sand eels. And some swear by whole squid or needlefish. While other anglers are content with two pound summer flounder, the serious fishermen are after those fish going five pounds or better, and they feel the bigger and different baits will do the job.

Anglers in southern Jersey often fish bucktails or a combination of live killie and jig with good success. They fish around the edges of march islands, channel drop-offs and deep holes. The bucktail should be just heavy enough to bounce off the bottom; 3/8 ounce being the average. Other baits such as squid strip, summer flounder belly strip and sand eels also work well in combination with a bucktail.

The advantage in working bucktails is being able to cover more water than by drifting. Cast the bucktail at various angles. Let it settle, then begin a slow, twitching retrieve in short hops along the bottom. Sometimes we'll cast out one rod and set it in a holder while we work another one. The "dead stick" offering will often catch as many fish as the one being fished by the angler.

The color of the bucktail can be important. We like white, but some days a yellow or red and white jig is the answer. Again, it pays to experiment.

Bucktails work best on a relatively clean bottom. Sea lettuce and weed quickly collect on a line and spoil the effort. The same applies to drifting or trolling. Summer flounder will not hit a week-draped bait or lure. You may be forced to try other spots, if there's a weed problem.

During the height of the summer flounder season you'll see hundreds of boats concentrated at favored locations, calling for precise boat maneuvering. We'd rather fish than steer the boat constantly like a taxi driver in traffic, so we avoid fishing with the "fleet." Instead, we'll troll slowly along the beach front, but it's often productive. When the wind is favorable you can drift parallel to the beach for miles.

Wherever and however you fish for them, summer flounder provide plenty of action and sport. They come in a variety of sizes and there's always a shot at the real heavyweight. Summer flounder put up a good scrap and anyone can catch them, including young children. They are ideal fish for introducing someone to salt water fishing.

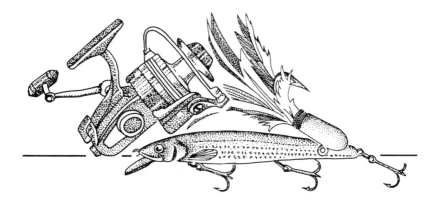

Chapter Five

SHARKS

Sharks are big, tough, nasty, smart and dangerous. That all adds up to some great sport fishing, if you can find sharks and fool them into taking your baits. Perhaps no other kind of offshore fishing has grown so rapidly as has shark fishing. However, shark fever has caused many anglers to set off ill-equipped, and misguided, in pursuit of these challenging fish. Without proper preparation and equipment their chances of success are slim.

Among the world record sharks recognized by the International Game Fish Association, the following were caught on the Atlantic Coast:

Species	Weight	Line	Angler
Blue	393 lbs	50 lb	Roy Carpenter
Blue	410 lbs	80 lb	Martha Webster
Blue	334 lbs	130 lb	Cassandra Webster
Mako	1080 lbs	50 lb	Jim Melanson
Porbeagle	238 lbs	50 lb	Bea Harry
Thresher	448 lbs	50 lb	Lynnette Pinturo
Tiger	1780 lbs	130 lb	Walter Maxwell

Sharks are plentiful along the Atlantic Coast and at times can be caught easily. But sharks can also be extremely wary and selective about what they will eat and how they react to a chum slick. As in any type of fishing, consistent success demands attention to detail; the correct rigging of baits, selection of proper tackle and accessory techniques and water temperature. All are important factors to consider when seriously fishing for sharks.

Sharks can be found in 15 or 20 fathoms of water, in 100 fathoms at the edge of the Continental Shelf or in shallow bays. A surprising number stay well inshore, offering some surprisingly good action on big fish in places like Chesapeake Bay, Delaware Bay, Barnegat Bay, Great South Bay and Cape Cod Bay. Because of space restrictions, chumming from an anchored boat is usually necessary under these conditions. The sharks will move with the tidal flow, following channels and passing through cuts in sand bars and other natural openings.

Shark season along the mid-Atlantic Coast gets under way in late May or early June. Blue sharks are usually the first ones to show up. Porbeagles, sometimes called mackerel sharks, will be close behind. When the water temperatures get into the high 60s, the star attraction appears - the mako.

Mako sharks are supreme game fish, rivaling marlin in their ability to run off line and take to the air. Their high-flying leaps will sometimes carry them 15 feet out of the water. And, in our opinion, makos are the best of all sharks for eating. Mako steaks rate on a par with swordfish, hence its nickname "Jersey swordfish" at the fish markets.

Other shark species available to sport fishermen include the sand bar or brown shark, dusky, tiger, thresher, hammerhead and the legendary great white. In Delaware Bay there is an excellent summer fishing opportunity for sand tiger sharks; a fish that hugs the bottom, has a mouth like a mako but lacks the jumping ability.

The Game Plan

When it comes to sharks, the difference between fast action and just spending a day on the water drifting and dreaming is knowing how to find the offshore structure. Hidden under the relatively calm, flat surface lie steep drop offs, ridges, trenches and deep fingers. This offshore structure draws baitfish and predators alike. Gentle upwellings of ocean currents bump into or rub against the structure causing eddies of warm, oxygenated water. Plankton thrive and attract schools of darting baitfish and shrimplike crustaceans that attract bluefish, which in turn attract sharks, especially makos.

Successful shark fishermen know the importance of working the structure and carefully plot their shark fishing forays to take maximum advantage of the changing bottom. The best technique is to drift over the structure while dishing out a soup of ground baitfish such as ground mossbunker or mackerel. As the boat drifts, pushed by the wind and current, the chum slick stretches out for hundreds of yards and eventually for several miles.

It's easy to pick out the best structure by checking a navigational chart. Bottom contour lines are pre-printed in pale gray on the charts but are hard to see unless enhanced by the fisherman. Trace over the lines with waterproof, fine line ink pens of various colors to more clearly show the 15, 20, 25 and 30 fathom lines. The bottom structure will literally jump off the chart with this simple modification making it very easy to plot the best offshore shark fishing areas.

The shark fisherman's day actually begins at the dock before the first light of dawn as attentive ears listen to the coastal weather reports giving not only the sea conditions but the direction of the wind. The strategy is to

Most shark fishermen chum with ground fish, such as menhaden or mackerel, and drift over changing bottom structure. Plastic storage crates make a good "automatic" chumming device.

plot the wind direction and then choose the bottom structure on the chart that will work best with that wind direction. The drift should start on the upwind side of the structure so the wind blows the boat on a path that covers the rising and falling bottom contours.

Sharks roam the wide oceans and they will shift their locations as wind and water currents change, as bait moves and as the water temperature changes with the passing seasons. Yesterday's hot spot may be tomorrow's desert so it pays to talk to other sharkers and your local tackle shop to see what patterns are developing.

The loran TD coordinates of the destination are entered into the loran and a course is run to take the boat directly to the edge of the first good piece of bottom structure. Once near the selected structure it's a good idea to stop the boat before getting into final position. Check the wind to be sure the weatherman is accurate and to see if the current will effect the drift. Adjust the starting position if necessary. Check the water temperature and watch the color scope or recorder for signs of bait. If the area looks alive with good fish signs, get set in the final position at the upwind start of the structure.

Tackle

3/0 to 6/0 reels, either star drag or lever drag style are good choices. Most sharks weigh around 75 to 150 pounds and are readily taken on 30 to 50 pound tackle. All sharks are strong, some are fast and some, like the mako, can leap wildly in the air, but most of them can be caught with much more fun when the tackle is on the lighter side.

A good all round outfit uses a stiffish stand-up style rod or a standard 30 or 50 pound class trolling rod. Don't use a stand-up style rod with a light tip action; it won't set the hook. We've caught makos up to 412 pounds on this tackle and tigers of better than 700 pounds.

Many captains and tournament winners use dacron line because it has no stretch to it; a big help when trying to set the hook in the tough jaws of a big shark. Other fishermen prefer monofilament because of its stretch which offers some cushioning when the fish is near the boat and makes a sudden lunge to get away. We use mono on the 30 pound tackle and dacron on the 50 pound tackle.

The Boat

The boat should have a fairly large, roomy cockpit with space for chum buckets, cooler of ice, baits, tackle and room for three fishermen to stand in comfort without being crowded. Gaffs and rods should be stowed under the gunwales until needed. Fuel capacity should be at least enough to allow for the run to the shark grounds and back with an additional 20% safety margin. Twin engine boats are preferred by many offshore anglers in case an engine ever goes down.

A VHF radio provides communication with other boats, a loran provides the navigation ability to pinpoint the drift starting point and a recorder or color scope shows the changing bottom structure, presence of bait and other fish. A temperature gauge is helpful.

Baits, Leaders and Hooks

The best mako shark bait is a fresh bluefish fillet since this is the primary food of makos in the summer months. Fresh frozen bunker, mackerel, butterfish or small bonito may also serve well. Sometimes a sandwich of a fish filet and whole squid will do the trick to fool a wary mako. Baits can be dressed up to look "alive" by adding colored vinyl skirts like the type used on tuna lures. Vibrant green, red or orange skirts dance with the rhythm of the rocking boat and breathe life into the baits.

Sharks will take whole or fillet baits. Hooks are size 8/0 to 12/0 depending on the size of the bait.

It is good practice to change the baits several times during the day, even if they've had no attack by a shark. Fillet baits get washed out and lose their smell. Whole baits get soft and washed out, sometimes hooks tear the baits, especially in rough water. A squirt or two of fish scent or the new color additives sometimes get extra interest from sharks on slow days.

Because of the sharp teeth of all sharks, wire leaders are absolutely necessary. Sharks also have a sandpaper-like skin that can quickly fray through fishing line so the leaders must be at least as long as the shark. Use 10 to 12 foot leaders made from 275 pound test braided cable. Another leader choice is single strand #12 wire but be aware that the single strand wire breaks easily if it ever kinks when a mako jumps and puts a twist into the leader.

The best hook is the Mustad #7699 offshore style with an offset to the hook point which helps the hook grab onto a jaw or flesh and a solid hookup is usually assured. Sizes 8/0 to 12/0 are used depending on the bait. Obviously a small fillet bait needs a smaller hook than a whole rigged two pound mackerel. Always use the smallest hook possible and use a file to sharpen the hook point to a triangulated, razor sharp edge.

Working the Drift

On a typical sharking expedition offshore, let's assume that we've located good structure between 15 and 20 fathoms and the wind and current are in our favor. What next? The first thing to do is establish a chum line. Ground fish, such as bunker or mackerel, is mixed with sea water in a bucket and ladled out every few minutes.

The chumming can be done automatically by placing a frozen chunk of chum in a plastic box with a grid bottom and sides and hanging it overboard. Blocks of frozen chum are placed in a net bag. The rolling of the boat will agitate the chum box so pieces of the thawing chum will break off and be carried away in the current. After a while the chum slick may be a mile long; a beacon of scent for sharks to home in on and, hopefully, trace to its source - you. Start the chum slick as soon as you are in position. Baits are positioned at three different levels because we're never sure at which feeding level the sharks will prefer on any given day. One bait is positioned about 200 feet from the boat suspended from a float to ride 70 to 90 feet below the surface. A second bait is placed about 125 feet from the boat about 40 to 60 feet down. The third bait is worked close to the boat with no float so it rides about 20 to 30 feet below the surface.

Rubber band wrapped around the float holds a loop of line so float won't slide along line until shark hits the bait.

The best floats are the red and white balsa type with a hollow tube run down the center. The line is run through the tube so the float slides up and down the line. A rubber band wrapped around the float will securely hold a loop of the fishing line so the float won't slide until the loop is pulled from the rubber band at the strike of a shark. Unlike styrofoam floats, the balsa type can be used over again so no debris is left behind on the water.

Reels are left in free spool with the clickers on. Line clips hold the line so the rocking action of the boat doesn't keep pulling a few feet of line off the reel at every wave. Stowed around the boat and ready for action are a gimbal belt, kidney harness, gaffs, bait knives, extra leaders, tail ropes and baits.

Sharking rod position

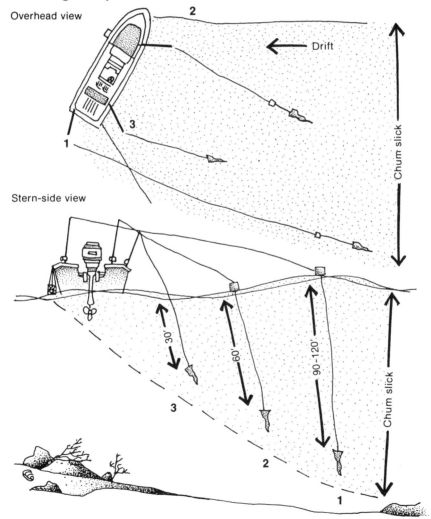

Overhead view

Drift

Chum slick

Stern-side view

30'

60'

90-120'

Chum slick

The Battle

The run off when a shark takes the bait and moves away from the boat signals the start of some great excitement. When a shark comes into a chum slick there's no telling how it will react to the baits. Some fish engulf the bait immediately, barely slowing down to do so. Others play with a bait, mouthing and spitting it out. Sometimes you can excite them by chunking, tossing small pieces of bait in with the chum. When the shark takes these chunks regularly, toss one in with a hook in it. We always keep a spare outfit rigged and handy for this purpose.

A pick up on one of the big baits will be announced by a steady run off of line. Don't be too anxious to set the hook. Give the fish plenty of time to swallow the bait. Keep your thumb on the spool to prevent an overrun and disengage the click. You want the shark to feel as little resistance as possible.

Sharks seldom oblige by swimming in a straight line directly away from the boat after taking a bait. This means the fishing line will be bowed or even double-bowed, depending on the shark's movements. This slack line will impede setting the hook. When you're ready to strike the fish, put the rod butt in a belt or chair gimbal, engage the reel and crank in any slack. Brace your feet and point the rod at the fish and wait until the line comes tight, then wait an extra second, and then yank back hard on the rod several times. You'll know immediately if you're in. A big shark will feel like you are tied to a freight train, so hang on!

While only the mako sharks jump, all sharks give a good account of themselves on 30 pound tackle. The terrific aerial jumps of makos are mind blowing, burned into the fisherman's memory bank for future daydreaming.

Depending on the size of the shark, and how it is hooked, you may be in for a half-hour fight, or one lasting several hours. Once the fish is hooked, have someone else reel in the other lines to keep from tangling. If the shark is a small one and fighting off to the side, you may want to keep one bait out hoping for a second hook up, if there are three or more fishermen aboard. One person should be standing by to do the gaffing, or to move the boat if necessary.

The final minutes of the fight are the trickiest. Only after the shark seems exhausted should it be drawn close. When a shark comes in too quickly or too easily, watch out! It still has plenty of reserve power and you don't want a rambunctious shark next to the boat. Don't try to gaff a "green" shark. Ease off on the pressure and wait until the fish moves off before leaning into it again.

With some of the double line on the reel the angler will have a stronger connection and can apply more pressure. Lead the shark alongside the boat.

Ideally, two or more "mates" will be ready to gaff a big shark. If you want to release the fish no gaffing is necessary. The mate will grab the wire leader and cut it a safe distance from the shark's jaws, and that's it. If you want to keep the fish as a trophy, to enter in a tournament or to eat, you'll have to secure it and kill it.

Sharks can twist in wild gyrations when stuck with a gaff and can bend cheap quality gaffs like wire coat hangers. Use the best. Any shark over 150 pounds should be secured with a flying gaff first. The flying gaff head has a rope to tie off on a stout cleat. The gaff handle comes off after the fish is struck. Incidentally, when gaffing a jumping shark like a mako, don't set the gaff in the forward half of the shark's body. Its tail could launch it into the boat. Instead, stick the gaff just aft of the dorsal fin to partially immobilize that powerful tail. Even so, makos have been known to become airborne, flying gaff and all. As the gaff man reaches out, he should sink the fly gaff just aft of the dorsal fin. Watch out! Your mako will be one ticked off fish and will splash furiously but that's part of the fun of sharking. Be sure the fly gaff line is secured to a cleat and then get a tail rope around the shark's tail.

When the leader man has hold of the wire the angler should leave the chair if seated and reduce the drag setting on the reel in case the fish pulls away under a renewed surge of strength. If the leader man can hold the fish the gaffer waits for a clear shot and plants his hook. He then gets the

CREW POSITION

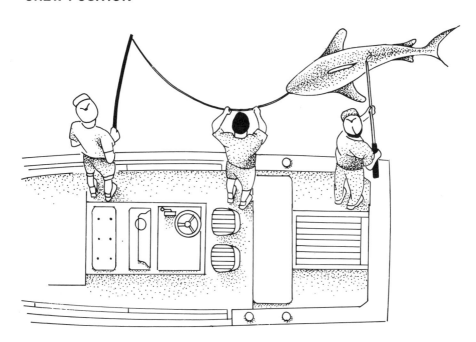

71

handle out of the way and pulls the shark in so a tail rope lasso can be applied. A straight gaff is used to hold the shark's head. With the fish stretched out and its head out of the water, the coup de grace can be administered by way of a bang stick, load of buckshot or rifle bullet into the brain area.

The flying gaff is then removed and the fish brought forward by the tail rope and secured to a bow cleat. We never bring a shark aboard until we are definitely, positively, 100 percent certain that it is DEAD. And even then we stay clear of its jaws.

Once tied off on a stern or spring line cleat, the fish is yours. Hung from the cleat, the mako will die and it will be safe to bring it aboard for the ride back to port.

Tag and Release

There is great concern that makos, and other sharks, are on the verge of being overfished by commercial interests. The concept of tagging and releasing all sharks not meant for the dinner table is a good one and will help assure a stable population sharks for future generations to enjoy.

There's a special reward, a feeling of participating with nature, when you tag and release a shark and let it swim away unharmed. Perhaps some day another fisherman will get the fun of battling one of the great game fish of the world just as you did.

Information gathered from tagging studies with the help of recreational anglers has helped Dr. Jack Casey of National Marine Fisheries Service gain valuable data about how sharks live, where they migrate and how long they live.

Tags are available from the NMFS, Narragansett Laboratories, RR 7, South Ferry Road, Narragansett, Rhode Island, 02882. They are free but the knowledge they provide is priceless.

Sharks as Food

Most sharks are good to eat but should be dressed out and put on ice as soon as possible. Makos keep well with frequent wetting, but other species take on an objectionable ammonia smell if unattended to. We stretch the shark along the gunwale, gut it out and cut off the head, fins and tail, then cut the body into convenient chunks to fit the cooler. Back at the dock we'll cut steaks about one inch thick, leaving the skin on to help hold the meat together while grilling over a charcoal fire. We treat them just as we would swordfish steaks.

Shark meat can also be boiled, broiled, fried or chowdered. As a general rule, sharks weighing less than 200 pounds are best for table fare. The meat of larger fish is coarser and tougher, according to some shark fanciers. It's a matter of personal opinion. We've had steaks off a 300 pound mako and found them delicious.

Some anglers smoke shark meat and pronounce it a gourmet's delight. Any firm-meat shark such as a mako, porbeagle, thresher or white should smoke up beautifully. Check at a local commercial smokehouse to see if they'll do it for you. Or, you can make your own smoker or use one of the small, portable electric smoke boxes sold in sporting goods stores.

As with any fresh fish, care should be taken during transportation. The trunk of a car gets mighty hot in the summer sun. Ice is the answer. But ice melts and you don't want the fish to get water-soaked. Pack the fish with ice but put the ice in its own plastic bag in the cooler. This eliminates a mess, keeps the fish better and allows for easy changing of the ice if need be on the drive home.

Shark meat lasts only about three or four days under refrigeration and should be eaten right away or fast-frozen for prolonged storage. Blue sharks, for some reason, have a shorter shelf life in the refrigerator. Blues should be eaten fresh no later than the next day; the surplus frozen as soon as you get home from the trip.

Individual palates differ but in our book the best-tasting sharks are: mako, porbeagle, thresher and blue - in that order.

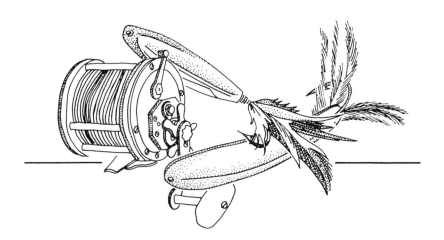

Chapter Six

TUNA, MARLIN AND SWORDFISH

These blue water species are at the top of the list for sheer excitement and angling thrills. Tuna, in particular, have captured the imagination of many coastal fishermen who now own twin engine outboard boats capable of running to the more distant fishing grounds where these fish are found. You don't necessarily have to travel all the way to the edges of the Continental Shelf, a distance of 60 to 80 miles depending on where you live, since tuna can many times be found much closer to shore. Often a run of only 20 or so miles puts fishermen right in the middle of excellent tuna trolling or boat fishing opportunities.

Angler interest in these pelagic species has grown tremendously over the past two decades. Part of the reason has been the discovery of large numbers of yellowfin tuna 20 to 40 miles offshore from the 20 fathom bottom contour lines on out to the 30 and 40 fathom lines. These fish are well within reach of fishermen who run their own boats or who charter fish on charter boats. Even party boats are getting in the action.

The other stimulant has been the development of fast, sea kindly hulls equipped with loran, VHF radios, radar, color scopes, and similar electronic gear which makes offshore navigation accurate and safe. Many fishermen who run Makos, Grady Whites and other twin outboard rigs are within striking distance of the offshore grounds.

Few experiences in fishing can match a day on the offshore grounds. Aside from the blue water, the herds of whales and porpoises and the feeling of adventure, there's the thrill of the hunt as the captain searches for signs of fish, the mate works his spread of lures or baits and the crew waits in anticipation of the first strike. When the action comes it is usually incredible.

Tuna crash baits like freight trains and first timers to the canyons are never fully prepared for the awesome power of these water-borne rocket ships. The sight of a white marlin dancing in the air is never easy to forget - thank goodness! The excitement and the heady thrills of battles with big fish combine into one of fishing's best examples of sport fishing.

Tuna

Shaped something like footballs with fins, the members of the tuna clan are all solid, speedy gamesters that have only one gear - full ahead. They can peel line off a reel at a frightening rate. They come in many sizes from five pound bonito to 1000 pound bluefins. All are dynamite on suitable tackle. The heavy weight giant bluefins have become scarce over the years, unfortunately, and most anglers concentrate on the smaller species both inshore and out at the canyons. However, each June a number of dedicated fishermen prepares their annual assault on the giant Atlantic bluefin tuna as these fish take up residence from New Jersey to Massachusetts. The bluefins could stay as long as a few weeks or be gone after a few days. This fishing is totally unpredictable.

Spreader bar rigs use rubber squids or fresh mackerel to imitate a school of bait. They drive giant bluefin tuna crazy.

The early season giant bluefin are trolled on spreader bar rigs, rigged with mackerel or squid, natural or artificial. The best of tuna skippers swear by the natural baits but many other tuna hunters take a good number of fish with artificial squids or mackerel rigged on the spreader bars.

The bars are about four feet wide and have anywhere from eight to eighteen baits hung from the arms and the center cable. Three rigs are trolled from 50 to 150 feet from the stern at about two to four knots, just enough speed so the rigs do not cartwheel or sink below the surface. When the strike comes, it is a humdinger. Even seasoned captains lose their cool as they shout "Fish on!!!"

Sometime after the initial run and certainly by the fall, most anglers after giants will chum from an anchored boat, much as they would fish for bluefish. In fact, bluefish are a nuisance to tuna fishermen. A soupy chum is used, usually ground bunker, is used by some captains while others prefer to toss handfuls of cut up chunks of bait to create an active slick. Live bait is preferred, with ling and whiting the favorites, but the realities of day to day fishing means most anglers use fresh dead mackerel, whiting, butterfish, bunker, ling or snapper blues. Live baits can often be caught on the bottom right under the boat. The baits are fished off of floats at several depths but one bait is usually fished on an active line that paid out by hand, then retrieved and paid out again so the bait is always moving.

Anglers work the lines while another cuts butterfish into chunks. A steady slick of chunk baits attracts giants to the hooked baits.

A heavy monofilament leader (300 pound test), not wire, is used because tuna don't have the dentures of sharks and they tend to be leader shy. Tackle for giants is usually 80 pound class or 130 pound class. Thousand pound bluefins are possible, though most will run 500 or less. Having a fighting chair aboard is a definite must for wrestling with one of these monsters. After the hookup, the anchor line is left on a buoy and the boat is free to follow the fish.

School bluefin are caught in good numbers along the coast from Virginia north to Massachusetts. Be careful not to take too many fish. Bluefin are regulated by the National Marine Fisheries Service and strict limits are enforced. The limits sometimes change, so I suggest you write to NMFS at their Gloucester, Massachusetts permit office and get a copy of the current regs and also to apply for a tuna permit in case you seek giants.

These small bluefins are taken on a wide variety of small trolling lures such as spoons, cedar plugs, plastic skirted lures and strip baits. Daisy chains of cedar plugs are very popular off Virginia while chains of tuna clones work their magic off the Jersey Coast. Spoons with a 3/4 ounce lead egg sinker wired to the nose of the spoon are old time favorites that have caught tuna for decades.

School bluefin and yellowfin tuna are caught on proven lures like cedar plugs, feathers, daisy chains of small lures, hex heads and spoons.

Small bluefins, false albacore and bonito will sometimes frequent the same waters as bluefish, with mixed catches not unusual in late summer and early fall. Both trolling and chumming are effective. The best baits when chumming are small fish such as spearing or sand eels on small hooks of size #1 to 2/0 hidden in the baits and tied directly to the mono line. A little weight may be needed to sink the offering so it stays in the slick level. Small split shots of 1/4 ounce rubber core sinkers do the trick to get below the surface layer.

When fish are active in the slick they will sometimes hit jigs and other lures. This is a perfect light tackle situation. Hook into a 10 pound school tuna on a one-handed spinning outfit and you'll be busy for quite a while.

Offshore Trolling

Trolling is another story. Because the boat is moving, and the fish may be charging in the other direction when it hits, stouter tackle is required. A 20 or 30 pound class outfit is adequate for inshore school tuna. Single tubes, plugs and spoons are common trolling lures. These are rigged on 5 to 8 foot mono leaders behind a trolling drail, a cigar-shaped sinker with swivels at both ends. Two flat lines, two over the stern corners and two outrigger lines is the usual arrangement. Multiple hookups provide plenty of excitement in the cockpit.

From Wachapreague to Cape Hatteras, spoons trolled off planers fool yellowfin and bigeye tuna of all sizes.

Favorite lure shapes include (top to bottom) concave chugger, flat face, elongated Yap style, angled face and bullet nose. They all make long jet streams of bubbles and catch tuna and billfish.

Moving a little farther offshore will turn up skipjacks, another small species of tuna. Skippies run five to ten pounds and like small spoons, feathers, vinyl skirts and tubes. If you run into a bunch of skipjacks and the water temperature is 75 degrees or slightly higher, be prepared for larger tunas - bigeye and yellowfin. The three species are often found in the same kind of water: 90 to 135 feet deep. While it is true that they are found in the greatest numbers out at the canyons, they will also move into shallower water in their never-ending search for food.

Out at the canyon proper the most popular way of fishing is fast-trolling artificial lures, like the types first developed in the Hawaiian Islands for tuna and marlin. The high speed lures from Mold Craft Soft Heads, Sir Ace Lures, Sevenstrand and a dozen other manufacturers are designed to swim erratically with a darting, skipping and diving action to create a commotion and attract game fish. Most are rigged on heavy mono with a single hook. Other good lures include Jap feathers, jets, daisy chains, squid spoons, cedar jigs, Jap bones, plastic squids and many varieties incorporating features of all these.

The beauty part of trolling artificials is being able to troll faster than when using natural baits, while mullet or ballyhoo, squid, eels or strip baits must be trolled fairly slow or they will break apart. And, natural baits require careful rigging and refrigeration. There's also the cost factor, and seasonal availability to consider.

Still, many of the best coastal fishermen, especially those who fish off Maryland and Virginia, prefer baits. There's no doubt that baits catch fish. Ballyhoo is the most popular bait, rigged on a wire or mono leader and with a skirted Sea Witch run down the leader over the nose of the bally to add color.

Artificials eliminate storage and deterioration problems. But the major advantage of fishing lures as opposed to baits is being able to cover more water by trolling faster, increasing the chances of finding fish in that tremendous expanse of ocean. It's fair to say that at least 75 percent of the fish caught out in the canyons are caught on artificials. All species of tuna, white and blue marlin, wahoo, dolphin and other pelagic predators fall victim to the metal and plastic lures.

The lures run from seven inches to twelve inches in total length and come in a rainbow of colors. Green, red, purple and blue are standards, but we've heard of good catches made on white, pink, yellow and black. Many skippers troll four to eight lines at a time so that the lures ride on the third, fourth and fifth waves of the boat's wash. When working right, the lures will be in the water about 80 percent of the time, the rest skipping and diving off the wave and into the trough.

Sometimes a large, hookless teaser is set in the wash close to the transom as an added attractor. One technique that has worked for us is to swim a lure on a flat line four or five feet behind the boat in the heavy white water prop wash. There have been times when this lure was high hook for

"W" trolling pattern

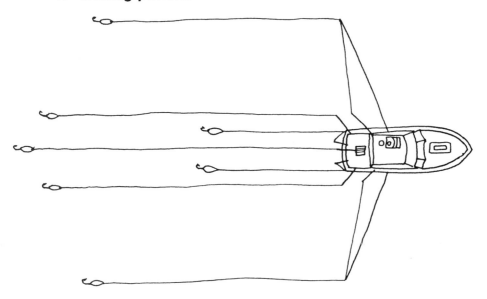

Lure position

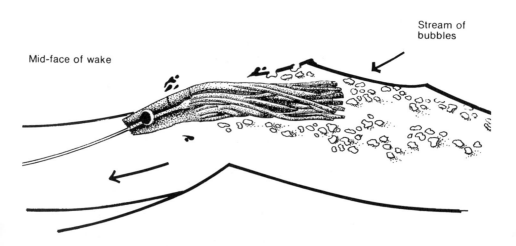

Stream of
bubbles

Mid-face of wake

the day. The boat's propeller(s) acts as a giant attractor. Very likely the fish have never seen a boat before and come by to investigate this new disturbance in their watery world. Then they spot the baits and remember they're hungry.

As a comparison of trolling speeds, three to six knots is routine when pulling natural baits; six to ten knots with lures. That's a big difference.

Lure hooks, of course, should be needle-sharp. There is no drop back as with natural baits. The fish crash the lure and are either hooked or off instantly. Fish in the 50 to 75 pound range are common, and 30 pound class or 50 pound class tackle is used. There's always a shot at a big bluefin, blue marlin or mako shark. However, most of the catch for northern boats will be made up of yellowfin and albacore tuna.

The pattern in the canyons seems to be that the yellowfin and bigeyes arrive early in May or June, depending on how far south you are. The albacore come up later when the water temperature reaches the 70 to 72 degree mark. Fishing in August and September can be fantastic and remain good through October, even into December off North Carolina's Outer Banks. One tip is to keep an eye on surface temperature. A difference of as little as one or two degrees on the low side from one spot to another can mean you're trolling in barren water.

Because of the great traveling distance involved in making a canyon trip, some boats stay out there over one or more nights, assuming of course their fuel capacity is adequate and weather permits. They drift at night with lights on.

If there's a snake in the fishing paradise, it's the weather. Seventy miles is a long way to buck heavy seas and headwinds. For obvious reasons, long-range weather forecasts are of prime importance to canyon runners. This is especially true in the fall when prevailing westerlies can roar and produce terrible conditions. Nevertheless, many anglers do make the trip gambling that a promised stretch of good weather will materialize and hold.

Chunking

Tuna fishing is always exciting but the chance to stand toe to toe with these amazing fish is especially thrilling. Called chunking, this method of bait fishing for tuna has proven successful from Virginia to Massachusetts. Depending upon where you actually fish, inshore or offshore, it's possible to use this method to catch yellowfin, bigeye, bluefin, long fin albacore and occasionally even billfish such as white marlin and swordfish, plus dolphin.

Most fishermen use tackle that is too heavy for the fish they intend to catch. Hefty rods and reels capable of handling 100 to 200 pound test line will usually "kill" the angler long before the fish is even beginning to tire. On the inshore grounds where most tuna will range from 15 to 75 pounds, 30

40 or 50 pound test tackle is ideal. In deeper water, 50, 60 or 80 pound tackle is usually preferred for the tuna running from 75 to 200 pounds.

Many big tuna have been taken on traditional star drag reels like the Penn Senators, but lever drag reels are the equipment of choice for charter captains and those who frequently fish for tuna. Two speed reels like the Penn 30SW and 50SW, and Shimano's Beastmaster series are preferred for 100 to 200 pound tuna and the ability to downshift to a lower gear saves the angler's strength while allowing the tuna to be lifted from deep water.

Rods with short lower butts and long grips ahead of the reel are ideal. Standard trolling tackle is usually unsuited for stand-up fishing except in the light tackle range. The short rods originated on the West Coast but local fishermen modified the basic concept to match the boats used in the Atlantic. Very short 4½ to 5 foot rods provide great leverage to lift big fish from deep water but offer no defense as tuna try to tangle lines in outboard lower units or inboard props and rudders. The best choice for East Coast tuna action are rods of 5½ to 6 feet to gain slight extra length to work the fish with maximum control.

Stand-up rods are rated for a range of pound test lines, such as 30 to 60 pound, or 40 to 80 pound line. A good rule of thumb when selecting a stand up rod for East Coast tuna is to use the lightest line rated for the rod. For instance a 40 to 80 pound class rod will work best with lines of 40 or 50 pound test.

Author fights an Outer Banks bigeye, stand-up style with gimbal belt and kidney harness.

Rigging for chunking will change with water clarity and how spooky the fish are from day to day. Most chunkers would prefer to add a heavier leader at the end of the line but when the fish are line-shy this isn't possible. Therefore, there are two choices; tie direct with no leader or add a leader to protect against cut-offs in battles that may last 15 to 45 minutes. Tuna can be notoriously line-shy so there are times when no leader can be used at all. We've had days when we had to go down to 30 pound test, tied direct to the hook, to score with line-shy tuna.

Most tuna chunkers prefer to use a leader at the end of the main fishing line and will select leaders about twice the strength of the main fishing line. With 30 pound line we use 50 or 60 pound test leaders. With 50 pound we go to 80 or 100 pound test.

A leader can be added in either of two ways. The first method uses a short bimini twist to make a two to four foot double line, then joins the leader to the double line with a surgeons knot. With this method the leader can be up to 10 feet long.

The second method adds a ball bearing swivel between the fishing line and the leader. A clinch knot secures the main line and leader to the swivel. In this case the leader should be four to six feet in length so the barrel swivel can be reeled right to the rod tip, placing the tuna within tagging or gaffing range without the need to handline any part of the leader. The swivel prevents line twist from spinning baits.

Several hook styles work well, including the Mustad 9175, 9174 and 94150; and the Eagle Claw #188. Use either bronze or silver finish hooks, sharpened to razor points. The size hook to choose depends on the size of the bait, not necessarily the size of the fish. Small chunks of butterfish work best with 3/0 to 5/0 hooks while a whole butter may get more hook-ups with a 5/0 to 9/0 size hook.

Hooks are attached to the leader or directly to the line with a palomar, improved clinch, or uni-knot. For bigeye tuna when heavy leaders are used, some fishermen prefer to use a small crimp to add the hook to the leader instead of a knot.

Chunking requires several sharp knives, cutting board, several five gallon buckets to store chunks and baits, two or more long handled gaffs, tail ropes, tuna bag, ice, boxes of hooks, coils of leaders, pliers, box of barrel swivels, split shot, egg sinkers, rubber core sinkers, anchor and line, leadering gloves, charts, note pad, tags, salt water wash down to clear decks and towels.

Butterfish, cut into chunks or fished whole is the bait most often used but bunker (menhaden), ling, whiting, large spearing and sandeels are also used. To hook a whole butterfish, insert the hook through the mouth and out the gill plate. Push the hook point cross ways through the body of the bait about 1/3 down the side of the butter fish. The leader should lie underneath the gill plate, the hook pulling against firm meat so the bait doesn't bend and the hook point is exposed. If the bait folds or bends the

Chunking Rigs

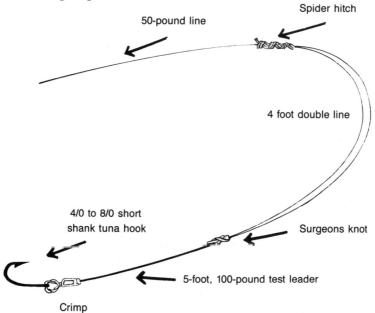

Spider hitch

50-pound line

4 foot double line

4/0 to 8/0 short shank tuna hook

Surgeons knot

5-foot, 100-pound test leader

Crimp

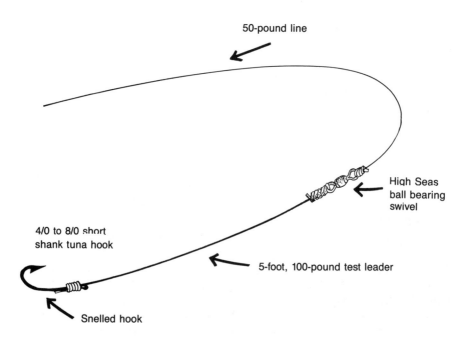

50-pound line

High Seas ball bearing swivel

4/0 to 8/0 short shank tuna hook

5-foot, 100-pound test leader

Snelled hook

hook is too far down the side of the fish.

Tuna follow the contours of the ocean bottom. Look for drop offs, ridges, sloughs, wrecks, lumps and the canyon edges. Warm water eddies usually hold fish. Whales, schools of bait and porpoises indicate "life" that may also attract tuna.

While whole butterfish are used as hooked baits, the chunk slick is made from sliced chunks of butters, bunker or sandeels; hence the name of the game - chunking. Depending on the size of the butters, three to five chunks can be cut from each fish. Butters are usually purchased frozen in 25 pound slabs packed in flat boxes. Each flat will last from one to two hours depending on how heavily the angler chunks.

We usually chunk lightly but occasionally toss in a large handful of bait if the action is slow. The idea is to attract the tuna to the boat where they can eat the baited hooks. Too heavy a chunk slick keeps the tuna far back and away from the boat and out of range of the hooked baits.

When tuna show in the slick and boil behind the boat, it can pay to toss extra chunks to get a feeding frenzy started. Any hooked bait tossed into the slick at this time will usually get smashed immediately.

NOAA navigation charts can be enhanced by using colored Magic Markers to trace over contour lines so bottom structure stands out for easy viewing.

On a boat with three fishermen, two anglers will fish while one will chunk. The chunker should toss several chunks in a pattern around the boat watching to see how the chunks drift with the tide or current. As the first set of chunks disappears from view into the water, another set of chunks is presented. The rhythm is continued until tuna invade the slick and attack the baits.

The rod is placed in a flush mount gun'l rod holder, the reel is in free spool with only slight tension on the spool to prevent a backlash at the strike. The angler stands along side of and slightly ahead of the rod and reel. Line is pulled hand over hand, a foot or two at a time so the bait drifts back into the slick with no resistance from the line but not too fast to cause excess slack line. After 30 to 80 pulls with no strike, the bait is retrieved. A fast retrieve may cause excessive line twist so go easy. A favorite trick of ours is to retrieve the bait with just enough tension on the reel spool to allow the line to be slowly wound on the reel. Sometimes tuna attack these backward swimming butters.

At the strike, the angler turns to the rod and reel, lifting tho taoklc from the rod holder with the left hand ahead of the reel the right hand on the butt below the reel. The right hand guides the rod butt into the gimbal belt, the left hand keeps the rod tip parallel to the water. The right hand slides the lever forward putting the reel into gear then reels until the line comes tight then the left hand lifts the rod tip smartly to set the hook. At the strike both

Working the lines

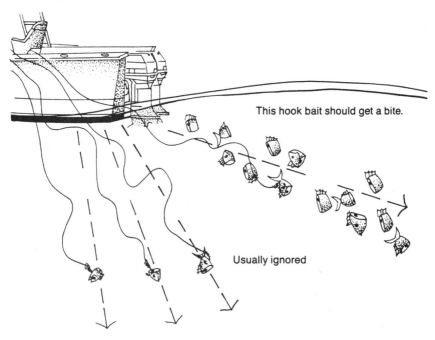

This hook bait should get a bite.

Usually ignored

hands are needed to hang on!!! With practice this takes a scant two to three seconds to work the strike smoothly and with a positive hookup. Too much delay may cause a lost fish.

For truly big fish that may take more than 10 to 15 minutes to land, a buddy should help the angler get into a kidney harness that attaches to lugs on the reel and provides support across the angler's back. By rocking back and forth and using legs and lower back, the fisherman raises the rod tip to lift the fish and lowers the rod tip to reel in line. This pumping action gains line quickly with little strain. Especially tough fish are short stroked with a rapid rocking motion gaining line a few inches at a time by putting the fish off balance.

Tuna caught while chunking are notoriously "green" when brought to the side of the boat. Their power is amazing and many captains have stories of gaffs ripped from strong hands as tuna tried to escape. Tagged fish should be estimated in length, tagged near the dorsal fin and the leader cut close to the mouth quickly with a sharp knife, not pliers.

Fish meant for the table should be gaffed near the head to save the most meat. A six to eight foot long gaff with a four inch bite of 1/2 inch stainless is about perfect. Heavy fish can be lifted into the boat with a tail rope. Once on board, a tap in the noggin with a billy club calms the fish as it's slid into the ice bag or cooler. Decks should be cleaned right away to get back in action quickly.

The chunker must continue chunking all through the battle and boat side antics. If not, a new slick will have to be started.

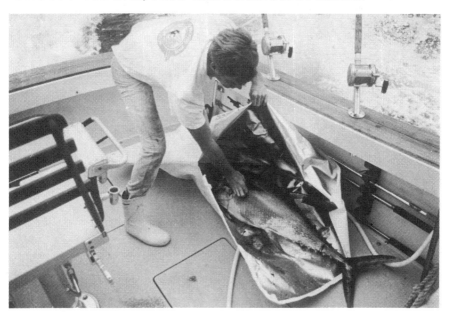

Insulated fish bags, stuffed with ice, are a handy way to protect delicious tuna from spoiling on the ride home.

It's easier and safer to drop the anchor from the stern, after tying the tag end to the bow cleat. As the anchor line comes tight, the boat swings around so bow is pointed at the anchor.

Use a special anchor at least one size larger than the safety anchor mounted on the bow. A ten foot chain helps grab bottom. The anchor line should be long enough to be two to three times the depth of the water. We rig two anchor lines; one of 400 feet to anchor in water of 120 to 180 feet and a second line of 800 feet for deep water of 250 to 350 feet. They are stored in large laundry baskets and washed after each trip.

It is important to anchor securely so the anchor and rode does not slip causing the boat to slide into another boat or another boat's slick. Use a heavy anchor and a long chain.

Lobster pots are private property and should not be disturbed without permission. The facts are, however, that many tuna fishermen use the lobster pot markers to "get on the ball" for the night's action. If you must do this, use a long line to attach the high flyer marker. Attach the line with a large stainless snap below the float at the bottom of the high flyer. Use a line of at least 200, preferable 300 feet in length to dampen the rocking action of the boat against the lobster pot line.

Try drifting. The tuna chunking action while on a drift can be spectacular and there's damage to anyone's expensive lobster gear.

Wahoo

Although wahoo are related to the tunas, I've placed them in a separate category because there are several things that make wahoo unusual. They aren't generally caught in great numbers, but there are times when they can be found in loose schools and a single boat may catch several fish. They are technically a mackerel and are the largest of this family. They are lean, mean fish machines capable of making exceptionally fast runs and they are absolutely among the finest eating fish you can ever serve for dinner. They have a set of teeth like razors and demand caution when handling on deck.

Typically, wahoo will average 20 to 40 pounds, but they do grow to much larger sizes. I've boated wahoo over 80 pounds and the world record stands at 155 pounds 8 ounces caught by Bill Bourne while fishing off San Salvador in the Bahamas. The women's 30 pound class record was taken off Cape May, New Jersey by Charlene Mascuch in 1977. Her wahoo tipped the scales at 108 pounds 9 ounces, a tremendous catch on relatively light tackle.

Fishermen off Virginia and the Carolina Outer Banks catch fair numbers of wahoo each season. The farther north you go, however, the fewer the wahoo. Boats from Delaware to Massachusetts depend upon the presence of a warm water, Gulf Stream eddy to bring wahoo within catching range. It is not unusual to hear of a few wahoo being caught in August and September when offshore waters reach the high 70 degree range.

Wahoo are hard fighters, they grow to large sizes and are absolutely delicious as dinner fare.

Wahoo are usually caught by accident, that is, when we fish for tuna we often stumble across a wahoo and are pleasantly surprised by the unique fish. They do seem to have a preference for darker lures and those wahoo that I've taken have been on black and red, or blue and red flat faced lures.

Some fishermen believe that wahoo hit best on sub surface lures and will therefore place one weighted lure in their pattern, a lure that may weigh four to eight ounces and will run several feet deep. Another popular style lure is the Boone Cairns Swimmer and the Murray Brothers Terminator. Both lures swim deep and can attract wahoo like bees to honey. Ed Murray showed me one of his Terminators a customer had returned with a note confirming the lure had caught over 50 wahoo. It was all chewed to heck but was still fishable and drew a lot of interest as visiting fishermen asked about the tooth-slashed lure hanging on the wall. It sure helped sell more Terminators!

Marlin

The grandest of the billfish along the mid-Atlantic Coast is the broad-shouldered blue marlin. They can exceed 1,000 pounds but the average blue weighs in closer to 250 to 400 pounds - still quite a handful. While white marlin might be considered abundant in some parts of their range, blues are scattered and seen much less frequently, even on the best marlin grounds.

Comparing a white marlin to a blue marlin is like comparing a leopard to a lion. The smaller animals may give away poundage, but never underestimate their fighting spirit. The average 50 pound white is an ocean jewel sparkling in the sun as it leaps time and again. It is the favorite fish of deep sea sportsmen who prefer to use light trolling tackle offshore. In fact, no fewer than 15 different tournaments celebrating the white marlin are held annually along the eastern seaboard.

At times a white marlin, or a blue, will crash a lure as if starved. Other times they will respond only if teased, especially when coming to natural baits. This uncertainty about what the fish will do adds to the allure of marlin fishing.

Marlin are individuals and their behavior is unpredictable. Unlike tuna, marlin tend to be loners. Since there are many more of the former in canyon waters, they usually find the lures before the billfish. Few fishermen will leave a school of cooperative yellowfins to resume blind trolling in hopes of finding an elusive marlin. This makes for a curious "problem," but a realistic one. It takes rare discipline and dedication to become a successful marlin specialist. It also takes a lot of money. After all, you're out there burning expensive fuel followed by more hours of trolling the first tuna that hits is most welcome, as are his brothers and sisters. For most anglers a marlin is a surprise bonus, or icing on the cake.

The tail-walking antics of white marlin are a memorable sight on the offshore grounds.

Billfish Baits

Marlin, especially the "white ones" are more attracted to baits instead of lures. My favorite rig is a ballyhoo fished on a mono leader with an egg sinker just ahead of the hook to make it swim like it's alive.

The monofilament rig is easy to make and at the same time it avoids the hassles of single strand wire that can kink badly. To make up mono rigs you need 7/0 or 8/0 Mustad #7731 round eye hooks, 125 pound test mono, Hi-Seas 1.2 mm crimps, #7 wire, 3/4 ounce egg sinkers, crimping pliers, rubber bands or copper rigging wire. For tuna, substitute 200 pound test mono and Hi-Seas 1.8 mm crimps.

Pull off 15 feet of leader. At one end, slide on a crimp, then the egg sinker and then the hook. Fold the end of the leader back over itself and push the tag end through the egg sinker. Slip the crimp onto the tag end and slide the crimp and sinker toward the hook until only a small loop is left at the hook eye. Before crimping the sleeve, cut a one inch length of #7 wire and bend it to form an "L". Slide one end of the "L" into the crimp

A swimming ballyhoo rig uses an egg sinker ahead of the hook to keep the nose of the bait down so it swims with life-like action.

Most ballyhoo rigs are finished off by sliding an Iland lure or a sea witch skirt down the leader and over the front of the bait.

so the exposed part of the wire forms a point at 90 degrees to the hook eye. Crimp the sleeve in place.

The rig can be fished "naked" or color can be added. Sea Witches are a favorite of many captains and are found in a wide variety of colors. Sea Witches are the nylon haired trolling lures with the longer hair of the facing forward. When the rig is trolled the hair folds back over the lure and bait, pulsating in a breathing rhythm. Small vinyl skirts can also be added or small lures like the Mold Craft Hookers, feathers or Tuna Clones.

With the bally in your left hand, bill pointing away from you, lift the right gill flap and insert the hook point. As the hook is pushed into the bait, bend the bait to follow the curve of the hook until the point exits just behind the pectoral fins. Push the small wire pin through the nose of the bally. Use a rubber band or a length of copper rigging wire to secure the nose and bill to the leader. Break off the end of the bill. Slide the skirt into place and you are ready to troll.

It's best to rig a few dozen baits ahead of time, stored in a small cooler half filled with ioo. Lay a towel over the ice then lay the rigged baits on the towel. Sprinkle with kosher salt to toughen the bait and the silver bullets are ready to fool tuna and billfish.

Swordfish

The swordfish is the most secretive of the billfishes, and it is believed that swordfish are largely nocturnal, feeding deep on squid and other bait. Yet, swordfish are fond of basking on the surface on calm days. Their distinctive dorsal and tail can be spotted at a long distance. They can be approached cautiously and a bait presented. They are not as apt to hit a fast lure and whole natural baits are preferred by swordfishermen. A large squid, mackerel or five pound skipjack rigged on large double hooks is pulled in front of the lazing fish. If the fish sounds it may mean that it's interested and will come up to slash the bait with that broad bill. Or it can mean the swordfish has been spooked. Fishing for swordfish on the surface can be extremely frustrating and unrewarding. Fishing at night, however, is another story.

Canyon anglers who drift after dark and fish squid baits in conjunction with Cyalume light stick 100 to 200 feet down do fairly well with swordfish. In fact, the New Jersey survey showed that conventional trolling produced swordfish only one percent of the time. Drifting at night, however, resulted in swordfish catches on 12 percent of the trips. These swords averaged 188 pounds each, but some brutes can weigh 500 pounds or more.

Night swordfishermen usually fish three weighted lines. One is set with the bait at 50 feet, another at 100 and the third down 150 to 200 feet. A Cyalume light stick is tied to the swivel with thin line or a rubber band that will break after a fish is hooked. The nightstick glows and acts as a beacon for wandering fish.

Leader length is 15 to 30 feet of heavy monofilament. Swordfish have very soft mouths so large hooks are used; 12/0 or 14/0. The bait may be a large, whole fresh squid, whole bonito or other small tuna, a skipjack fillet strip bait or a live bait.

Reels are left in free spool with the clickers on. It's a relaxing kind of fishing. The rods are in holders and all the angler does is sit back and wait for that electrifying sound of line being pulled off a reel.

As in any kind of bait fishing, the lines should be checked occasionally for weeds and to replace the baits with fresh ones. It pays to experiment with different baits at different depth. Radio chatter from other boats may tip you off to the best combination that night. You may fish all night and not get a touch. Or a fish may hit the first bait as it's sinking.

Swordfish are prized as food and few are released. Marlin, on the other hand, are being tagged and released in greater numbers each year, with more sportsmen coming to realize these fish are more valuable alive in their natural element than hanging from some dock scale.

You may find other games out at the edge of the shelf. A stray sailfish, wahoo at times, a rare kingfish up from the Carolinas, and a variety of sharks could provide surprises. The extremely colorful dolphin (the fish, not the mammal more correctly called a porpoise) are relatively abundant at the edge of the shelf. From small school fish called "grasshoppers" to hefty fish of better than 30 pounds, the dolphin provide excitement and good eating.

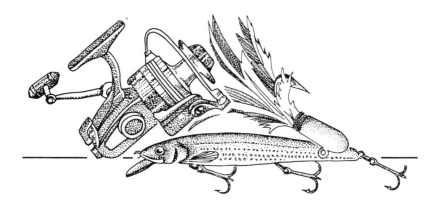

Chapter Seven

BLACKFISH AND SEA BASS

These two bottom fish have always been crowd-pleasers. And, no wonder, there are usually plenty of them around, they're easy to catch and good to eat. Both have similar habits although differing considerably in appearance. The sea bass is a distant relative of striped bass with a striper-like head and mouth, but its body is dark and chunky with oversize fins. The blackfish always reminds me of a bulldog - stout, compact with a no-nonsense set of choppers in its mouth.

They can be caught in rivers and bays where rocky or gravel bottoms are available, or around bridges where they make the pilings their home. They are also numerous on many inshore areas, especially where there are rocky jetties like Delaware's extensive breakwaters around Lewis Beach or the many jetties that dot the coastal beaches and inlets.

Fishermen willing to make short offshore runs to the deeper water wrecks finds sea bass and blackfish in good numbers and in some terrific sizes. The world's record blackfish was caught off Wachapreague, Virginia in 1987 by Greg Bell and weighed 24 pounds! Records aren't kept for sea bass but catches of better than six pounds have been reported.

Sea Bass

The Black Sea Bass (Centropristas striatus) is found from Massachusetts to northern Florida, with the center of fishing activity concentrated from New York to North Carolina. The species is migratory, spending the winter offshore and moving close to shore and into bays and rivers during the warm weather months. The larger sea bass remain on offshore wrecks down to 100 feet, whereas the smaller ones move into bays and sounds but tend to stay in the deeper channel waters.

A mixed bag of blackfish, sea bass and a few porgies is a typical late summer catch from rocky bottom or mussel bed areas.

Even a big sea bass seldom weighs over five pounds. Most average a pound and a half, with bay fishing reaching half that size. Where light tackle can be used, sea bass are sporty to catch, putting up a scrappy struggle. However, the facts of sea bass fishing often necessitate using several ounces of sinker weight, especially when fishing over a deep wreck with a strong current being pushed by the wind. Conventional boat tackle with 20 pound test line is most practical for ocean fishing.

The easiest way to catch sea bass or blackfish is to go aboard a party boat that specializes in seasonal bottom fishing. The skipper will know which wrecks and bottom structure are producing fish, according to what's running at the time. He'll position and anchor the boat so his fares will drop baits into good water. Meanwhile, deckhands will pass out bait, usually sea clams for sea bass.

Rigging is kept simple because some losses are inevitable when fishing on wrecks. It pays to use two hooks on short leaders. Sea bass are bait stealers so, if you miss with the first bait, you may catch the fish on the second. And, double-headers are possible.

The basic rig is the old reliable 3-way swivel with a short length of sinker line, 12 inches of leader and hook, with a second leader hook tied in with a second swivel about 24 inches above. Sea bass do stick to the bottom but will come up a few feet for a bait.

The sinker weight should be heavy enough to feel it bounce on the bottom, but not excessive. Hook sizes of 2/0 or 4/0 are fine since sea bass have relatively large mouths. Leaders are usually of 20 to 30 pound test, but a handy tip uses a lighter pound test line to attach the sinker. When hooked into the rocks or a wreck, the lighter line breaks and the rest of the rig is saved.

Rigs for bay or river fishing for sea bass are similar but scaled proportionately for the smaller fish. Look for sea bass on hard bottoms containing rocks, broken stone or shellfish beds. They also hang out near wrecks, dock pilings, piers and trestles that have been there long enough to support many barnacles and mussels.

Blackfish - sea bass two hook rig

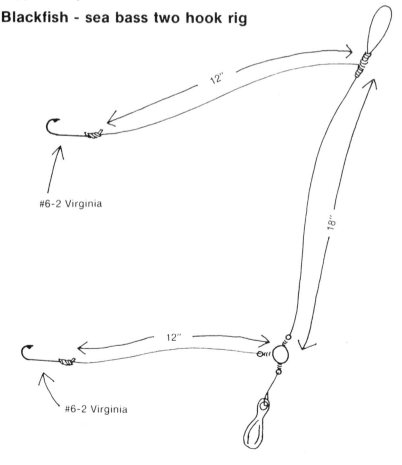

12"

#6-2 Virginia

18"

12"

#6-2 Virginia

Anchoring position

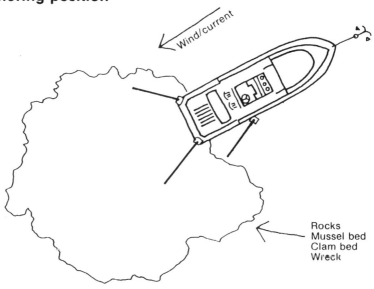

Rocks
Mussel bed
Clam bed
Wreck

When you feel a nibble, give the fish time to mouth the bait. But don't wait too long or you'll be left with a bare hook. Work out the timing for yourself. Nobody can describe exactly how to tell when it's time to lift the rod tip. But if you wait until you feel a couple of good tugs, that's usually the signal to strike. You're not hooking a shark, so only a short, quick snap of the rod is needed.

Sea bass have 10 sharp, spiny rays along the dorsal and sharp gill covers so some care should be exercised when handling them as you remove a hook or transfer them from the cooler to the cleaning table.

Sea bass are excellent on the table. The flesh is firm and white and suitable for many kinds of preparation. I prefer to fillet and skin the sea bass, but some folks choose to scale or skin them and bake them whole. The hazardous dorsal spines can be removed by running a knife along both sides of the back, close to the spines and then lifting the dorsal fin out. Small sea bass could be considered as salt water panfish, well worth their cleaning regardless of their size.

Blackfish

In New Jersey it's called a blackfish. In New England it's known as a tautog. In Virginia they're called taug or chubs. Ichthyologists call them Tautoga onitis. Whatever you choose to call them, blackfish are a very interesting fish and a pleasure to have in our waters. Most fishermen know this fish as the blackfish or "tog". No matter what you call them they are great sport and great eating at the dinner table.

This member of the wrasse family appears rather dull with a plain, leathery-looking hide and a goofy expression. However, inside that ordinary exterior is a fish that will challenge any jetty jockey or boat fisherman. Blackfish can grow to weigh over 20 pounds, but the average is probably closer to four pounds. Whatever their size, they possess surprising strength. Blackfish are challenging because of where they live and how they feed. They love rocks, the more jumbled, the better.

An old tog will know every inch of its rock pile and at the first hint of trouble will dash into the nearest opening. The fish are in the rocks because that's where the food is. Tog eat crustaceans and shellfish, with crabs and mussels heading their menu. The mouth and teeth of a black-

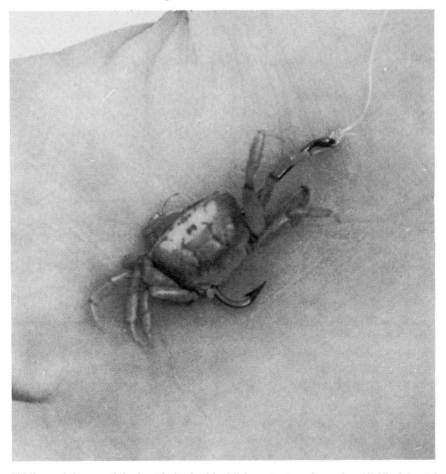

Fiddler crab is one of the best baits for blackfish, or tautog. A number 1/0 Virginia style hook is preferred.

103

fish are perfectly adapted to nibbling at mussels slinging to slippery rocks, or crunching any crab caught in the open. Its lips are rubbery and thick, hiding a set of big buck teeth backed by crusher teeth. They can grind up a hard crab and spit out the pieces of shell in a wink. The crab meat, of course, stays inside the tog.

The blackfish could have been designed by hook and sinker manufacturers, then given a bonus. Expect to lose rigs, lots of them, when you go blackfishing. If you're not getting snagged regularly you're not fishing right.

Tautog often take up residence around dock pilings and are readily caught by shore-based anglers.

You've got to put the bait in the tog's lap to ring its dinner bell. And you'll need tackle stout enough to turn its head and keep it coming after you've hooked the fish. Let a tog have the advantage of diving under a rock and that's all she wrote. Say goodbye to the fish and your rig.

We don't mean to scare you off blackfish, but there are places where the fish has the upper hand to start with. Offshore, blacks frequent wrecks, broken bottom and mussel beds. They also like jetties with a good depth around them at high tide, bridge abutments, inlet breakwaters and any rocky islands. Find an area with lots of mussels and chances are the blackfish know about them too.

Although not strictly school fish, tog of the same size tend to be found together. In some places they'll all run around three pounds; in another spot they may average five or six. Ten pounders are fairly common and we've seen several 12 and 14 pounds come off of party boats.

The Atlantic Coast is home to some highly talented party boat skippers who can put a 70 foot boat over a wreck with the precision of a bricklayer. They have a mental picture of the bottom on their fishing grounds based on years of experience. Private boaters can also get in on the wreck action. A depth recorder is essential to pinpoint specific bottom acreage. Bow and stern anchors will keep the boat from swinging out of position.

Anchoring Near a Bridge

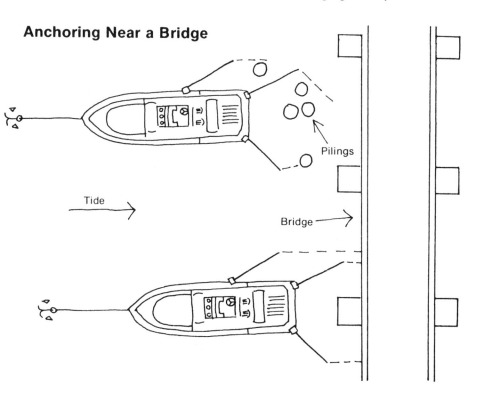

Tide →

Pilings

Bridge →

Wreck fishermen use a standard anchor, a grapling hook and marker buoys to find offshore wrecks and to hold the boat in position.

Blackfish regulars often use concrete blocks or other "throw-aways" for anchors in case they have to leave them down there. They'll also use a thinner, cheaper rope on those occasions.

We've mentioned that blackfish have comparatively small mouths for their bulk. You need a hook that will accommodate a half a green crab bait, penetrate quickly, yet not tear the soft flesh around the fish's mouth. We've used the Virginia style hooks for many years and prefer them for all our togging. Others go with the Pacific style bass hook. Try them both and decide for yourself.

Hook sizes (Virginia style) #7 to 1/0 will cover most blackfishing situations. The larger sizes are tied on when we're fishing an area known for larger blacks, and the small size for fishing coastal rock piles and inlets. In any case, carry at least a dozen rigs and plenty of dipsey or bank sinkers in several sizes.

I use a simple rig, just like the one for sea bass, except I leave off the top hook. A second hook is too likely to snag on the rocks. The list of blackfish baits is a short one. Clams, worms, mussels, green crabs, fiddler crabs and sand bugs are most common. Each area has its own favorite tog bait. Try what the local experts use and how they rig it. We've had good luck with green crabs; fiddlers, too.

The fiddlers are fished whole after breaking off the big claw. Most green crabs are too big to be used whole, so cut them in half, or even quarters if very large. Remove the legs and claws and peel off the top shell. Run the point of the hook through one of the leg sockets to secure the bait.

Green crabs can be bought at bait shops in good tog country, but many anglers catch their own fiddlers. They look for small round holes about the size of nickels in muddy marsh banks at the waterline. A pitchfork is jabbed into the bank and shaken. If the crabs are home, bright yellow claws will emerge from the holes. Grab the claw and the crab is yours.

There's an art to hooking blackfish. Old-timers claim you have to hook them before you feel the tap. That's an exaggeration, of course, but it takes concentration. Usually there'll be a little tap as the tog nips at the bait. He's tasted it and passing it back to the crushers. When you feel a solid pull, rear back on the rod. You'll miss many fish, everybody does, but other times you'll feel that exciting power of a blackfish as it tries to pull its way back to the rocks.

Blackfish are excellent eating. Most togs are skinned and baked whole, or used in fish chowder in chunk form. Some anglers, myself included, prefer to fillet and skin the fish as they would any round fish. Make a cut along both sides of the dorsal fin and behind the gill covers to the pelvic fins. Cutting downward will free the slab of fillet with a few bones attached to the belly cavity. Cut these away. Lay the fillet skin side down and work a knife edge between the skin and the flesh at one end. With a sawing motion push on the knife and the skin should come away easily.

I cut the fillets into pieces to fit the fry pan and cook them as we would flounder. Fillets can also be steamed, broiled or baked. Many anglers claim blackfish are among the best eating of all our saltwater fish.

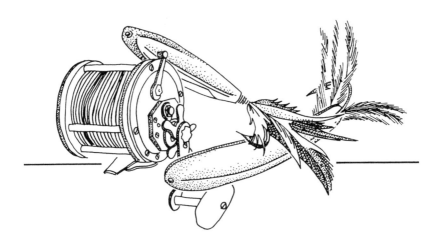

Chapter Eight

COD AND POLLOCK, LING AND WHITING

This group of bottom fish are usually found in cooler waters from Delaware to Massachusetts. They range in size from the smallish whiting and ling that rarely exceed a few pounds to the cod and pollock that grow to tackle busting size of better than 60 and 40 pounds, respectively. These are the "big boys" for the party boat fans and they draw customers from far and wide. Many small boaters also fish for them and they can provide great sport at many offshore wrecks. Often thought of as winter fish, the cold layer of bottom waters found in 30 or more fathoms of depth will hold these fish all through the summer months. If you can find offshore wrecks, you can bet you'll find some action.

Cod have been rumored to exceed the one hundred mark and a number of hefty fish have been documented by commercial fishermen. The all-tackle world record is held by Al Bielevich for an impressive 98 pound 12 ounce cod that was taken at Isle of Shoals off New England waters in 1969. The heaviest pollock ever weighed in by a rod and reel fisherman was caught off Brielle, New Jersey in 1975 by John Holton. His big pollock tipped the scales at 46 pounds 7 ounces.

On the inshore grounds, all of these fish are most abundant through the fall, winter and early spring. As long as they're not iced in at their berths, party boats fish all winter. Modern party boats have heated cabins and even heated rails to lean against. If the seas are moderate and the wind slight, mid-winter fishing can be pleasant if the angler dresses properly.

Long johns, insulated boots, wool pants and shirt, gloves and hat, a parka and a large thermos of scalding bouillon are called for. On some days you won't need all that clothing, but it's best to go prepared. You can always shed some, but if you leave it behind and need it you're out of luck. It's not much fun to have to sit in the cabin watching others catching fish.

Cod

Thankfully, cod are making a comeback in local waters; no doubt a result of the 200-mile limit imposed on foreign draggers and haul seiners. The offshore wrecks host the biggest cod, partly because of the greater food supply at those depths, and partly because of less fishing pressure there. On open bottom, cod show a preference for rough, sandy and rocky surfaces with shellfish beds. Until cod increase in numbers and fill those old habitats, most anglers will head for familiar wrecks. Some of these lie a considerable distance from shore and several large party boats make special long-range trips, and advance reservations are necessary. It's first-come, first-served on routine, daily trips.

Most of this is deep water fishing and stout tackle is needed. Cod regulars like jigging sticks built on 30 pound class blanks, and they'll use

Heavy jigs that weigh from 8 to 16 ounces are used for deep water cod and pollock.

a 3/0 or 4/0 size fast retrieve conventional reel filled with 40 pound test monofilament line.

Cod are taken on bait herring, sand eels, clams - or on jigging lures and tubes. Jig sizes are determined by the depth and tide. Ten to 16 ounces are normal. The banana-shaped jigs are used in combination with two or more surgical tube teasers in red, yellow or fluorescent red or green.

The jig is lowered until it hits bottom then reeled up a few feet and worked by raising the rod quickly and lowering it so the jig falls on a slack line. Cod may hit on the rise or fall. A cod may look sluggish but will charge what appears to be a small group of baitfish.

The other standard method is using a high-low double-hook rig with bait. Sinker weight is usually 8 to 16 ounces and bait holder hook sizes range from 7/0 to 9/0. Some cod experts use only one hook on an 18-inch leader attached four feet above the sinker, claiming they get hung up less and catch just as many fish their way.

Cod High-Low Rig

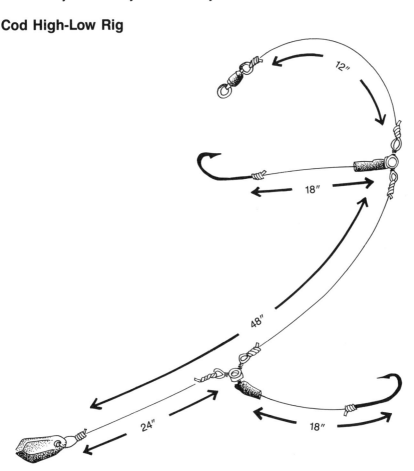

Cod High Rig

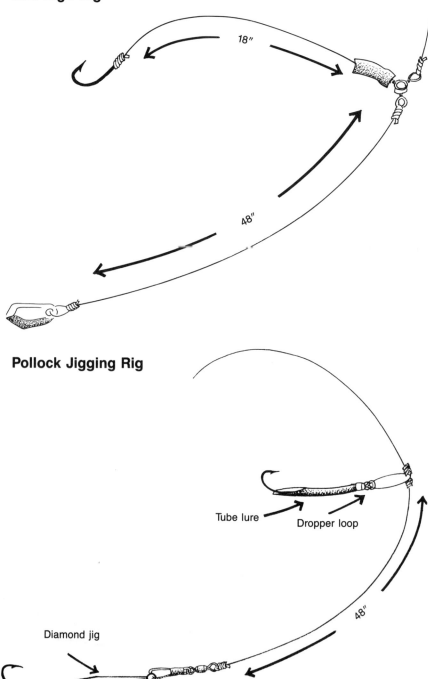

18"

48"

Pollock Jigging Rig

Tube lure

Dropper loop

48"

Diamond jig

Pollock

Many deep water bottom fishermen consider the pollock to be the ultimate catch. They fight hard, hit artificial jigs readily and grow to respectable size. Believe me, a 25 or 30 pound pollock can fight like crazy and they are therefore, a lot of fun to catch.

Unlike the cod that has more northern range, pollock show up in catches of Delaware and Maryland party boats when they wreck fish in the winter months. They have been known to be found as far south as North Carolina but their primary range is Maryland to New England.

Pollock will take many of the same baits and lures as cod but they also take positions in the upper water levels above a wreck, while cod are usually found much closer, even in the wreck. Pollock are frequently caught as a heavy jig is first dropped down to the wreck, many times the jig only makes it 30 to 50 feet below the surface before it is walloped by a pollock.

Years ago when pollock were much more abundant, before the intense commercial fishing fleets overfished most of our offshore species, pollock could some times be found crashing baits on top, splashing a lot of water and looking much like feeding bluefish. For this reason old timers often nicknamed the pollock, Boston blues. This still happens today, but not as frequently.

Pollock, large or small, are fine eating. Be sure to ice the catch immediately.

Ling & Whiting Rig

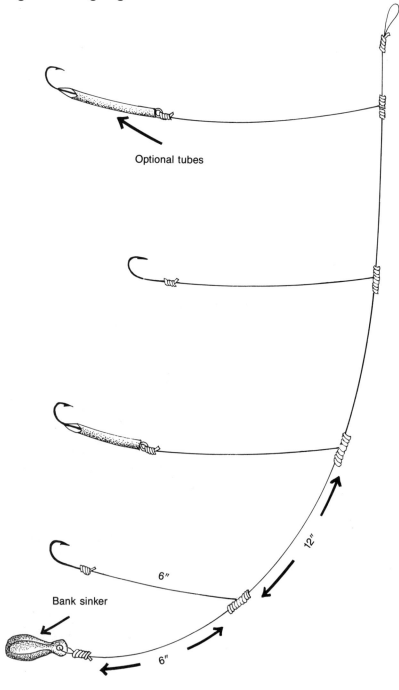

Optional tubes

Bank sinker

6″

12″

6″

Ling/Whiting

Officially, ling are red hake, and whiting are silver hake, but let's not get involved in proper names. They compliment each other like franks and beans and anglers lump them together when talking about bottom fishing. Ling hug the bottom but whiting are usually found slightly higher in the water column. Drop a jig to the bottom and a ling will jump on it, keep the jig a few feet off the bottom and whiting will attack it. Whiting are more active, sometimes coming within range of shore casters. It's common to catch them from piers and jetties on cold winter nights. Whiting are more predatory than ling and will chase baitfish.

I like to fish for them in late November and through December from my own boat. The fish are in shallower water and lighter tackle can be used; the same outfit used for jigging weakfish. Often, we'll use multiple-hook rigs and load up for the freezer. Neither species is known for its fighting qualities, but both are delicious eating, especially smoked whiting. For frying, I prefer ling for its sweeter taste.

Fishing for ling and whiting from a party boat is basic sinker bouncing. Keep one bait near the bottom for ling and tie the second two or three feet higher for whiting. Squid strips, clams or a piece of herring or whiting belly are all good.

A standard boat rod and reel with 20 pound test mono is all you need. A favorite bluefish chumming outfit will do fine for this fishing. Sinker weights from three to six ounces and a supply of 4/0 hooks complete the rig.

Fish the rig so that it just touches bottom and give it a little lift now and again. The slight movement seems to draw more strikes. When you feel several steady pulls, set up with the rod and crank the fish to the surface. Swing the fish over the rail and grab it with a hand towel. Ling tend to be slimy and whiting have sharp spines. A burlap bag tied to the rail is handy for holding your catch.

There's one thing about fishing in the wintertime, you don't have to worry about fish spoiling from the heat. However, temperatures could hit the 70s on an early spring day with bright sunshine and no wind. Then it pays to clean and cool your catch as the day progresses.

You'll probably go back for a repeat trip once you've tried ling and whiting fishing. It's not fancy, but it sure beats painting the kitchen or cleaning out the garage on a winter's day.

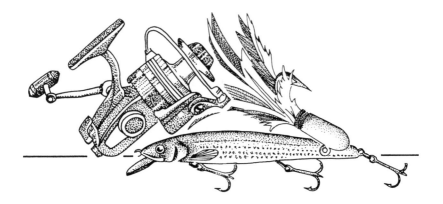

Chapter Nine

RED DRUM AND BLACK DRUM

Fishing for these giant members of the croaker family is pretty much centered in the mid Atlantic region from Delaware Bay down the coast into Chesapeake Bay and especially along the North Carolina Outer Banks. They are caught accidentally in southern Jersey waters, but they are rarely ever caught further north. The huge size of these fish, however, draws anglers from New England and the Midwest in a spring time quest for these hefty, hard fighters. Check the license plates at Delaware Bay or Chesapeake Bay marinas during black drum season and you are likely to find fishermen from Michigan and New England along with the local boys.

They seem to get more attention from surf fishermen, and indeed, the red drum is one of the all time great catches to be made while fishing from the beach. Black drum are more numerous than many anglers believe, and in Delaware Bay and Chesapeake Bay they are usually caught from boats by bait fishermen.

One of the prettiest places in the world to catch both species is the Virginia Outer Banks from Chincoteague south to the Bay Bridge Tunnel. These Outer Banks are owned primarily by the Nature Conservancy and will remain forever wild and natural. You have to get to one of the island by boat, then pull the boat up on the beach and hike across the islands to the surf on the east side, but it is well worth it. This is one place in America where you can fish without seeing many people, and the solitude is exceptionally pleasing.

Red Drum

Known by many names, the red drum is one of the premier game fish along the Atlantic Coast. Depending on where you fish for him, this fish may be called channel bass, red, redfish or just drum, although the last name may cause some confusion with its close cousin the black drum. The weakfish and seatrout are also related to the channel bass and the males of these species can all make croaking noises to call one another.

Dave Duel caught the biggest red drum on record at Avon, North Carolina. His remarkable catch weighed 94 pounds 2 ounces. Virginia waters gave up the men's 8 and 12 pound class records with fish of 69 pounds 3 ounces by John Everett and a 57 pounder by Hans Gabler. These fish came from Gwynn's Island and Wreck Island, respectively.

Red drum are most common from Delaware to Florida. Years ago there was a viable red drum fishery in south Jersey and each spring a number of good sized reds would be caught in the surf at Cape May and also in Great Bay at Graveling Point. Some still are caught in these waters but they are far from numerous, a rarity rather than a common occurrence. Montauk surf fishermen of the 1940s and 50s used to catch an occasional red drum but these, too, are now just a memory.

If you want big red drum, it's best to fish from Chincoteague, Virginia south to Virginia Beach or the Carolina Outer Banks. Smaller fish can be caught in the lower reaches of Chesapeake Bay and occasionally in Delaware Bay. Several years ago I caught a puppy drum while bucktailing for weakfish at Brandywine Light in Delaware Bay. The surprise catch was duplicated by another nearby boat but that was the only two fish caught on

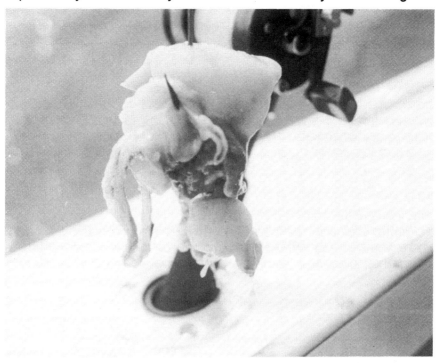

A big glob of surf clam is sure to entice a red drum, or black drum, to take the hook.

that tide. Perhaps there are more there, but the weakfish get the attention and few reds are caught.

Comparatively little is known about the red drum by biologists and efforts are underway to increase the store of knowledge about these fish. Commercial pressure in southern waters of Florida and in the Gulf of Mexico put severe pressure on the spawning schools and the fish was nearly wiped out when the Cajun recipe, Blackened Redfish, hit the yuppie crowd. The demand was so great, it took years for the fish to recover.

Although Gulf of Mexico reds do not seem to migrate, Atlantic Coast reds seem to migrate from the Mid Atlantic waters to Florida as water temperatures change. The fish may spawn in Florida, then begin migrating northward as they grow in size and age.

Red drum are considered bottom fish, and therefore feed mostly on crustaceans, mollusks, worms and small bait fish. Popular baits will vary depending on where you fish but favorites include clams, crabs, blood-worms, sand fleas (sand bugs), cut mackerel, cut bunker (menhaden) or cut mullet. Live baits, such as the drum's tiny cousin, the spot, can also be very effective. Smaller drum will take shrimp, squid, cut fish belly strips and worms.

Channel bass will also hit lures. Favorites include spoons, bucktails, and slow plugs like the Mirro-Lure. Smaller fish seem to take artificial lures more readily than the larger fish. Fly rodders also seek the school sized fish and can frequently take them on streamers.

My own experience with red drum has shown that bait is by far the better producer of fish. While fishing the surf, many beach-bound fishermen will heave a bait out to a cut in the bar and while waiting for a possible strike, will cast lures just to stay occupied. One night in the surf at Oregon Inlet I caught three drum, all on bait. The tide lasted a good five hours and I took a fish about every hour or so. The rest of the time I cast lures, had only one hit on a lure and can't be sure it was drum.

School drum, the puppy drum size fish of two to five pounds, will readily take lures. I've had several good days of fishing with bucktails tipped with squid and a plastic tail or a Mirro-Lure that saw a good number of fish brought to the boat. My own experience showed a slower retrieve than what I used for seatrout was the best bet.

Red drum usually stay close to the beach, moving into the sloughs along the beach through cuts in the outer sand bars. The end of the rising tide and the first half of the falling tide are considered to be the most productive times to fish. Reds will often hit best on the night tides. Perhaps the low light makes them feel safer, but no matter the reason, the dark hours are generally better.

There's always the exception to the rule and there are many reds that have been caught at high noon. On a trip to Virginia's Hog Island with Eric Burnley and Jerry Gomber, the mix of red and black drum they caught were all at mid morning to high noon. It was the tide that was the most important, not the time of day. Still, at the local launch ramp we saw a boat come in that had fished the night hours and they had a tremendous catch of drum.

Look for red drum in the bays where deep sloughs meet deep channels. The drum will move from the deep to the edges of the shallower water on the rising tide. The key to success is to fish the tide correctly. At low water, look for the fish to be holding in the deepest water. At high tide, follow the deep channels to where they dead end in deep sloughs. This is usually where you'll find the red drum.

Tackle should match the area you fish. Surf fishermen lobbing cut baits and using four to eight ounces of lead to hold bottom in a strong tide will want a nine to ten foot heavy action surf rod. Often called Hatteras Heavers, these stiff rods are capable of handling not only big fish, but the heavy sinkers needed to fight the surf currents. In quieter waters where the currents were not so strong a more limber rod of nine to eleven feet would be appropriate. Small drum can be handily caught in the surf on medium action surf tackle for more sport. One of my favorite outfits is an old Harnell blank of nine feet length with a light tip that casts small cut baits or lures like spoons and plugs with 15 pound test line.

Because the fish may reach tremendous size and because casting distance can be critical to reach the fish, conventional reels offer the ruggedness needed to battle the fish and minimal line resistance while casting. Spinning tackle is generally used when the fish are known to be in close in a slough or when the smaller fish are sought with smaller baits, rigs and lighter line.

Boat anglers anchoring on the edges of sloughs will use a medium action rod of 6½ to 7 feet length with 20 to 30 pound line. Some of the biggest drum are caught by bottom fishing and you may need some hefty tackle to turn a big fish.

School drum call for lighter tackle. From one handed baitcasting outfits to light spinning gear or a light two handed plugging rod are good choices. My own rod was made from a cut down 7 foot popping rod. Trimmed to 6½ feet, it became stiff enough to work a bucktail effectively and has enough power to really drive a hook home.

When plugging, I prefer slow retrieve baitcasting reels to help keep the lure moving slowly. With many of today's spinning reels opting for fast retrieve ratios, it takes a concerted effort to be sure the lure travels slowly when using a spinner.

To rig for surf fishing, I use a heavier leader attached by adding a small barrel swivel at the end of the main fishing line, then tying on the four foot length of 40, 60 or 80 pound leader. The heavier leaders are used when I know there are oyster beds where we are fishing, which can have many sharp edges to cut off a lighter leader.

When plugging I use 12 or 15 pound test line, add a short double line to add a three foot section of 25 pound mono. The leader is attached to the double line with a surgeons knot. No wire leader is ever necessary when red drum fishing.

Black Drum

They resemble the red drum but are thicker through the shoulders with a pronounced humpback. Forty and 50 pounders are common and it's not unusual to see several fish in the 60 and 70 pound class weighed in each season. The world's record is a monster of a drum taken off Lewes, Delaware by Gerald Townesend in 1975. It weighed 113 pounds, 1 ounce! What a catch!

These heavy weights enter Delaware and Chesapeake Bays towards the end of April to spawn, and fishing action starts about mid-May and continues through June. Some drum stay in the bays the entire summer but summer fishing is not always as productive as the spring run.

One of the appeals of black drum fishing is the chance to set a world record in one of the lighter line classes. The IGFA allows a double line up to 15 feet long. If you're serious about record hunting, by all means use one. A Bimini twist or spider hitch will produce a double line. Add five feet of 50 pound mono or plastic-coated braided cable leader, attached with an Albright knot.

Drum rig

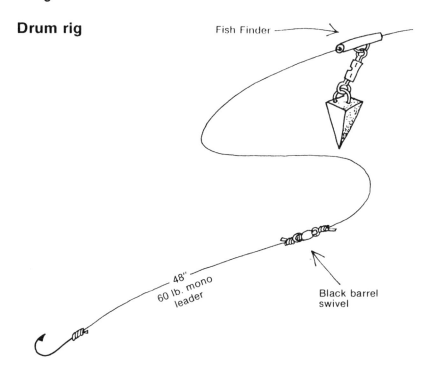

Fish Finder

48"
60 lb. mono
leader

Black barrel
swivel

These big fish take a bait gently, so a fish finder rig is advised. Run the leader through the eye of the fish finder and tie on a 10/0 eagle claw style hook with bait-holding barbs and an offset point. About two feet up the leader slide on a small cork a bit larger than the eye on the fish finder. This keeps the bait two feet from the sinker and allows the fish to move off with the bait and not feel any sinker resistance.

Bait for drum is usually a big glob of sea clams. Some anglers wrap thin cotton sewing thread loosely around the clams to help them stay on. And, some add a half a shedder crab to the hook for dessert. Fresh shedders are best, but frozen ones will do. Drum eat plenty of shellfish. They also eat lots of Delaware Bay crabs.

The take of a drum will feel like a small fish fooling around. Since there may be hours of waiting, the rods are placed in holders; reels in free spool

Anchoring in a slough

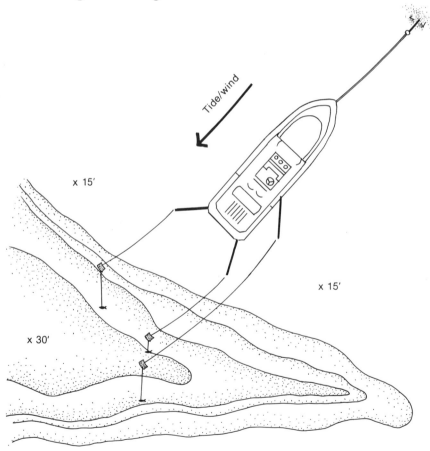

with clickers on. There'll be a few tentative clicks. Pick up the rod, release the click and feed out line. Let the fish move off about 15 feet, then engage the reel gears, wait until the line comes taut and strike hard. Careful you don't fall over backwards if you miss the strike.

Tackle will depend on the line test. Standard tackle would be a reel like the Penn #60 with 30 pound mono and a rod to match. Many drum fishermen prefer to use large spinning reels. Most important is that the drag be smooth. It will get a workout.

Many anglers fish after dark, while just as many report catching fish during daylight hours. It's a toss-up; go when you can. Party boats and charter boats from both sides of the bay do a lot of night fishing, but if you'd rather not be out in the dark, don't hesitate to try after sunup.

Drum follow channels and move back into finger sloughs on a turning tide. Most boats anchor, particularly when boat traffic is heavy, and put over an anchor line buoy in case they have to get off the ball and follow a fish. Drum make a few long runs then settle down to slugging it out deep, making you work for every inch of line. You may be onto a fish for 20 minutes or an hour. When a drum gets sideways in the tide it's like pulling against a barn door.

Eventually, the fish will tire, with luck, before you give out. When the fish is rolling on its side near the boat, reduce the drag setting. A drum can turn on a sudden surge of reserve power all big fish seem to have when they see the boat and break off. Wait until the fish is completely under control before sinking the gaff. Then all hands drag the brute aboard.

Not flashy, not acrobatic, not even handsome, the black drum still has a loyal following among anglers. They appreciate his brute strength and size and the fact that here's a big gamefish that can be reached by the average guy in a small boat. Not too small, though. Delaware and Chesapeake Bays can get treacherous and you want to be able to get in quickly if conditions turn ugly.

Black drum are good to eat, tasting more like veal than fish. Some of our drum have had parasites buried in the flesh. We've been told they are harmless despite their unappetizing appearance. We just cut them out during cleaning. Most drum will be parasite-free.

One curious thing about drum is that they actually do make a drumming sound using their large air bladder. It may be a "mating call." Sometimes on a still, quiet night you can hear them under your boat. It is an eerie, but beautiful experience.

Incidentally, one last tip. If you catch what you feel is a record fish, place your line sample in a Ziploc bag with water in it when you send it to the IGFA. Wet line always tests out at a slightly lower pound test than when dry.

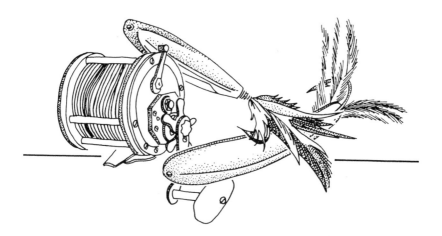

Chapter Ten

MACKEREL: BOSTONS, SPANISH AND KINGS

The mackerel of the Atlantic Coast come in two sizes; small and large! The Atlantic mackerel, often called the Boston mackerel, and Spanish mackerel are the diminutive members of the clan, while the king mackerel is the "big daddy" of this trio. Boston mackerel, more correctly named Atlantic mackerel, are found all along the coast from Virginia to Maine. The schools are often huge and anglers can catch a good supply of macks for food, as well as bait that can be frozen and used later in the season for sharking, bluefishing, surf fishing and flounder fishing.

Spanish mackerel are found from Florida to southern New Jersey, rarely above Montauk, and are taken by trolling, sometimes by casting. They get mixed in with bluefish at times, or schools of little tunny. They are a great light tackle fish and are numerous in the summer months.

The king mackerel, also called kingfish, is found from Maryland to Florida, and is only occasionally caught above Delaware or south Jersey. The biggest kings are usually caught out of Key West, Florida. Most kings of the Virginia and Maryland Coast will weigh in the 10 to 30 pound range, but each season sees a few "smoker" sized kings of better than 40 pounds taken on rod and reel.

All three mackerel are fun and exciting to catch. The Atlantic mackerel is the harbinger of spring, the other two bring on thoughts of summer, fast running fish, tight lines, doubled over rods and excited anglers.

Atlantic Mackerel

These miniature tuna are found along the coast from fall through spring, moving north as the waters warm. Virginia boats get them in February and March while New Jersey and New York fishermen look for action in April and early May. In New England, it is possible to catch mackerel up until June if the waters stay cool.

They come equipped with many small teeth and are colored green on the back with dark irregular stripes across their back and sides. The silver bellies make great summer flounder baits and strip baits for trolling larger tuna.

Wind direction influences their movements; a strong northerly will slow down the migration, a southerly speed it up. Steady easterly winds can push the fish inshore, westerlies offshore. The professional boat skippers are out every day fishing and listening to radio traffic. They usually know where the action is. Your best shot at catching mackerel is shipping aboard a head boat during the height of the run. The individual boat fisherman is also privy to radio chatter between boats, can check daily reports in the newspapers and talk to other fishermen to get an idea of where to fish.

Party boats, with many anglers aboard, usually drift or anchor and set out a chum slick to draw the macks. Individual anglers in private boats can drift the area and jig at different depths to locate fish. Just be sure that you don't run across or disturb the party boat's slick. A graph recorder will indicate any macks under your boat.

I like to get in several mackerel trips and stock up on baits for the coming season. I use them for shark, tuna and bluefish bait and, they also make great bait for crabbing. With the price of bunker these days, we try to cram the freezer.

Mackerel fishing is fun, particularly with freshwater tackle. This would cause problems along a shoulder-to-shoulder party boat rail resulting in horrendous tangles. On your own boat you're the boss. Typical boat gear, the same as for the sea bass or ling, is needed on head boats. If you want to fill a potato sack with macks use a multi-hook jigging rig. Tie on a diamond jig of two to six ounces and add two or more short tube teaser on 1/0 hooks about a foot apart. To speed up unhooking the fish, replace the treble hook on the jig with a single hook.

Mackerel can be spooky and veteran party boaters make up their rigs using 10 to 15 pound test mono, which is less visible in the water. Until somebody gets a hit, try jigging at several levels from the bottom to fairly shallow. If the action is really slow, try putting squid strips on the hooks to

Besides being tons of fun, mackerel fishing assures a freezer full of bait for the coming season.

"sweeten" them.

Commercial mackerel jigging rigs, sometimes called "Christmas trees," are available in tackle shops. Just add a diamond jig to the bottom and you're in business. When you hook a mack, let it swim around and more should latch on. Don't overdo this on a party boat as macks will run sideways around your neighbor's line.

At times straight up-and-down jigging doesn't work. Now is when a fast retrieve reel comes in handy. Let the jig drop to the bottom then crank it up as fast as you can. Mackerel are easy to catch on an average day, but it's good to know some different techniques.

Along with the fun of mackerel fishing comes the mess. Mackerel have tiny scales that come off easily and stick to everything. This is one reason why regulars wear sea boots and foul weather pants. Mackerel also bleed freely. Try and stay ahead of the mess on your own boat with frequent wash-downs. Once the scales dry fast they're the devil to get off. So don't let the fish flop around on deck. With two or more fish on the line this can be difficult, but if you plop them into an open sack or big garbage can the boat will stay a lot cleaner. On a party boat, of course, deckhands are the ones on clean-up detail.

This full barrel of mackerel will be used for baits when sharking, fluke and bluefishing, or surf fishing during the coming season.

Spanish Mackerel

Larger than the Atlantic mackerel, Spanish mackerel may reach weights of better than ten pounds. Bob Cranton caught the world all-tackle record a short time ago in 1987 when he landed a 13 pounder while fishing out of Ocracoke Inlet in North Carolina. The fish was caught in among larger kingfish and it hit a strip of mullet draped with a blue and white sea witch.

Spanish are also taken from the beach in the surf, from piers, from small boats in the sounds and bays and from inshore boats trolling in 10 to 20 fathoms of water. They are occasionally taken in much deeper water, but are seldom seen at the offshore canyons.

They are easy to identify with their bright yellow spots on the sides of their silvery bodies. They are found from Delaware south to Florida although when inshore water temperatures soar in the summer months, they may be caught as far north as Montauk. The best fishing occurs from the lower reaches of the Chesapeake Bay through the Carolinas.

In sounds and bays, schools are located near deep channels and they can be cast to with light spinning gear. Ten to twelve pound line is about perfect to cast bucktails tipped with a belly strip or small spoons and

Spanish mackerel have become more numerous during the last few years and provide great sport on light tackle.

swimming plugs. A quick retrieve is usually preferred when working buck-tails, with short sweeps of the rod tip to make the lure dance. Spoons call for a steady, but fast retrieve.

Delaware and New Jersey boats catch them mixed in with schools of bluefish, bonito and little tunny when chumming at inshore ridges and baiting up with spearing, smelt or chunks of menhaden. They make a delightful change of pace and stir a lot of interest on the party boats.

Many fish are lost because of the sharp dentures found in Spanish mackerel so a short trace of wire leader is a good idea, even when using plugs or bucktails. However, Spanish have notoriously good eyesight and get spooked by bulky terminal tackle. I've found a six inch length of #5 wire attached to the main fishing line with an albright knot to be the best compromise. It may spook a few fish, but it is not too easy to see and most Spanish will strike the lure or bait when using a light leader like this. Avoid those factory made leaders with the shiny snaps and swivels.

An excellent bait in the Chesapeake is fresh shrimp. For $5 you can buy a pound of bait, that provides at least 40 baits; more if the shrimp are cut into chunks and added to a bucktail to add some smell. Other good baits include squid strips and strips cut from already caught Spanish mackerel. Mullet strips work too.

King Mackerel

These large members of the mackerel family can reach a length of over five feet and weights that can top 100 pounds. The king mackerel is an important commercially caught fish and there lies a conflict; overfishing has introduced the need for catch limits in order to maintain the stocks at stable levels. Recent effects to manage these fish seem to be paying off.

They are a warm water mackerel and are rarely caught above Delaware, but New Jersey boats report a few fish each summer. Cape Cod occasionally reports a small number of kings, apparently because it juts out towards the Gulf Stream and may get a bath of warm water in the summer months. The prime season runs from the summer months through the early fall. Smaller kings are called "snakes" and provide the bulk of the fishery, while larger kings of better than 20 pounds are called "smokers", a nickname they earned either from their ability to smoke a drag on a reel or because they are perfect size for hanging in a smokehouse.

Kings do get big. The all-tackle record is a 90 pounder taken out of Key West, Florida by Norton Thomton. Most kings we see along the Mid Atlantic Coast seldom get above 40 pounds but each season does see a few king mackerel of 50 and 60 pounds weighed in to get local anglers excited about the prospects of landing a trophy fish. They can be taken while drifting with live or cut bait, or when trolling.

Kingfish Trolling Rig

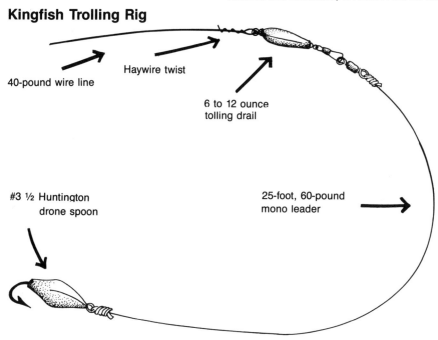

Haywire twist

40-pound wire line

6 to 12 ounce
tolling drail

#3 ½ Huntington
drone spoon

25-foot, 60-pound
mono leader

King Mackerel Balloon Rig

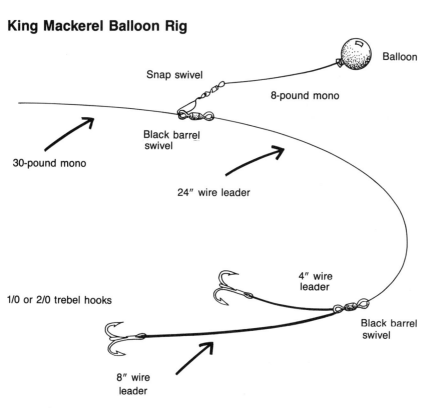

Balloon

Snap swivel

8-pound mono

Black barrel
swivel

30-pound mono

24" wire leader

4" wire
leader

1/0 or 2/0 trebel hooks

Black barrel
swivel

8" wire
leader

131

Live bait specialists prefer a menhaden rigged with a stinger hook to catch short strikers. Using a length of wire is a must, or you will lose every bait. The aerator set up is similar to the type used by striped bass fishermen as described in Chapter One. Be sure to remove any dying or bleeding bunker which may cause the rest of the baits to perish, too. Save the dead baits for last. Kings will take a dead bait at times. To rig, use a short shank tuna hook, like the Eagle Claw #188 style. Pass the hook through the nose or just ahead of the dorsal fin. The stinger hook should dangle free and not be embedded into the bait. The bait is then slow trolled in an area where kings have been sighted or recently caught.

Tackle need not be overly heavy. A reel capable of handling 20 or 30 pound line is about right, unless you are specifically targeting big smokers, then 40 pound would be a better choice.

It may help to set the drag at just above free spool so the line can't backlash when a king hits the bait. They often take off like madmen immediately and you don't need an overrun and tangled line at that moment.

King Mackerel Bunker Rig

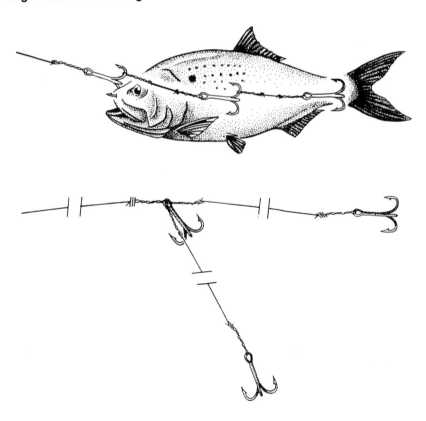

To maintain proper depth, some captains use balloons tied onto the line so the fish can only swim so deep before being snubbed by the balloon. Kings will most often be found nearer to the surface so very deep running bait would therefore escape his fate of a mackerel hors-d'oeuvre if it could get near the bottom. When the mackerel hits and takes off with the line, the balloon pops and the line can be reeled in with nothing in the way.

When fishing live bait, or fresh dead baits, you can either slow troll or drift. Slow trolling is accomplished by shifting the boat in and out of gear as needed to work against the current or move the boat over good structure or schools of fish. Drifting works well when the fish are scattered over a wide area. Some tournament fishermen use fresh ground menhaden as chum to help draw the fish to the baits.

Although generally considered to be an offshore fish caught in waters of 10 to 20 fathoms, or deeper, king mackerel will surprise beach and pier fishermen with infrequent runs along the edge of the surf. Live bait fished off balloons works just as well from a pier as from a boat and this method is a favorite of Carolina pier anglers.

A friend of mine fished the surf at Chincoteague a few years back in late August and was surprised several snake kings mixed in with a school of Spanish working in the surf just beyond the bar near The Point. He caught a pair of kings within a short cast from the sandy surf; an unusual catch to be sure.

Other fishermen prefer to troll for kings and use spoons, rigged baits like ballyhoo and mullet or large swimming lures. Trolling tackle can be of 20, 30 or 50 pound gear but the lighter stuff usually gets the nod as the most fun to fish with. Wire line is used in some areas along the Virginia Coast to take spoons down deeper, about 15 feet below the surface, and this greatly increases the chances of hook ups. One hundred yards of 40 pound monel or stainless wire, spooled on a Penn 113H is standard gear.

Trolling during the late summer and early fall can be especially productive as the kings move into shallower water, chasing schools of menhaden. Later, as the inshore water quickly cools, they head back to the deeper water.

If you find bait, the kings won't be far away. Also look for bottom structure like ridges, hills and wrecks that will hold not only the bait, but the kings too.

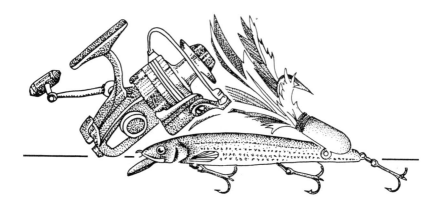

Chapter Eleven

COBIA AND AMBERJACK

Here are two of the hardest fighting game fish of the coast, yet if you live north of Virginia you may not get to catch either of them, unless you head south for a vacation. They are found from Florida to the Delmarva Peninsula, and may occasionally be found off the coast of New Jersey or the south shore of Long Island. I caught a cobia about ten years ago in Delaware Bay. It was a small one of only 14 pounds, and I heard of several other boats that caught cobia that same weekend. An unusual catch, but delicious eating!

Amberjack may be more numerous north of Virginia than many fishermen realize. On a charter trip for tuna off Cape May, New Jersey, we found amberjack of 10 to 15 pounds schooled below a lobster pot marker. Above the amberjack were school dolphin, little green hornets that we were catching for the cooler for next week's barbecue. One bait drifted deep, untouched by a dolphin, and an amberjack grabbed it. We thought we had a huge dolphin and were quite surprised to boat a 23 inch amberjack. I've spoken to other charter captains who have also encountered amberjack while shark fishing in waters off Montauk, New York and Ocean City, Maryland.

The best cobia fishing occurs in Virginia, as does the best action for amberjack. The water temperatures below Wachapreague, Virginia in the summer months seem perfect for these fish and they provide excellent angling opportunities for charter boats and private boats alike.

Cobia

Cobia are a terrific game fish. They fight hard, go crazy at the side of the boat, are challenging to catch, and are great eating. They have a lot of nicknames such as ling, lemon fish, crabeater, and cabio. Most of the IGFA records are for cobia taken in Florida waters but one exceptionally large cobia came from the waters off Oregon Inlet, North Carolina, a 97 pound fish caught by Mary Black quite a few years back in 1952. Most cobia off Virginia, Maryland and Delaware will weigh in the range of 5 to 25 pounds.

The biggest cobia I ever saw personally was a 57 pounder taken near the Chesapeake Bay Bridge Tunnel off the Naval Amphib Base at Little Creek. Several of us who were stationed at the base would charter a boat out of Lynnhaven for a day's fishing. That was some fish and took the angler nearly a half hour to land it.

Cobia can be taken on a wide range of tackle, including salt water fly tackle, spinning, plugging and heavier bait fishing tackle. A typical rod and reel for bait fishing would match a medium action 6½ foot rod with a reel like a Penn 112H or 500M filled with 20 to 30 pound test line. This equipment would handily beat cobia up to 50 pounds.

Live bait such as pinfish or menhaden (bunker) work just fine, although some cobia specialists prefer live eels. Snapper blues, live spot and small crabs are other good baits. Dead bait can be productive and the favorites include crab chunks, chunked baits, squid and shrimp.

Smaller fish will be a lot more fun on plugging tackle with a stiff popping style rod and a reel capable of handling 400 yards of 12 to 15 pound test line. The equivalent spinning gear is preferred by many fishermen, although the plugging gear is considered to be best. Rig with a length of 50 to 60 pound leader at the end of the line to avoid fraying the lighter line and losing the fish.

They will readily take a streamer fly so fly rodders are especially keen on finding cobia. An 8½ or 9 foot fly rod capable of handling a 9 or 10 weight, salt water taper fly line is a must. The reel should be able to hold the fly line plus 200 yards of backing. Cobia can make strong runs so be prepared for a spirited battle on the light gear.

You will find cobia in loose schools roaming along the beach or in sounds and bays in deep holes or channel cuts. Memorial Day weekend is the unofficial start of the cobia season as local fishermen gear up and head for the beaches and bays. After several years of low cobia populations, these fish are responding to size limit regulations and they seem to be making a big come back. In recent years, large numbers of school fish have been caught. Anglers should be aware of the need to release the many small cobia they catch to provide for the future of the fishery.

Cobia apparently spawn in late June in the deep waters nearer to the Gulf Stream so the fishing drops off for the bigger fish at this time, but picks up again in July.

Live bait fishermen look for the bottom structure to give away the likely areas where cobia will lie, then they fish the bait down deep, right on the bottom. Cobia also like to hang around buoys, markers, pilings, and floating debris. The best tactic when approaching these fish is to idle up near to the marker or buoy, then shoot off a cast to get the lure, bait or streamer fly right near the fish. Don't drop it right on their heads, but off to the side a few feet so the fish aren't spooked.

If the cobia are hungry, you may have a wild time as several fish attack the offering at the same time! Usually it is the largest fish in the group that gets to eat the bait as it exercises its leadership role of the school. That's delightful for the angler, since we all like to catch the biggest fish!

On the dinner table, cobia are absolutely delicious. In fact, many fishermen consider the cobia to be the very best eating fish to be found anywhere on the coast. OK, that might be debatable, but one thing is sure, they do taste great. The meat is pure white when cooked and flakes well. On a barbecue, broiled or baked, cobia ranks high on the list of dining treats.

This hefty cobia was caught on spinning tackle and hit a tube lure cast towards a marker buoy.

Amberjack

Pound for pound, amberjack may be the toughest fish in the ocean. They can pull like there's no tomorrow, and a big amberjack can make you wish you never tangled with it. Your arms will ache, your back will burn and you sweat bullets until the fish is finally brought to the boat and released. They are worthy opponents and a delight to catch.

Amberjack are in a large family of fish that scientists call the Carangidae, fishermen call "jacks". The jack crevalle is perhaps the most famous of the jacks, but the amberjack is the largest member of the family. It is easily distinguished by its brown back, silver sides and black bar that slashes across both eyes.

They are found nearly world wide, and are reported to reach 200 pounds although the all-tackle record is a fish of 155 pounds taken on the Challenger Banks of Bermuda by Joseph Dawson in 1981. Marion Hutson holds the eight pound class world record for an amberjack of 83 pounds 12 ounces that he caught off Virginia Beach. That's some outstanding fish on light tackle.

Amberjack are not usually considered to be ideal table fare so most of the fish are released unharmed. Dr. Jim Wright of the Virginia Beach area frequently fishes for amberjack, and has won many awards for his conser-

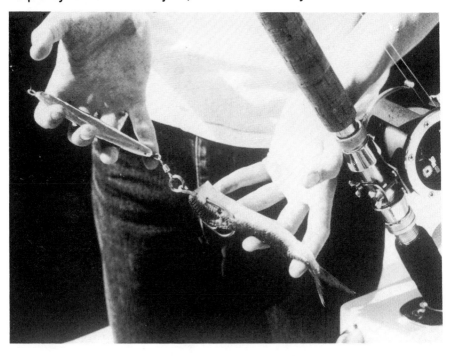

Amberjack can be taken on bait rigs and on heavy jigs sweetened with a fillet of ballyhoo.

vation efforts in tagging amberjacks. In recent years, more anglers are realizing the enjoyment of catching amberjack and the number of fishermen seeking this important fish are expanding rapidly. With increased pressure from rod and reel angling, it is ever more important to release these fish.

Look for virtually any offshore wreck and you'll likely find amberjack. As mentioned, their range is primarily south of Delaware, but several years ago when waters just south of Montauk at the famous Texas Tower were unusually warm, a number of big amberjack were taken off the tower wreckage. Fish any wreck south of Cape May in the summer months and it is very likely that amberjack will be in residence.

Amberjack are not finicky eaters and will accept most any dead bait that is neatly rigged. Too many large hooks or bulky leaders may make the fish wary, so keep it simple and the chances for hook ups increase. Favored baits include chunks of menhaden, butterfish, ballyhoo, mullet and mackerel. Use a strong hook of 5/0 to 8/0 size, 2X or 3X strong. I've had 40 pound jacks make quick work of standard hooks. I use the same Mustad #7731 that I use for rigging ballyhoo for tuna to rig a bait for amberjack.

Deep jigging with heavy bucktails or large diamond jigs can be a fun way to fish. Add a strip of fish belly, a small squid or a pennant made cut from a towel and soaked in bunker oil to add some spice. Again, be sure the hooks are sturdy. Amberjack will make short work of a light hook, ruining the lure and losing the fish.

Perhaps the most sporting way to catch amberjack is to chum and tease them to the surface. The chum slick draws them from the depths, a live bait splashed on the surface gets them all fired up and eager to eat. It's then simply a matter of dropping a chunk bait, a plug or a fly in front of the frenzied fish and it's an instant hookup.

Light tackle specialists use this technique to fool amberjack into leaving the safety of the wreck. Once the jacks are in the slick and being teased, the boat is allowed to drift away from the wreck. When the angler thinks he is far enough away from the wreck, he baits the fish and can play the catch without danger of "Mr. Muscles" getting back into the safety of his rusted metal home.

States like Virginia and New Jersey are becoming more active in sinking ships on artificial reef locations. As more ships are added to the ocean bottom, the chances at amberjack fishing increase.

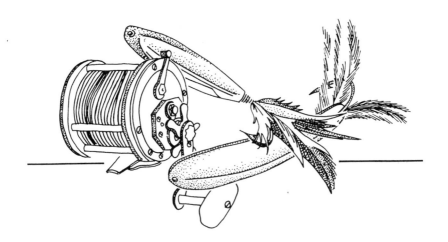

Chapter Twelve

FISHING KNOTS

Tying good knots is a frequently overlooked skill yet the right knot, properly tied, is THE vital connection between the fisherman and the fish. Unfortunately even the best of knots cause a slight weakening of the line; the wrong knot, or a poorly tied knot, can cause a severe loss of line strength. The choice of which knot to use is an important decision every fisherman makes when tying on a snap swivel or a lure, or when joining two lines together, or when adding a shock leader at the end of the main fishing line.

There are several excellent pamphlets distributed by line manufacturers such as Berkley Trilene, Stren, Maxima and Ande that detail how to tie knots but a description of how or when to use them is left up to the fisherman to decide.

In this chapter we'll take a look at the most often used knots, what they are best used for and how to tie them. Fancy-wrapped custom rods and precision reels are of little value if the knot in the line which joins the lure and the tackle is inherently weak or poorly tied.

The best knots retain as much of the original line strength as possible. These same knots hold firmly without unraveling and are quick and simple to tie.

Over 200 knots have been developed over the years to fit fishermen's needs, but most of us can get along with the following selection of basic knots which can be used to tie a wide variety of rigs.

Skillfully tied knots are relatively easy to accomplish with the following tips:

1. Make neat knots. All twists or spirals should be uniform so that when you draw the knot snug, the turns all tighten to the same degree.
2. Pull knots tight with steady, even pressure. Don't jerk a knot tight.
3. Wetting the knot with saliva before tightening helps the coils come together smoothly.
4. Use a fingernail clipper to cut line. A knife is bulky, hazardous and can accidentally nick or scrape the knot or line.
5. Don't be stingy when tying a knot. Use enough line to make the loops and twists easily, with a few inches left over.
6. When tying knots in double lines keep the lines parallel and avoid any twists, unless otherwise specified.
7. During a day's fishing, it pays to check the line frequently to be sure it is at its maximum strength. If your line feels rough or frayed, check the rod guides and reel for rough spots. If the line breaks at the knot repeatedly, check the hook, snap or lure connection. A damaged hook eye or rough spot on a lure eye or snap swivel can cut a line.

Knot tying is a skill that is learned only through practice. Try knot tying at home, using heavy monofilament for easier handling and to see how the knots are formed.

Improved Clinch Knot

The improved clinch is the knot preferred by most fishermen when adding something to the end of the line. It is easy to tie, very strong and is widely used by fishermen everywhere.

Tests at DuPont's Stren laboratory have shown the improved clinch knot provides 95 to 98% of the breaking strength of the line depending on how carefully it is tied. It is important to make at least five twists around the standing part of the line. Fewer turns will make a weak knot but any more than seven twists may also weaken the knot because of the excessive effort then needed to draw the knot tight. Too many coils may also cause the knot to jam so it can't be drawn up tight no matter how hard you pull.

Draw the knot down with no loose or overlapping coils which cause a dramatic loss of line strength. It also pays to lubricate the knot with saliva when drawing it tight so the coils don't fray against one another or build up excess heat. Don't yank it tight, just pull firmly with no jerks.

It is also important to add the last tuck of the tag end of the line under the loop formed when the tag end is brought back towards the snap swivel eye. The extra tuck is what makes the knot "improved" over the old clinch knot. Leave out the extra tuck and the knot loses about 25% of its strength. That extra tuck prevents the line from slipping, the main reason for knot failure.

The improved clinch knot is best used with lines up to 30-pound test but for heavier lines its close cousin the double improved clinch knot can be used. Fold about 24 to 30 inches of the line back on itself, then tie the knot with the two strands of line in exactly the same manner as if they were one strand.

Some offshore fishermen are getting away from tying long lengths of double lines (which we'll discuss in a few more pages) and instead are using the double improved clinch knot to tie the snap swivel directly to the end of the line. The lack of a leader doesn't seem to hinder fish-fighting ability and there's no bulky bimini twist or spider hitch to become jammed in roller guides.

Trim the tag end close to the knot but leave a 1/4 inch or so exposed. Under the pressure of casting lures or playing a fish, the knot may slip slightly. Too closely a trimmed tag end may slip under the coils under heavy strain and cause the clinch to unravel.

When tying the clinch knot in a heavy leader, say a 60-pound mono leader, it may be tough to get five coils to draw up tightly. In this case use only four coils. The slightly weakened leader is still stronger than the main fishing line.

It is a good idea to re-tie the improved clinch knot frequently. Tournament fishermen re-tie the knots after each trip or after landing an especially heavy fish. The coils of the knot begin to chafe and cut into one another each time the knot is flexed under pressure, say from fighting a fish. In time, after hundreds of pulls, the knot will fail because of this flexing, chafing action.

With little practice this knot is among the simplest to tie and can be done even at night without the aid of a flashlight.

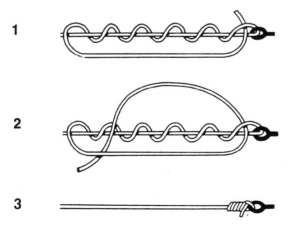

1

2

3

Palomar Knot

The palomar knot was developed by tournament fishermen on the freshwater bass pro circuits. They needed a connection that was not only exceptionally strong but which was also easy and quick to tie. It had to be able to withstand the shock of a slamming, cross-their-eyes type of hook setting that seems to be the hallmark of a hawg fisherman. The knot has become popular with saltwater anglers. Its use is similar to that of the improved clinch knot and in many ways it is easier to tie than the improved clinch, especially when tying on hooks which are usually relatively small in size as compared to a large plug or a saltwater trolling lure.

When tying the palomar knot, the final loop is pulled over the terminal tackle or lure being attached to the line. A plug or lure that is very large or bulky just won't fit conveniently through the loop. The palomar is therefore, most often used to tie on a hook, a snap, a bucktail, a small spoon or plug, a barrel swivel or a streamer fly.

The ease of tying and the palomar's ability to withstand tremendous shocks of setting the hook on big fish has widened the use of this once "freshwater only" knot to the saltwater angling clan. Many tuna chunkers use the palomar as the primary knot of choice when tying a tuna hook to the end of the leader. Even in the low vision of nighttime fishing, when chunking is frequently done, the knot can be tied by feel after only a little practice.

Surf fishermen now use the palomar knot when tying on snaps or snap swivels, trout and salmon fishermen use it extensively for trolling and for drifting baits. Many light tackle saltwater anglers who cast bucktails or spoons to fish like seatrout or weakfish, fluke, dolphin, mackerel and puppy drum find the palomar to be the best knot when using lines of 8 to 12-pound test.

The palomar tests out nearly the same as the improved clinch but is far better when used with heavier lines. The palomar can handle 60 to 100-pound test saltwater leaders with no problem but seems to fall off in strength when used with ultralight lines such as the 2 and 4-pound test lines that a trout fisherman might use. Ultralight lines seem to work better with the improved clinch knot or the Uni-Knot which we will discuss next.

The palomar knot is very reliable and rarely slips once drawn up properly and snugged into place on the snap swivel or hook. Its criss-crossing coils spread the strain of the pull against the line over several stress points. Like the improved clinch knot, the palomar should be re-tied after each day's fishing or after each big fish.

It is necessary to wet the knot with saliva before drawing it tight to lubricate it and assure a firmly tied knot. When tied with dry line the crisscrossing coils that add to the knot's durability may cut into and chafe one another causing a substantial loss of knot strength. The knot's shock resistance may be severely reduced causing the loss of a fish right at the strike.

I watched a video which advocated the use of a cigarette touched to the tag end of the line to put a small crown or nub on the line to prevent the tag end from slipping under the knot coils. The heat from the cigarette will surely add the small nub but it may also weaken the coils that get close to the glowing, and very hot end of the cigarette. And, if the knot was properly tied it will not slip anyhow so there's no need to melt the tag end.

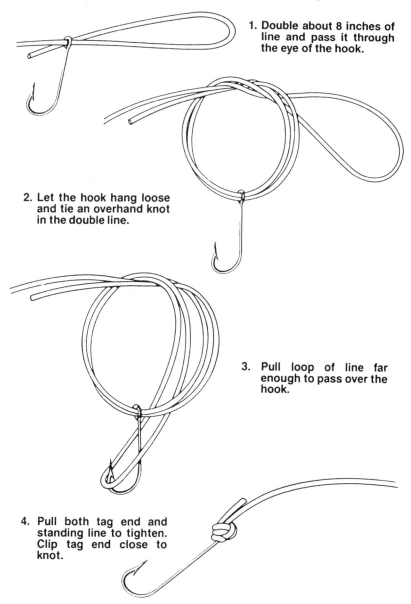

1. Double about 8 inches of line and pass it through the eye of the hook.

2. Let the hook hang loose and tie an overhand knot in the double line.

3. Pull loop of line far enough to pass over the hook.

4. Pull both tag end and standing line to tighten. Clip tag end close to knot.

Uni-Knot

The Uni-Knot is the last of the trio of knots used for tying terminal tackle or a lure to the end of the line. In many ways it is the best knot to use although slightly more complicated to tie than the improved clinch or the palomar. A major advantage is the knot's consistent high strength of 97 to 99% of the breaking strength of the line. A poorly tied Uni-Knot will usually test out better than a poorly tied clinch or palomar.

The knot gains exceptional strength because it adds an extra lay of the main fishing line beneath the knot coils. This effectively cushions the cutting forces as the knot is flexed and tensioned when casting or fighting a fish. The knot is durable and does not have to be re-tied after each fish or each day's fishing, although better fishermen will always re-tie as a matter of habit, just to be sure.

Its inventor is Vic Dunaway, a top notch light tackle angler from Florida and editor of "Florida Sportsman" magazine. Vic is a master at many types of fishing and is equally well at home deep jigging a reef for grouper or flats fishing for bonefish, or live baiting sails, or fly rodding for tarpon. As a thoughtful, innovative fisherman he clearly understood the need for good, strong knots but was not always satisfied with the traditional knots most everyone used.

His Uni-Knot was born from discussions with fishing guides and captains who used knots similar to the Uni-Knot but which had no name and needed some fine tuning. Vic perfected the knot and actually developed it into a system that can be used to join two lines and snell a hook. If you want to learn the entire Uni-Knot system write to E.I.du Pont, Fishing Line Division, Wilmington, DE 19898 for a copy of "Powerlines to Better Fishing". It's free.

The Uni-Knot is especially good for light tackle fishing but it is a universal knot that even the big game angler can use to tie snaps or hooks directly to the line.

As you follow the directions and get to step three you'll find that the knot's coils come snug as the line is drawn up before the coils slide down the line to jam against the eye of the lure or snap. Be sure to wet the line

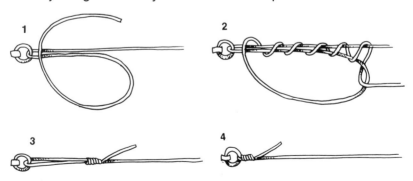

so it is properly lubricated and to be sure the tightened coils don't fray the main line as the coils are drawn down.

For added action when fishing bucktails, don't draw the knot all the way against the eye of the lure. Leave a small loop in the Uni-Knot so the bucktail can swing and hop more freely. A friend of mine who uses the Uni exclusively, keeps a small wooden dowel on his center console that he puts into the loop before drawing the knot tight. As the coils slide down the line to the eye, the dowel leaves a neat 1/2-inch loop.

Under the pressure of fighting a fish the loop will collapse against the eye of the lure so the knot will have to be re-tied after each fish - if you want the loop.

Simplified Blood Knot

Here's a basic knot used to tie two pieces of line or leader together when the lines are equal, or nearly equal, in diameter.

1. Take the two line ends and tie a simple overhand knot and pull it tight. This will be clipped off later.
2. Form a loop where the two lines meet, with the overhand knot hanging free, as shown.
3. Pull one side of the loop down and begin taking turns with it around the standing line. This is easier to do than describe. Keep the place where the lines join open so the number of turns on each side is equal.
4. After making eight or ten turns, reach through the center opening and pull the overhand knot through. Put your finger in this loop so it doesn't slip out.
5. Hold the overhand knot with your teeth, take your finger away and pull on both ends of the line, creating tight coils.
6. Let go with your teeth and pull hard to set the knot firmly. The overhand knot loop will stick out at 90 degrees. Clip off the excess close to the joining knot.

1

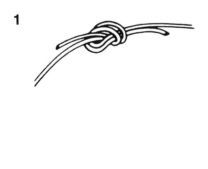

2

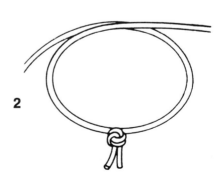

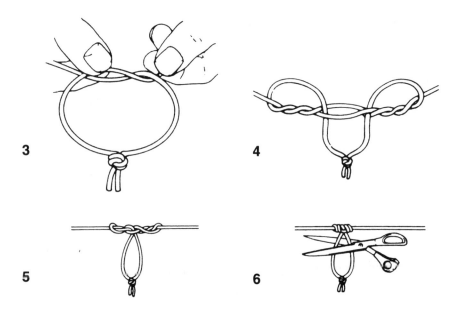

Spider Hitch

The two knots used to make double lines, the spider hitch and the Bimini twist, are favored by fly fishermen, tuna trollers, light tackle bluefish experts and everyday ordinary fishermen like you and me whenever we want to add a leader to the end of our line. Surf fishermen, bottom fishermen, party boaters and back bay casters also find uses for tying a double line.

Offshore anglers use a double line to add strength and protection at the end of the main fishing line. A 200-pound mako can be horsed at boat side once a few turns of the double line are on the reel. In essence the pound test of the fishing line has been multiplied by two once the double line is on the reel spool. The double line also protects from break-offs if a big yellowfin rubs the line against a hull chine or if the mate misses with the gaff or tag stick.

Light tackle fishermen, whether they cast bait in the surf or toss swimming plugs to blues, redfish or seatrout need a double line to add a leader to the end of the fishing line. The knot of choice for adding the leader is the surgeon's knot, which we'll cover in a few more pages. It gets high ratings for being easy to tie but it isn't known as a strong knot since it only tests at 70 to 85% of the breaking strength of the line. Adding a leader with the surgeon's knot directly to the main line will in reality weaken the main line by 20 to 25%. Because of the knot, 30-pound test will be reduced to 24-pound test, 20-pound becomes 15-pound, 12-pound is reduced to 9-pound test.

The double line doubles the strength of the main fishing line so when the leader is added with the surgeon's knot the weak link in the leader to double line connection is still far stronger than the main fishing line itself. Twenty-pound test line becomes 40-pound test at the double line. A 75% reduction in strength at the surgeon's knot still gives the equivalent of 30-pound test which is 10-pound test greater than the main fishing line.

If the surgeon's knot is so weak, why use it? Alternative knots, like the Albright and nail knot are rather difficult and time consuming to tie. They test at 90 to 95% of the breaking strength of the line which is better than the surgeon's but still a reduction in the strength of the main fishing line. Once the double line is tied, the surgeon's knot is so much easier to tie, it wins as the knot of choice.

Of the two knots used to tie a double line, the spider hitch is far easier to tie and is especially well suited to lighter tackle of 6 to 30-pound test. Beyond 30-pound line, the knot gets difficult to tie and below 6-pound test it doesn't seem to hold its strength.

The spider hitch will test at 98 to 100% of the main fishing line so little or no line strength is lost in the transition from single to double line. Like all knots it should be wetted with saliva when drawn tight. Draw the coils down slowly and be sure they are even before snugging the coils tight. When first learning the spider hitch there is a tendency for the coils to wrap back over themselves so watch for this. If the coils don't look like the accompanying diagram, try the knot again.

The spider can break under sharp impact, another reason why it is the preferred knot when using light tackle. Light lines and light drag settings translate into relatively light pressure on the knot. The spider should be re-tied after each big fish and at least after each day's fishing. The pressure and flexing of the knot under strain of casting and playing fish will slowly weaken the knot. The older it gets, even by a few hours, the weaker it gets. It's a good idea to get into the habit of re-tying terminal connections and leaders after each fishing trip anyhow so the spider will rarely fail you if you always tie fresh knots.

The length of the double line varies depending on the fishing. Trollers use 15 to 30 feet of double line, according to IGFA regulations if they choose to fish to these standards. Diamond jiggers, bait fishermen or plug casters might use only a 3 or 4 foot double line, then add a 4 to 10 foot leader. Fly fishermen use double lines of only a few inches to add leaders.

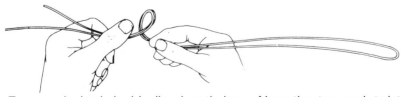

1. Form a desired double line-length loop. Near the tag end, twist the strands into a small reverse loop.

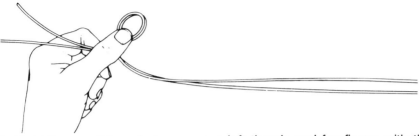

2. Hold the small loop between your left thumb and forefinger, with the thumb extended well above the finger.

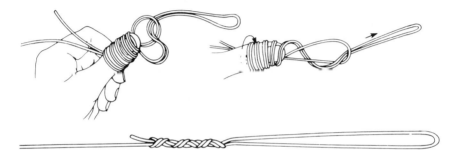

3. Wind the double line strands around your thumb and loop strands, taking five parallel turns. Pass the end of the original big loop through the small loop, pull the slack out, and put the five turns off your thumb. Pull the tag end and standing line strands against the loop strands to tighten the knot. Then pull the standing line only against the loop for final tightening. Clip off the tag end.

Bimini Twist

Also called the 20 times around knot, the Bimini twist was first used by big game fishermen who needed to add strength to the end of their Dacron lines. A doubled section of line at the end of the line would be twice as strong as the main fishing line. Once a few coils of the doubled line were on the spool the angler could then use hand pressure to increase the drag setting to horse a big fish at boat side. Often those last few feet are the hardest when battling a big bluefin or marlin. The doubled line and its increased strength gave the angler more control so the leader man and gaffer could do their job.

Today's fishermen use the Bimini for light tackle as well as big game fishing. It is used in lakes and back bays, for seatrout to striped bass and it has become one of those universal knots that freshwater and saltwater anglers find a use for.

Many fishermen never learn the Bimini twist because someone told them the knot was difficult to tie. Anyone who uses the Bimini regularly will agree that while there's no doubt this knot isn't the easiest to tie but it sure isn't the hardest either. With practice the Bimini can be tied in only a few seconds. My son, Rich, has had some fun in the cockpit of our charter boat with newcomers by tying the Bimini in less than one minute. All it takes is a bit of practice.

Properly tied, with neat rolls and twists, it tests at 100% of the breaking strength of the main fishing line making the Bimini the best knot to use when a double line is needed. It is ideal for use with lines of 10-pound test or stronger and is especially well suited to big game fishing with 50, 80 or 130-pound test lines and can be tied in Dacron or monofilament.

Fly rodders like it for building leaders. When a Bimini is tied at the end of the fishing line it creates a loop of double line. Fly leaders are joined to butt sections by interlocking the Bimini loops.

For many fishermen who have taken the time to learn the Bimini it is the knot they always use when adding a leader to the end of the line. Leaders are tied into the main fishing line by first doubling the line with either a spider hitch or the Bimini. The leader is then added by using the Surgeon's knot to between the leader and the Bimini double line.

A short Bimini of two to six feet as used for adding light tackle leaders can be tied according to the accompanying illustrations. The longer double lines of 15 to 30 feet as used by big game trollers or shark fishermen require a second person to help tie the knot. Have a buddy walk off the required length of doubled line so he is at the end, or bend, of the loop. You should be holding two legs of line; the main line and the leg of the loop. Hold your end tight and have your buddy make 20 twists in the line. It's easy to do this by placing the wrist of one hand through the loop and then twisting the wrist until 20 line twists are built up.

After the twists are in place, hold your end steady by squeezing the main line and the tag end of the line between your fingers while your buddy walks towards you spreading the two legs of the double line between the fingers of one hand (place one leg between the thumb and forefinger, the other between the forefinger and middle finger).

As he walks toward you the separated line is allowed to drop to the floor or deck. When only a few feet away from you the tension on the twists will build and he can then grab one leg in each hand. Your buddy will pull the legs apart much like the knees separate the legs in the illustrations. As tension on the twists continues to build, feed the tag end of the line so the knot rolls over itself. Once the twists start rolling over the knot ties just like in the illustrations.

Don't let the illustrations fool you. The Bimini only looks tricky. Tie it four or five times and you'll quickly get the hang of it.

1. Measure off a little more than twice the length of double line desired and double back forming a very long loop. Hold the standing line and tag end and have your assistant rotate the end of the loop 20 times, putting twists into it.
2. Your helper can slip the loop over a stationary post, get inside the loop and force or "walk" the twists toward you until they are about 12 inches from the tag end. Sit in a chair, put your feet on the two lines and spread your legs slightly to put tension on the twists.
3. The twists will be vertical in front of you. Hold the standing line in one hand just slightly off the vertical angle. Hold the tag end at a right angle (90 degrees) to the twists. Keep tension on the loop with your knees. Gradually relax the tension on the tag end so it will roll over the column of twists, starting just below the upper twist.
4. Spread your legs slowly to maintain pressure on the loop. Guide the tag end line into a series of tight spiral coils as it continues to roll over the twisted line.
5. When the spiral of the tag end line has completely rolled over the column of twists, maintain your knee pressure on the loop, release the standing line and place a finger of that hand in the V or "crotch" where the loop "legs" project from the knot to prevent slippage of the last turn. Take a half-hitch with the tag end around the nearest "leg" of the loop and pull it tight.
6. With the half-hitch holding the knot, relax some knee pressure but keep the loop stretched taut. Take the tag end and make a half-hitch around both legs of the loop, but do not pull it tight just yet.
7. Make two more turns with the tag end around both loop legs, winding inside the bend of line formed by the loose half-hitch and toward the main knot. Pull the tag end slowly, forcing the three loops to gather in a spiral.
8. When the loops are pulled nearly to the knot, tighten them to lock the knot in place. Clip the tag end but leave the 1/4 inch sticking out of the knot.

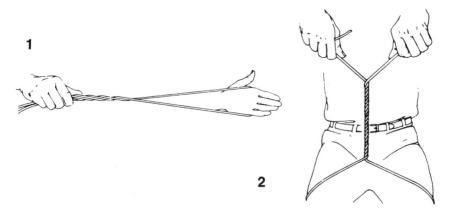

1

2

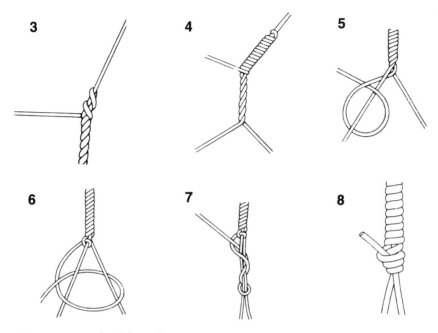

Surgeon's Knot

This knot can be used to join two lines of different diameters. It is easy to learn, easy to tie and convenient for adding heavy leaders for diamond jigging, livelining big baits, tuna chunking, surf casting and plug casting.

1. Lay the line and leader parallel with an overlap of about eight inches.

2. Treat the two lines as a single line and tie an overhand knot, passing the entire leader through the loop. Leave the loop open.

3. Make a second overhand knot, again passing the whole leader and overlapped line through.

4. Hold both overlaps and pull in opposite directions to make the knot. Then pull the line only against the leader to set the knot. Clip the surplus ends close to the knot.

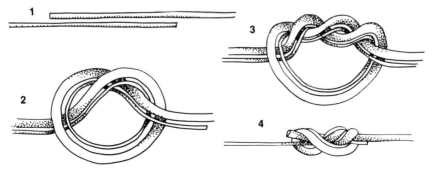

Albright Knot

Here's the ultimate way to add a very heavy leader to relatively light line, or to add a mono leader to a haywire loop formed at the end of a wire line or leader. It's more difficult to tie than the surgeon's knot, but can be mastered in a few tries.

1. Double back a few inches of the heavy line (or wire) and pass about ten inches of the lighter line through the loop.

2. Wrap the light line back over itself and both strands of the heavy line. This is a bit easier if you hold the light line and both leader strands with your left thumb and forefinger, and wind with your right hand.

3. Make ten snug, neat wraps then pass the end of the line back through the original big loop, as shown.

4. While holding the coils in place, pull gently on both strands of the heavy line, causing the coils to move toward the end of the loop. Take out the slack by pulling on both strands of light line. When the knot is snug pull hard on the main light line and main heavy line. Pull as hard as you can for a good solid knot. Clip both excess tag ends close.

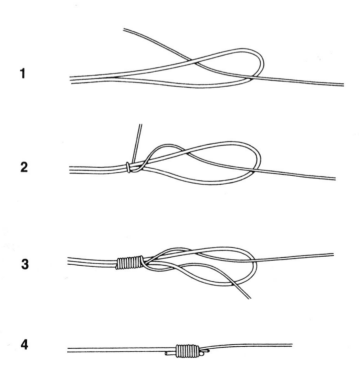

Dropper Loop

This is one way of tying in a second hook on a snell. Although this is not a strong knot, it is useful for small saltwater species and when using heavy 30 to 40-pound leaders for bottom fishing.

1. Form a loop in the line.

2. Pull one side of the loop down and begin taking turns with it around the standing line. Keep the point where the turns are made open so there are an equal number of turns on each side.

3. After eight to ten turns, reach through the center opening and pull the main loop through, as shown. Put your finger through this loop so it won't slip back.

4. Hold the loop with your teeth and pull both strands of line, creating tight coils.

5. Let go of the loop and pull hard to set the knot. The tightening coils will cause the dropper to stand out perpendicular to the line.

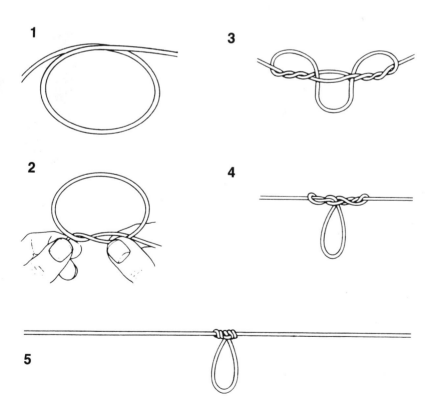

Surgeon's End Loop

Use this knot to tie a loop in the end of a line for attaching leaders, sinkers or other terminal gear quickly.

1. Double back a few inches of line and tie it into an overhead knot.

2. Leave the overhand knot open and bring the doubled line through once again.

3. Hold the standing line and tag end and pull on the loop to tighten the knot. The size of the loop formed can be controlled by positioning the loose knot and holding it while the knot is tightened. Clip tag end.

1

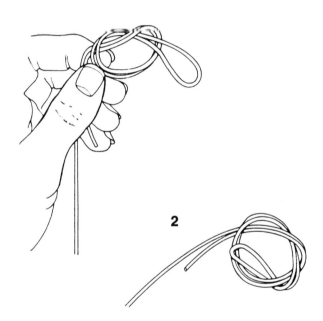

2

3

Offshore Swivel Knot

Big game fishermen use this knot for attaching a snap or swivel to the long loop formed when tying a double line with the Bimini twist and the spider hitch. A primary advantage of this knot is its ability to resist uncoiling even if one leg of the double line loop is broken during a fight with a big fish. Even though the double line is weakened, it will not unravel at the offshore swivel knot and will provide about 90% of the line's unknotted strength, thereby preventing the escape of a trophy fish.

1. Slip the loop of the double line through the eye of the swivel. Turn the loop a half-turn to put a single twist between the loop end and the swivel eye.

2. Pass the loop with the twist over the swivel. Hold the end of the loop, plus both strands of the double line. Let the swivel slide to the other end of the double loops now formed.

3. While still holding the original line loop and line strands with one hand, use your other hand to rotate the swivel through the center of both loops at least six times.

4. Continue to hold both line strands tightly but let go of the end of the loop. Pull on the swivel and the twists will tighten.

5. To draw the knot tight, hold the swivel with pliers and push the twisted loops toward the swivel eye while pulling tight on the line strands. Having someone else hold the double line helps at this stage.

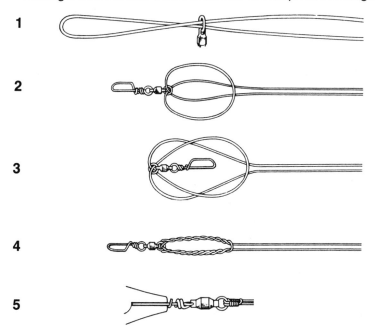

1

2

3

4

5

Haywire Twist

The haywire twist may sound like a middle America farm dance but it's a knot every fisherman who uses wire for leaders or line should know. Bluefishermen make up chum hooks with short traces of wire leader. Shark and marlin fishermen use it to make wire leaders. Fresh and saltwater wire line trollers use it to connect the wire to a leader and backing. Trollers who pull rigged ballyhoo for tuna, marlin and dolphin use the haywire twist. Fly fishermen use it when adding a short length of wire when casting streamers to toothy blues, king or Spanish mackerel. With few exceptions, most fishermen use the haywire twist some time during the fishing season.

I've only come across informal tests of the strength of this wire knot so information on how strong it should be is somewhat sketchy. Unlike knots used with monofilament lines where Berkley and DuPont have done extensive testing, no such lab information exists on the haywire but there are some things about the strength of the knot we know from fishing with it. Its strength is usually superior to the main fishing line being used so the haywire will nearly always be stronger than the mono it is joined to. For instance, when used to make bluefish chum rigs, and depending on the wire being used, the wire and haywire will be two to four times as strong as the fishing line.

The exception is when wire is used as the fishing line itself as when trolling wire for striped bass, blues or kingfish. In this case the haywire may cause some slight loss of strength in the wire line. I've tried testing the haywire with a Hunter Spring Scale and have found that 30-pound test Cortland stainless steel wire will usually break at or above the 30-pound rating and it will break at the knot nearly every time. My non-scientific, workbench tests seem to show the haywire is very close to the strength of the unknotted wire line.

The informal tests did show a definite loss of strength when the knot was incorrectly tied. Using less than three twists of the wire caused the haywire to slip under high pressure as might happen when battling a big mako shark. Less than three locking coils caused the knot to break at the coils or allowed the knot to slip under high pressure. To be on the safe side always use at least five twists and five locking coils when tying the haywire twist.

Soft stainless wire makes tying a haywire twist an easy job because the wire is so soft and bendable. Tying a haywire into much stiffer leader wire, sometimes called piano wire, especially a hefty #12 wire is much harder. There is a trick to it that once learned makes tying this knot very easy, even with those extra heavy duty wires of #12 to #16. After making the loop and while holding the loop end between the fingers of the right hand, begin making the twists by pushing both hands towards each other. Each time the hands are rotated 180 degrees, a half twist is bent to the wire. The pushing motion helps the knot fold each twist neatly intertwined with one another. Ten rotations will put five complete twists into the wire.

The tightly spaced locking coils are much easier to make but it is important to make a smooth transition from the last twist into the first coil. Too abrupt a bend into the coil may cause the last twist to deform with a loss of knot strength.

Wire leader coils come in sizes from #3 to #16. To practice, use a #9 wire. It's large enough to handle easily but not so stiff that it can't be worked with untrained hands and fingers.

Never cut the tag end of the wire line with pliers. The cutting edge of the pliers will leave a razor sharp edge at the end of the wire that can ruin a mates hands and cause severe cuts. Bending a crank handle into the tag end allows the wire to be easily broken so it breaks cleanly with no protruding sharp edge to slice a finger.

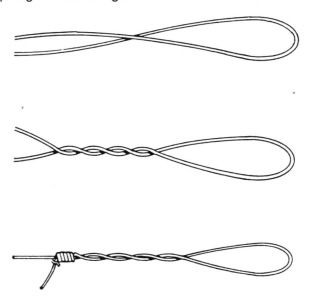

1. Pass several inches of the tag end of the wire through the hook eye. Bend the tag back next to the standing wire to form a small loop.

2. Hold the loop firmly with the thumb and forefinger of your left hand. Form a wide V between the two wire strands. Both sections of wire must be twisted simultaneously, or else the tag will simply wrap around the standing wire, producing a much weaker connection.

3. Make at least 3 1/2 twists in the two wires. Next, bend the tag end so it is 90 degrees to the standing wire.

4. Hold the already twisted section and wrap the tag end around the standing wire in several neat, tight, parallel coils.

5. Bend the last inch or so of the tag to a right angle, bending away from the standing line, not over it, to form a "handle."

6. Hold the twist steady and rock the tag end back and forth. It should break quickly, leaving a smooth end at the twist. If the wire is cut at this stage of the twist, it will leave a sharp burr that can cut your hand.

The haywire twist is an easy knot, often made difficult by lack of practice. If your first few don't turn out so hot, have patience and try a few more. Once you get the knack of it, you'll never lose the technique. It's like riding a bicycle; you just never forget how to do it.

Offshore Loop Knot

This knot is used to put a loop in the end of a cable or monofilament leader or to attach a hook to the end of a leader. It must be formed with crimps, and double crimps are preferred for greater strength.

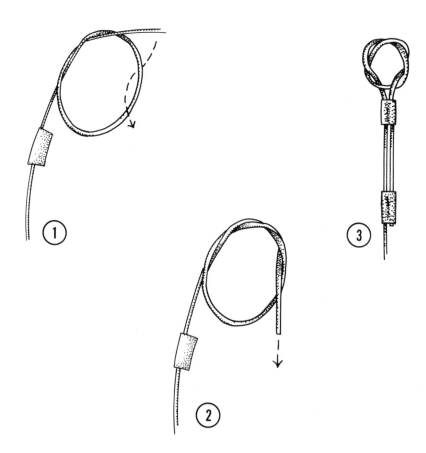

Snelling A Hook

Years ago factory-snelled hooks were common but today fishermen prefer to buy loose hooks and leader material of their own choice and tie the snells themselves to suit bait fishing needs. One distinct advantage of the snell is that it will never allow the hook to twist at an angle to the leader as might happen with a clinch, palomar or Uni-Knot. The snell can be used with hooks having an upturned or downturned eye by passing the line through the hook eye. Hooks with no turned eye can still be used but do not pass the mono through the eye.

1. Pass one end of the leader through the eye and past the hook bend. Pass the other end of the leader through the eye in the opposite direction, leaving a large loop.
2. Hold both lines along the shank. Use the line hanging from the eye and wind tight coils around the shank and both lines, starting at the eye and working toward the bend. Make 5 to 10 neat turns.
3. Hold the coils and pull on the long leader end until the entire loop disappears under the coils, and pull the coils snug.
4. Hold the tag end with pliers and the leader in your other hand, and pull in opposite directions to tighten the snell securely. Clip off the tag end and tie a surgeon's end loop in the end of the leader.

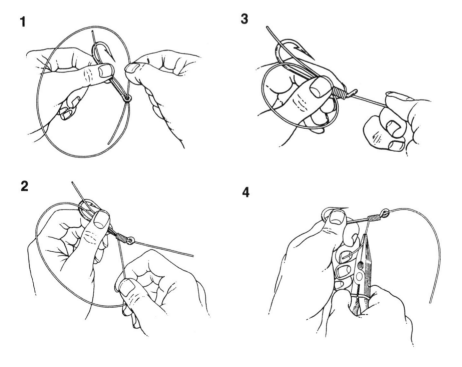

1

2

3

4

Line Splices

Most Dacron lines sold today are of the hollow core design and can readily be spliced to form double lines or to join two lines together. If you have a Dacron line that isn't hollow, you must use the Bimini twist or spider hitch to build the double line just as with monofilament.

Joining two lengths of Dacron is easy with this splice. Since the lower coils of line on a spool don't get much use, many anglers only replace the top 100 to 200 yards of line at the start of each new season. The splice is just as strong as the unspliced line.

1. Insert needle in line A about 4″ from end for a distance of 1″ and pick up end of line B.

2. Pull back through line A and detach needle.

3. Approximately 1″ from splice, insert needle in line B. Pick up loose end of line A in needle.

4. Pull back through line B.

5. Smooth splice by pulling both loose ends to work splice together.

6. Trim. Roll splice in fingertips to make neat.

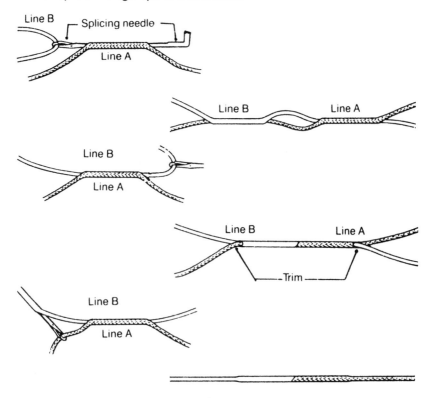

How To Make A Spliced Loop

Here's a quick, easy way to make a double line loop in braided Dacron line.

1. With end of line towards you, insert the splicing needle about 6″ from the end. Run needle about 2″ inside line, then out, and catch line with hook.

2. Bring the line back through and detach needle. Hold loop with thumb and forefinger of the left hand. Use the right hand to work the outside covering back over the line so that it literally turns itself inside out.

3. Start 1″ from the end of loop, insert needle in line toward loop; hook needle into loose end of line, pull back through the smooth out. Trim loose ends.

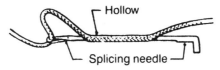

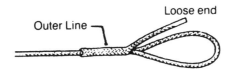

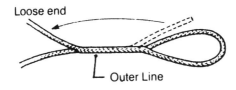

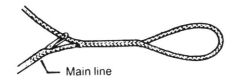

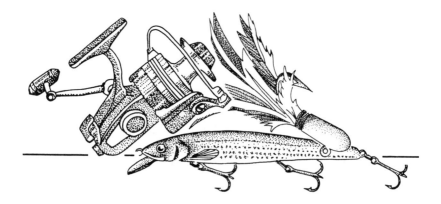

Chapter Thirteen

TRICKS WITH LURES

Fishing with lures is the ultimate challenge for many saltwater anglers. While there's no doubt that live bait can be extremely effective, the act of casting and manipulating the lure, to breathe life into an inanimate hunk of wood or plastic, is what makes fishing so interesting to many, many fishermen. And, lures can be just as good at the game of fish catching as natural baits when conditions are right.

There is a rhythm to lure fishing that comes after a lot of practice. The slow dance of a swimming plug, the pulsating dart of a bucktail and the seductive "pop" of a surface plug can only be learned through actual fishing experiences, so the goal is to fish often and experiment with the magic of lure fishing. The more you fish with lures, the better you get.

There are thousands of lures on the market and they probably all catch fish at one time or another. However, there are relatively few that earn the respect and habitual use of charter captains and guides. Traditional favorites like bucktails, nylons, spoons, jigs, swimming plugs, nylons and tubes are still catching fish today because they have proven to be effective lures for decades. Still, it's always fun to try a new lure - it may just be that "secret weapon" we all dream about, that will catch fish like no other lure ever invented.

The Art Of The Bucktail

The bucktail is truly one of the great casting lures of all time. They can be trolled but they are the most fun to fish when the angler uses rod and reel to impart life to the lead and deer hair by casting to the edge of a marsh sedge, a school of feeding fish or jigging over a wreck. Saltwater fish of all sizes eat them. From spike seatrout of only a pound to immense amberjack of close to 100 pounds, a properly presented bucktail is hard for a hungry game fish to pass up. The key is in presenting the lure to the fish so they want to attack it.

The right rod will help the action of the bucktail. A rod with a weepy tip action will not provide enough dancing and motion to the bucktail's action to be effective so a rod with a stiffer tip is usually preferred. Conventional tackle is the choice of many casters for inshore use, for deep jigging bucktails over wrecks and for casting where accuracy is vital. Conventional gear works best when the bucktail is retrieved in short hops and darts by working the rod with wrist action alone. Spinning tackle is especially handy when casting to schools of breaking fish and where the jigging action that catches best is a long sweep of the rod tip.

Bucktails are sold in a wide variety of shapes and fishermen along some parts of the coast get stuck on one style bucktail over another that seems to catch fish the best. The tried and true lima bean style is universally used. The ball shaped jigs, open mouth, torpedo and bullet shape all have their fans depending on which bay, sound or coastal area is being fished.

Perhaps more important than shape is the balance of the lure. The position of the eye on the bucktail will add to, or take away from, the action of the lure. When connected to a round bending snap like the Duo-Lock or Berkley, the bucktail will either hang level or with the tail of the lure at a down angle. Level bucktails when cast out and away from the boat or beach will have minimal up and down bouncing action. These style bucktails are best retrieved in sweeps. A bucktail that is tail or head heavy will have more of a dancing action and tend to hop in a more pronounced up and down motion. The hopping bugs are usually best when casting bucktails to the edge of a drop off, a channel edge, a deep hole or a shoal.

The rhythm of the jigging action can also be important. Sand eels dart and zip from side to side so a bullet shaped jig retrieved in a series of short sweeps will imitate the silvery baitfish better than a slow hopping action. Spearing, shrimp and sand fleas move in shorter darts and often appear to hop along as they move with tide and current. A lima bean or musketball bucktail retrieved in shorter hops will get more interest than a long sweeping retrieve. The variety of retrieves is nearly endless and it pays to experiment with different actions on every fishing trip.

Speed of retrieve is important, too. Spring-run weakfish, seatrout and striped bass are still feeling the effects of cold water and will not feed as aggressively as in the warmer summer months. A fast retrieve will be ignored no matter how hungry they may be. To slow the retrieve down, anglers who drift and cast bucktails make their cast into the direction of the drift. The drifting boat moving towards the retrieved bucktail tends to slow the lure down.

Bluefish chasing a school of bait will laugh at a slow moving lure. Give them too much time to examine the lure and they'll probably be able to tell where you bought it and how much you paid for it! A fast moving jig will get more results.

The level of retrieve, or the depth of the lure in the water column, is also critical. Surface feeding blues are exciting to cast to, yet a lure retrieved near the surface may get few strikes. Allowing the lure to sink at least a few feet will get more strikes. Weakfish, white perch, striped bass, seatrout and summer flounder need a lure retrieved near or on the bottom. The tail-hanging bucktails can be hopped or bounced along the bottom with deadly results. Work the rod tip in short vertical lifts to get the bucktail dancing. On the down stroke of the rod, the lure should hit the bottom and bounce up on the next rod lift.

I've never been completely sure about the effects of color but I've seen many occassions when one color bucktail did work a lot better than another color. On a trip to Delaware Bay for weakfish I was using a white bug with a purple worm and watched my buddy next to me catch fish after fish on a yellow bug with a green tail. I switched over to a lure like his and still couldn't catch! I then switched to a slightly heavier bug, again in white

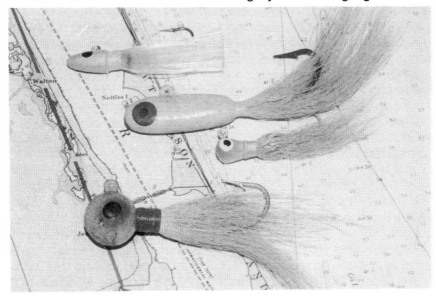

The universal lure for the entire East Coast, bucktails come in many shapes, sizes and weights to suit any fishing situation.

and then matched him fish for fish. Still, color may play a big part in the day's success so I always have a selection of colors in my doodlebug box.

The weight of the bucktail can be critical. We only need enough weight to hit the bottom. Too much weight may ruin the action of the lure. Not enough weight will leave the bucktail at the mercy of tide or current and never allow it to get to the fish. Surface or near surface retrieves call for enough weight for casting convenience. Bucktails bounced on a channel edge or deep shoal need enough weight to cut through the current to get to the bottom. Naturally the weight of the bucktail should match the tackle being used. A three ounce bucktail is hardly the lure for a one handed casting rod meant for 3/4-ounce lures.

The use of bucktails as fishing lures goes back to ancient times as evidenced by the discovery bucktail-type lures being found preserved in ancient Egyptian tombs. Thousands of years later, the bucktail is still doing yeoman duty all along the coast catching lots of fish.

Spoon Feeding

Spoons are an often overlooked lure in many fishermen's tackle boxes. Years ago that wasn't the case. I remember looking into the trays of my grandfather's tackle box and seeing the nifty spoons all lined up and ready for action. His biggest fish, a freshwater muskellunge from up in New York state was taken on a spoon. While spoons are still used today, they often seem overshadowed by more modern swimming plugs.

I still like spoons, as do many light tackle fans in saltwater, and they can be just as effective today as they were decades ago. Sometimes considered a bass lure, the old time Johnson Silver Minnow can be deadly on weakfish, seatrout and bluefish. I once out-caught a fishing buddy on striped bass by casting a Johnson Minnow into the marsh sedges off Connecticut's Norwalk Islands while fishing for schoolie striped bass. The pork rind tail no doubt added to the fish appeal. The biggest fish of the day was a real surprise at just over 15 pounds but it was a ball on the light spinning tackle.

Small bluefish like to eat spoons, too. Once on a windy day that forecast 8-foot seas offshore, we wondered what to do with a visiting outboard motor factory rep from Wisconsin. We eased on down to the inlet, staying inside the jetties and the nasty water that lay beyond. Casting 3/4-ounce Krocodile spoons with light spinning rods and did a leap job on 3 to 4-pound tailor blues. It seemed like every cast had a strike. The fish tore 6-pound test line from the reels, bent the rods hard and thoroughly impressed our visitor. The spoons had just the right flash and wobble to grab the attention of the blues and with a single hook at the tail end, unhooking the mini choppers was a breeze.

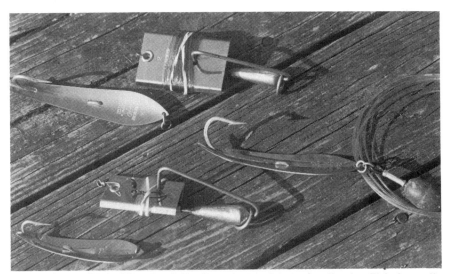

Spoons are an old-time favorite trolling lure that work just as well today. Fish them off planers, behind a trolling drail on a 15-foot leader or add an egg sinker at the head of the spoon to get them down deep.

Spoons are also favorite lures for trolling. Depending on where you fish, spoons will catch blues and bass, school tuna, bonito, king mackerel and Spanish mackerel, little tunny, weakfish, seatrout and school channel bass. In shallow water coastal sounds and bays spoons can be trolled directly on monofilament line. If a little more depth is needed a trolling drail tied about six to ten feet ahead of the spoon will get it down several feet. Figure five feet for every two ounces of weight at a slow troll.

Along the surf or on the inshore grounds a few miles off the beach, the best bets are planers, downriggers or wire line to get the spoons to the feeding level of the fish. Early season blues will sometimes be located right near the surface and a four ounce drail is all that is needed to get the right depth but by summer when the fish lie deeper in the water, holding nearer to the bottom deeper trolling methods are necessary.

Spoons can be jigged in shallow water along the beaches. Weakfish and striped bass are often fooled by a thick bodied, heavy spoon cast into the surf. Work the boat a few yards from the back side of the crashing surf and allow the spoon to sink before working the retrieve. Work the crank a few turns then stop to let the spoon flutter to the bottom, then reel again. This reel and flutter, reel and flutter jigging action can be a sure thing at times.

Spoons come in all sizes from an inch to nine inches. Some have thin, light-weight bodies, others have thick heavy-weight bodies. Some have painted bodies or reflective tape added for color and flash. Others sport nothing more than their shiny silver or gold plated finishes. Match the size to the bait, the weight to the depth and spoons will catch fish for the next hundred years.

Surgical Tube Lures

Here's an old-time lure that is used along most every part of the East Coast to catch fish from the Florida Keys to New England. Depending on where you live, they're called snakes, eels, tubes or hoses. Charter skippers in Massachusetts, Montauk, Sandy Hook and Chesapeake Bay have perfected them over decades of use and in the hands of the best fishermen, tube lures are deadly. Most tubes are trolled, especially the unweighted types used for weakfish, striped bass and bluefish. Tubes with lead heads and bead chain-mounted tails can be cast to bluefish, cobia, small sharks and striped bass. Tube lures are vital ammunition in the arsenal of lures needed to catch fish consistently.

Tube lures are made from surgical tubing available from most any pharmacy or from the newer plastic tubings used for low pressure water lines, soda fountains and various industrial applications. The plastic tubing is available from plumbing supply stores. Special coils of pre-colored tubing are also available in many tackle shops that also sell surgical tubing and the plastic industrial tubings. The three types of tubing are sold in several diameters to make little skinny tube lures to big, fat striped bass cow killers.

An advantage of the natural surgical tubing is its ability to absorb clothing dyes, like Rit and Tintex, to make some fascinating colors. An old cooking pot filled with several quarts of boiling hot water will make a concentrated dye mixture to soak the tubes in. Once washed and cooled they are ready to go fishing. Striped bass fishermen have traditionally favored the deep, muted tones of wine red and purple for use as single tubes or as tubes for umbrella rigs. The natural amber color of undyed surge tubing is another terrific color especially when fishing over a light colored, sandy bottom.

Surgical tubing does not readily take to very bright colors, so for a flashy look the nod goes to the pre-dyed tubes with their brilliant finishes. The colors have been factory dyed under controlled, high temperatures and are available in vivid lime green, orange, yellow and hot pink.

Clear plastic tubes are much stiffer than surgical tubes and do not take colors at all. Instead, tube manufacturers add color by inserting silver or colored mylar strips inside the tubing. The resulting color schemes are often very life-like. The harder plastic is not so supple as the surge tubing and requires more time to shape the lure. Some fishermen feel the tough plastic tubes stand up to bluefish better than the softer latex surgical tubing.

Tubes must spin in the water to be effective fish catchers. Slow swimming fish, like striped bass and weakfish, only react to slow trolling speeds and a very gentle swimming motion from the tube. Surgical tubes are usually best for bass and weaks because of the natural suppleness of the tubing. Many charter captains rig their tube lures with a heavy mono leader so the 8 to 16 inch lures swim with a slow rhythmic action caused by the natural curved shape. Tubes that have become straight from hard use or poor storage in a tackle box, can be re-curved by placing them in a coffee can, coiled neatly, and leaving them in the sun to "bake" for a day. When removed from the can they'll have their old natural shape back again. In New England these soft tubes are fished with a sandworm draped on the tail hook for added appeal.

Other captains assure perfect action by rigging the tube with a length of wire through the tube. Chesapeake Bay captains bend the wire into an "S" shape by wrapping the tube around a gaff handle to get the right swimming action. The wire offers the chance to fine tune the tube lure to get an action that suits any trolling speed, any water conditions and for different species of fish.

Bluefish like a more aggressive action in the tube. The wire leader down the center of the tube prevents cut offs from the sharp teeth of the bluefish and allows the tube to bend into shapes that swim more erratically and with amplified spinning motion. While bass and weaks like the gentle, slow spin, bluefish much prefer the wild, twisting action of a tube lure bent into a larger curve.

Jointed tubes have been a favorite of mine and I especially like them because they can be cast to surface breaking fish, cast near large offshore buoys where dolphin, blues and cobia may hang out and I've had some neat fishing by casting them to small sharks in shallow water. They

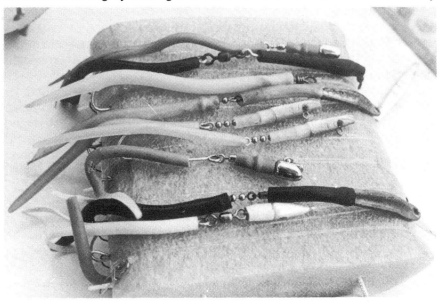

Jointed tubes will catch a variety of game fish while trolling. They are available in bright and dark colors and in many lengths.

can be used in the surf or from jetties and several manufacturers of jointed tube eels sell them with swim heads that work in a side to side wiggle action just like a rigged eel. From Stamford, Connecticut to the Florida Keys, jointed tube lures have been winners for me.

They are perfect for use as the center tube on an umbrella rig. I tie them on three to four foot leaders so the tube trails behind the tubes mounted on the arms of the umbrella. Jointed tubes work just as well on a coat hanger spreader bar, too. Of course, they can also be trolled as single tubes and I've caught blues and bass, king mackerel, weakfish and school tuna on the jointed tubes. When trolling I use tube lures that have a head with the mounting eye offset to the side, not straight pulling tubes that can cause some horrendous line twist at bluefish trolling speeds. The offset mounting eye serves as a keel so the tubes won't spin unless worked at very high speeds.

Tube lures imitate slim profile bait like sand eels, squid and eels when trolled slowly. The faster spinning action gives them a larger silhouette as they imitate menhaden, mullet and other small fish.

Versatile Diamond Jigs

For fall fishermen, diamond jigs are one of the most important lures to catch bluefish, striped bass, weakfish (seatrout), school tuna and also fish that live on the inshore wrecks like pollock, cod and ling. For more southern anglers, the diamond jigs are gaining in popularity for bluefish, amberjack and school tuna. Captain Eric Burnley, a friend of mine from Virginia Beach, has taken blackfish on diamond jigs. The appeal of the lure is universal and it's hard to find a fish that won't eat a well presented diamond jig.

Jigs come in several styles and sizes and have been around for perhaps a hundred years. Old timers used to make their own and fished them on hand lines. The most popular production jig is still the slab sided jigs made by Bridgeport Lures of Connecticut. They have 4 sides and are nearly square in shape when viewed from top to bottom. They are good catchers of cod, pollock and alligator blues and in the smaller sizes catch mackerel, whiting, ling and seatrout.

The now defunct Ava Lure Company popularized a 4-sided jig that looked like it had been run over by a truck. Rather than being square in cross section the Ava was flattened more like a diamond shape. Called the A series, the Ava spawned a whole slug of imitators all using the A label to identify the weight of the lure. Typically available in 2, 4 and 6 ounce sizes the jigs are labeled A27, A47, A67 and so on up into the heaviest A16 sizes. For many years it was THE jig to use on party boats for blues and weakfish.

Other versions of "diamond jigs" may not even have slab sides but are

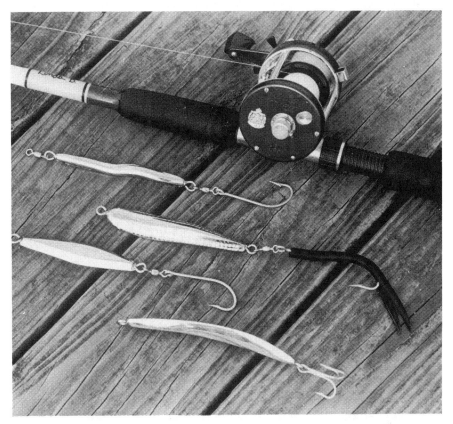

Slab-sided jigs are the traditional "diamond" jig, but there are other shapes and styles that catch deep water game fish, too.

rounded in shape or bent to swim on the retrieve like the Bridgeport Sand Eel jig and the Wobble Jig. Acme Kastmasters and Hopkins Shorty jigs are other good metal lures that can be jigged with success. There are probably other diamond jigs that I'm forgetting or that I haven't seen and the best sources for jigs that work in any part of the coast are local tackle shops.

The actual technique of fishing with diamond jigs calls for the lure to be dropped to the bottom then retrieved in either a fast zippy action back to the boat or a jerking action that makes the jig dance. Bluefishermen usually put the reel in free spool and let the jig fall to the bottom then retrieve with no jigging action. Seatrout may hit better on a slower action with lifts of the rod tip. Tuna hit large diamond jigs when jigged with long sweeps of the rod tip. I've caught amberjack with a similar action while fishing Florida wrecks.

When fish hit the jig they usually do it like they mean it. I had a visitor from Ohio on the "Linda B" one time while jigging bluefish. He asked, "Will

I feel the nibble?" He thought we were making fun of him when we told him to hang on the rod real tight so it wouldn't go over the side. He mumbled something about how he caught big walleyes and they fought pretty good. Next thing we hear is a shout as the guy is struggling to hold onto the rod while his first East Coast bluefish was yanking for all it was worth at the other end. "They do pull hard", he later admitted.

Conventional reels are the best for diamond jigging if you jig frequently. A spinning reel is designed for casting and retrieving and not for winching in bottom hugging big fish. This isn't a knock on spinning reels, they can do things that conventional reels can't do; but in this case the spinner is best left at home. Lifting a 10-pound bluefish from 120 feet of water is tough. Battling a 30-pound amberjack is even tougher. A 100-pound yellowfin is gut-busting pleasure.

Rods should be on the stiff side. Many fishermen go to custom rod builders to get the action they need since many factory rods do not offer firm tip actions, something very necessary to set the hook with authority. The so-called West Coast style rods make lifting the fish easier but may lose fish after the strike because the hook isn't well set. In between all the fast taper rods there are some factory-made sticks from Fenwick, Daiwa, Penn and others that have the required stiffish action. Some factory rods with limber tips, or extra fast taper tips, can be improved for East Coast use by trimming the blank to the first guide. Glue on a new tip top and you're in business with a better jigging rod. Wire leaders should never be used. The metal body of the jig is built-in leader that prevents cut offs from toothy blues or king mackerel. A leader may actually foul the jig by folding back on it as the jig is dropped into deep water as it tangles around the lure.

Jigging can be done while at anchor or while drifting. I prefer drifting for blues, bass, tuna, seatrout and other species that hold over a fairly wide stretch of the bottom. Wreck-hugging fish may require the boat to be anchored. In the spring, when the fish are scattered over wide areas, trolling is the best bet, but in the fall many species of fish gather in tight schools holding close to major bottom structure so this is the perfect season to work the jigs.

The help of a LORAN, a graph recorder or color scope will pinpoint the bottom structure and the feeding level of the fish. The recorder will also tell you how to fish the jig. When fish marks are randomly spaced from top to bottom in the water column the jig can be retrieved all the way back to the boat after being free spooled and dropped to the bottom. It may be possible to get a strike at any level.

When the fish are holding near the bottom it can pay to only partially retrieve the jig about 10 to 15 cranks of the handle then free spool the lure back to the bottom. This keeps the lure down deep where the fish are located and avoids retrieving the jig through the upper fish-less water.

Trolling Nylons

The basic nylon lure is simple - a lead head, much like a bucktail head, and has a trolling eye located at the forward center or slightly above center of the lead casting. The head can be bullet, ball, torpedo or cut mouth Smilin' Bill style. At the rear of the head is another eye to which a length of brass chain is attached. The hook, usually a 5/0 to 8/0 size, is attached at the end of the chain. Long strands of nylon Fish Hair are attached to the lead head, wrapped in place just like a bucktail lure. The nylon strands are long enough to cover the hook and chain.

Nylons come in a wide variety of colors. Favorites include the green and yellow combination, red and white, blue and white, purple and white, all white and a new blaze orange offered by Andrus Lures. I've caught them on many colors, but the brighter colors seem to get more attention from the blues. I like the green and yellow, red and white, and blaze orange the best.

Other versions of nylons are available too. The plastic skirted Hoochies that are used so much off Delaware can be good alternatives and Sevenstrand now offers a bluefish sized clone lure, appropriately called the Bluefish Clone, that is another sure winner. I began using the Sevenstrand lures a few years ago soon after they were first introduced and they caught fish real good. Although not actually nylons, in the manufacturing sense, charter skippers would lump these plastic-skirted lures in the same category, so we will too. They are trolled exactly the same way as a nylon.

A distinct advantage of nylons is their durability. The lures usually cost somewhere around $4 to $7 depending on the size of the lure, yet they'll last a long time. One year from May through June with nine bluefish charters I used a selection of six nylon lures to catch nearly all the fish for an average catch of 75 fish per lure. If you want to calculate economics that's only $.07 per fish! We replaced straightened hooks and the lure heads were chipped, but the nylon hair was still virtually like new. Nylons are nearly indestructible.

Nylons can be fished on monofilament, on planers, on wire line with downriggers. Which method you choose is decided by the graph recorder. In mid-May to late June it is not uncommon to find bluefish holding on the top layers of water never more than a few feet below the surface. A set of four nylons run with two off the outriggers and two off the transom will usually yield a good catch of fish. One year in June, off Delaware, we caught blues so fast that all we could handle were two rods. We never got more than two rods set in the holders before a bluefish would waffle one of the two nylons already being trolled.

It's important to fish the correct depth where the fish are located. When the fish are holding between 10 and 40 feet deep, as in early summer, the choices would be planers or wire line. Which you use is probably determined by where you live along the coast. North of Delaware many fishermen lean toward wire line while the south Jersey, Virginia and North Carolina crew prefers planers.

Even when using wire or planers I still may run a nylon off each outrigger. Blues hooked on a deep line will sometimes be followed by their brothers and sisters as they are played to the surface. On many occasions another fish can be hooked on a top water lure dragged off the outrigger. As the boat is slowed to play the fish, the nylon will sink slightly because of the slower boat speed so it is right in front of the rising blues.

Downriggers are the solution when blues are located more than 40 feet down. In the fall when the blues are usually found closer to the bottom than to the top, we've trolled nylons on downriggers and scored well.

Nylons don't require wire leaders because the lures have their own built in leader provided by the brass chain running under the skirt. At a typical length of 9 to 15 inches in length, and since blues always hit the tail of the lure, there's no need to run an extra length of wire ahead of the lure. In fact, that extra wire may inhibit the action or fish appeal of the lure.

When replacing hooks, purchase open eye hooks that can then be crimped onto the brass chain. A long shanked hook offers a little extra leverage when unhooking a bluefish and can speed up the unhooking time as compared to a short-shank hook that almost always requires pliers or a hook disgorger to remove the hook.

Nylons, spoons and diamond jigs are famous for catching chopper bluefish like this one caught by the author's dad over a deep water ridge.

Umbrella Rigs For Striped Bass

There are two styles of umbrellas that seem to pull striped bass consistently; the larger gorilla rig and the mini rig. The gorilla has six arms with teaser tubes mid-length on each arm and bead chain mounted tubes on the outboard ends of each arm. The outside tubes have hooks, but not the teasers. A single tube is attached on a 3 to 6 foot length of 40 to 60-pound, mono dropped from an eye at the center of rig so the tube trails behind the other tubes.

The mini rigs are smaller versions of the gorillas. They still have six arms with tubes mounted at each end, but they lack the teaser tubes and the arms are therefore shorter. The minis have much less drag as they are towed through the water and are easier for most fishermen to launch into position. Like the larger gorilla rigs, a single tube is always dropped back off the rear center eye.

The appearance is much like a school of baitfish passing by with the trailing tube looking like it's trying to catch up with its baitfish brothers or like a small bluefish chasing sand eels. We'll never really know what the bass thinks it is, but we do know that both rigs work.

The colors of the tubes can be very important. Striped bass seem to prefer the more subdued colors like dark red, wine purple, black and dark green. Bluefish on the other hand like the more gaudy bright reds and greens, yellows, white and silver tubes. There is always the day to prove the general rule wrong, but bass will most often hit the darker colors.

Tube shape and length is also important. Bluefish will hit best on tubes with a more pronounced spinning action. I even bend the hook shanks to make the tubes spin more wildly. Bass are the opposite and most strikes will come on tubes with softer action. Slightly longer tubes with a bead chain at the head end to assure slow spinning are the better bass tubes.

Years ago off Sandy Hook, a fishing buddy, Vince Grippo, began using Cape Cod spinners just ahead of the trailing tube. The spinner is the same type used by sandworm trollers but it worked nicely with umbrella rigs, too.

A favorite trick of charter captains was to use a contrasting color for the trailing tube. If the rig is armed with wine-colored tubes they add a green, amber or white tube at the center. The tail tube becomes more visible and therefore gets most of the strikes.

I have three favorite colors that take striped bass year after year; red, green and wine. I'll fish three rods and put a red rig on the port, green rig to starboard and the wine rig down the center. To keep the lines from tangling on turns the two side rods are mounted in side rod holders to keep the rod tips 90 degree from the sides of the boat. The center rig has a 4-ounce drail added just ahead of the rig to take it down just a bit deeper to keep it away from the side lines on a turn.

Bluefish will hit the red and the green rigs, but rarely mess with the wine rig. Most all the striped bass hit the red or the wine rigs, but I leave the green rig in the pattern because occasionally it takes a big fish. In fact my second 50 pounder fell for a green tubed gorilla rig.

Umbrellas are almost always fished on wire. I've tried them on downriggers and they work okay, but the wire line system offers more control when fishing for bass and blues over changing bottom structure. For instance at Shrewsbury Rocks with 150 of wire, when the high reef rises to only 15 feet of depth, a simple push of the throttles increases boat speed and raises the rigs over the reef. With downriggers the trolling weights have to be manually lowered and raised as the bottom changes.

Most fishermen will use 40-pound test wire, either stainless or monel. Stainless is less expensive but can kink easier. Monel is softer but wears out faster. Either will get you through at least one if not two seasons before replacement is necessary.

I rig the wire to a small black swivel to attach it to the backing. Another small swivel attaches the 60-pound twelve-foot leader to the wire. The umbrella rigs are attached via a large Duo Lock Snap to the end of the leader.

To calculate trolling depth, estimate that for every 50 of wire line in the water, the lure will go down about 5 feet of depth. Mark the wire with tape or dental floss to be sure how much line is in the water. I use red tape at 150, 200 and 250-foot increments since I rarely ever use less than 150 of wire at a minimum.

This school striped bass hit the trailing tube on an umbrella rig trolled a few hundred yards off the beach over a sand bar. School fish should be released to protect the future of this great game fish.

Trolling speed for bass is S-L-O-W, 3 to 4 knots is about right, but 4 to 6 knots for bluefish. Since there is an overlap in acceptable speed for both fish, you can catch bass and blues from 3 to 6 knots, but if bass are the target, you'll definitely catch more of them at slower speeds. Some twin engine boats have to troll on one engine to get the boat down to striped bass speed.

Tricks With Plugs

Plug casters are perhaps the most inventive of fishermen. They are always tinkering, altering or improving. Anyone who uses plugs a lot seems unable to resist the chance to try something new, some new way to make the plug cast better, swim better, look more alive or dance a bit more seductively. Whether you fish from a boat or plug the surf, changing the action of swimming plugs can bring more strikes, more fish.

"Let all fishermen praise chicken feathers" I once heard a tackle shop owner say. Dyed on brilliant yellow, hot red or bleached pure white, saddle hackles (as fly tiers call them) can add a new dimension of life to a swimming plug. I use a siwash stainless steel hook with an open eye, adding two or three feathers to each side of the hook. I use a pair of vise grips to grab the hook and hold it while wrapping the feathers with thread. The pliers are held in place on a workbench vise.

After tying in the feathers, a few dabs of fly tyers head cement secures the threads. Once the cement is dry the hook is added to the tail end of the swimming plug, replacing the standard treble hook. Pliers crush the open eye in place around the hook mounting eye of the plug.

You can use large plugs or small. The Atom Jr and the ancient Surfster work especially well when retrieved slowly so the tail of the lure rides high in the water causing a small wake. The feathers, soft and supple when wet, move with a snake action that is very life-like. Fished at night along the jetties or in quiet bay waters, these plugs have a well deserved reputation for fooling striped bass and weakfish.

Smaller plugs can be modified in the same way. A yellow-backed Bomber with a yellow feather tail and single hook proved itself for me on many early morning bass forays. The plug scored on fish with uncanny ability, but stopped catching after a bluefish tore the feathers from the hook. Its fish catching ability was restored by simply adding new feathers.

A fishing guide showed me some swimming plugs he modified by removing the tail treble hooks and replacing them with single hooks. To the single hook he added a plastic tail, like the Mr Twister style, which added a new dimension of action. These plugs were used primarily for weakfish, casting in quiet back bay waters at dusk. The tail inhibited the swimming action, but added the vibrating tail which proved deadly.

Plug action can be modified by bending the towing eye of the plug. A rusty pair of needle nose pliers is often found in a plug casters jetty bag or tackle box. The amazing effect of modifying the eye was shown to me by a member of the Rhody Fly Rodders, whose name I lost in the cobwebs of time, as we cast for seatrout at the mouth of a tidal creek. He had bent the plug eye to the left to make the lure swim more to the left to take greater advantage of the left flowing current. His plug stayed in the prime water a few seconds longer than mine did and he was definitely scoring more fish; his four to my one. Like many good fishermen he didn't show me his secret until the tide stopped and we were back at the car. Under the glare of a flashlight he showed me what he had done.

Bending the eye can save a "bad" plug. Manufacturers go to great lengths to assure quality and consistency in their plugs but who knows what may happen once the plug leaves the factory? A surf tackle shop owner I know got a great deal on a box of plugs that had damaged packaging. The price was right and he offered them for sale at good savings to his customers only to have one of them complain that the plug swam funny. Looking closely at the lures he saw that nearly every one of them had the eye bent severely to one side. A quick touch up with the pliers and they were all back in perfect shape.

Minor tune ups may be needed while you are fishing. I've had many plugs that changed their action by being banged on jetty rocks, thumped on the deck of a bass boat, or from being jammed in a tackle box or plug bag. All it takes is a fine tuning adjustment with the pliers to correct any odd action and the plug is once again swimming A-OK.

Most plugs can be made to swim deeper by bending the eye upward, or they will swim closer to the surface by bending the eye down. This works most dramatically with larger plugs like the Atom Juniors or wooden surf plugs that have the eye set sideways in the front of the lure. Smaller plugs where the eye is set vertical in the front of the plug are not as affected by the eye angle change.

Retrieving the plug at a slow speed will keep the lure closer to the top, a faster retrieve digs the plug deeper into the water. Bluefish may appreciate the deeper, faster retrieve while striped bass and weakfish may find the top water, slow retrieve more to their liking, particularly at night, dawn and dusk.

The best action for any swimming plug is usually obtained by tying the line directly to the lure, no snap at all and definitely without a snap swivel. If a snap must be used, look for the type with a rounded bend like the Duo-Lock or Berkley Cross Lock rather than a snap with a tapered end that restricts the movement of the plug's wobbling action.

Among my favorite plugs are the swimmers, like the Rebel, with the glued-in-place plastic lip, but they sometimes tumble when casting against the wind. To get around this problem, wrap lead wire around the tail hook to add a small amount of weight. With a few wraps of lead wire, like the kind sold in fly tying shops, the extra weight rockets the plug out on a cast so the tail is always pulling first with no tumbling and twisting. If you don't have any lead wire, use a small split shot on the hook shank crushed in place with pliers.

Momentary "anti-tumbling" control can be added with the tip of the index finger of the hand that holds the spinning reel. As the plug zips away from the rod tip it usually has plenty of inertia to send it on its way with no tumbling. It's halfway through the cast that a breeze can cause the flipping action of the plug. If the angler drops the index finger along side the spool to slow the coils of line flowing from the reel spool, slight tension will be applied to the line adding some additional control to the plug. Although a slight loss in distance may result, the added control assures every cast will result in a properly working plug.

If you fish for blues, once a school is located the plugging action can be quite fast. Unhooking the catch quickly is essential to catching a lot of fish. To make unhooking easier, I replaced all the treble hooks with single hooks on my bluefish plugs; poppers, swimmers and spoons. Both Mustad and Eagle Claw sell hooks with open eyes that can be added to a plug in a few seconds with the pliers.

Sometimes the plugs work better without the swimming lip or with the lip bent into a new shape. Use pliers to snap the lip off one or two swimmers to create a plug that skitters across the surface rather than digging in with a swimming action. Work the rod tip in short sweeps, with the tip held low to the water so the plug seems to dart and skitter each time it is pulled. This action seems to drive bluefish crazy and I have caught several striped bass with this method, too.

A bent lip can also make the plug do strange, fish-catching things. To bend the lip, hold the plug near a butane torch to heat the lip enough so the lip can be bent back to dramatically alter the plug action. This is a trick used for barracuda in the Keys and I've been delighted to use it up north for bluefish, striped bass and weakfish.

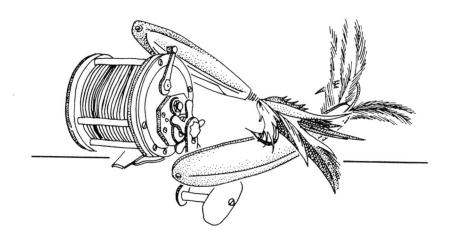

Chapter Fourteen

FISHING WITH ELECTRONICS

Modern technology plays a vital role in today's sport fishing electronics. Tiny computer chips, space age materials and innovative designs have miniaturized sport fishing electronics making them easier to install on a greater number of boats at reasonable cost. Years ago, LORAN receivers were so large only Navy ships had room to install them, today they fit the palm of your hand.

Walk along the dock of any sport fishing marina and you will find few boats that don't have at least a graph recorder or flasher, a VHF radio and a LORAN receiver. No longer considered toys for the well-heeled anglers in offshore cruisers, even 20 to 29-foot mini-fishing machines sport temperature gauges, color scopes and radar, while LORAN sets and VHFs are considered "must have" items for many small 16 to 19-foot skiffs.

Electronics that may seem like something out of a "Star Wars" movie will actually help you catch more fish, navigate with more safety and run your boat more fuel efficiently. The bottom line is that electronics are good values and help you catch a lot more fish.

Fish Finders

A modernized version of the World War II Navy SONAR units used to detect submarines, these so called fish finders use the same basic technology to find bottom structure and schools of fish. To experienced fishermen, they are more valuable as a tool to peer into the depths to locate structure. Once the structure is found, the schools of bait and game fish are not usually far away.

A sound signal is transmitted from the SONAR unit through a transducer mounted on the transom or through the hull. The signal bounces back to the transducer when it strikes the bottom or any fish in between. A graph recorder will mark the bottom and schools of fish on a roll of paper. As the paper moves, a profile of the changing bottom will become a permanent reference. Flashers show the bottom with flashing lights on a dial face but have no way of permanently recording the bottom nor fish that you may find. New LCD units use tiny dots to show bottom contours and fish.

Fish finders are of three basic types; the graph recorder with its paper print outs, the LCD or Liquid Crystal Display with a screen made of hundreds of dots called pixels, and the color scope which is much like the TV screen in your living room at home.

The paper recorders etch the image of the bottom and any fish in between by sparking a scratch into the surface of the special paper. The image is permanent and can be referred to in the future, a feature many wreck fishermen like because it provides a "picture" of the wreck that can be filed in a notebook. LCD fish finders work much the same way, but the paper is replaced with a screen composed of pixels. Fish and the bottom contours are marked by black dots as the image slowly moves across the screen. The color scope fish finders mark the bottom and fish in a display of many different colors so you can quickly distinguish between bait and game fish, and even between different species of game fish because of the size of the images and the colors of the images. The LCD and the color scope fish finders do not provide a permanent image. As the display moves across the screen, the old image is continually lost while the next

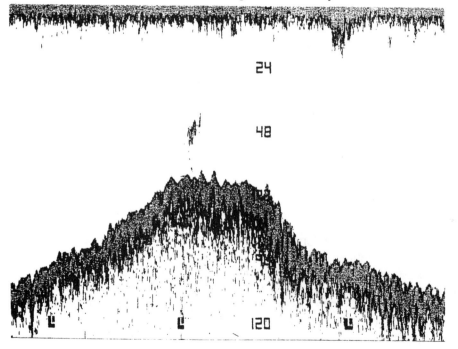

The recorder is your vital link to finding the structure and then the fish.

new image is being shown.

While some anglers still use the term "fish finder" the real advantage of a recorder is its ability to record the bottom structure. The top of the water may all look relatively level and calm, but down below there is an ever changing panorama of hills, valleys, ridges, drop-offs, deep holes, flat shelves and lumps. These major changes in the bottom are called structure and this is what you are looking for. Fish move along structure as they change feeding locations or to adapt to changing light levels, presence of bait and changing water temperature. The structure serves as a "highway" for fish to travel along. Find the structure and you will find the fish.

To effectively use a recorder, LCD or scope, it is helpful to have a good chart of the area you usually fish. Use magic markers to trace over and enhance the bottom contour lines already printed on the NOAA charts. The local ridges, lumps, holes and sloughs will show up dramatically on your chart.

Run a compass course, or use your LORAN, to get to the structure. Just before you arrive, turn on the recorder to begin marking and plotting the changing bottom. Once you arrive on the structure you should begin to mark fish. If you don't, run a zig zag search pattern or move to the next nearest structure.

The recorder can tell you how to fish. For instance, if you were looking for bluefish and found them over a steep drop off, the recorder can tell you whether to deep jig or troll. If the fish are marked high and are scattered, a typical spring bluefish situation, then you would troll. If the fish are marked down deep almost on the bottom as typically happens in the fall, you would diamond jig.

LORAN

For many years LORAN was available to only the affluent fishermen. That has changed dramatically with the latest LORAN receivers becoming smaller in size and ever lower in price. Some LORANS are now in the $200 range! For an offshore fisherman, a LORAN could save enough fuel in one or two seasons (because it can steer a very straight course) to easily pay for itself! And, it will help you to navigate to the best offshore hot spots increasing your catch.

In very simple terms LORAN is a radio navigation system. Instead of playing Jimmy Buffet or Willie Nelson it "plays" numbers and displays them on the front of the LORAN receiver. The numbers represent the difference in time of arrival of 2 radio signals called secondaries matched to a single master signal. The numbers are measured in millionths of a second called micro seconds.

These time differences are nicknamed TDs and they are printed on coastal navigation charts. Along the Northeast Coast, depending on your

Chart overlays

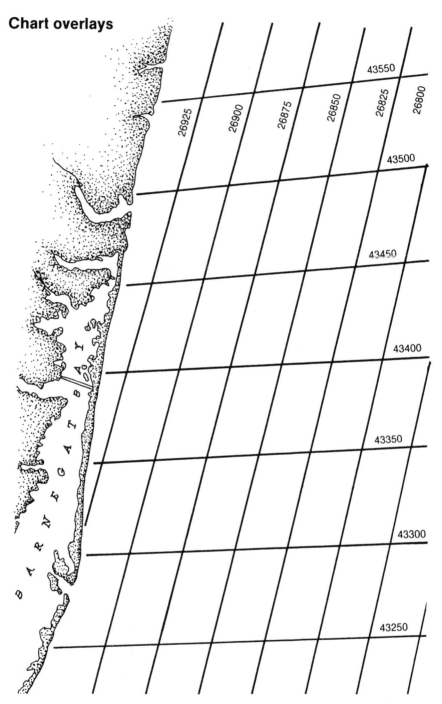

The Time Differences (TDs) displayed by loran receivers are also Lines Of Position (LOPs) and are printed on most coastal charts.

actual fishing location, we use the 25,000 to 27,000 TD lines which run north/south and the 43,000 - 40,000 lines which run east/west. By reading the numbers displayed by the LORAN and matching them to the chart, you can determine your exact position to within 50 feet of accuracy!

LORAN is a tiny computer that does more than just tell your present location. By pressing the key pads on the front of the unit you can program it to plot courses from an inlet to any offshore hot spot. It will not only plot the course, but also calculate your speed, the time of arrival and distance to go.

LORAN has opened many new fishing areas to coastal anglers. Years ago we relied on shore ranges to pinpoint good fishing locations rarely leaving sight of the land. Now we can range 10, 15 and 20 or more miles offshore to good bluefish, tuna, billfish and kingfish spots, and find wrecks no bigger than 200 feet around.

Temperature Gauges

Knowing the water temperature is important to all kinds of fishing, inshore and offshore. A pocket of warm water along the beach may hold weakfish, fluke or small blues. Offshore anglers look for warm water eddies to locate tuna, sharks and marlin. Bay anglers may find better fluke action at one end of the bay than the other because of a difference in temperature.

The best temperature gauges read to tenths of a degree and the probe should be mounted so it is in the water at all times. The fanciest even have a paper print out that rolls out the fave of the gauge with imprints of the

PREFERRED WATER TEMPERATURES

Amberjack	65-80	Marlin, Blue	70-88
Seabass	55-68	Marlin, White	70-85
Blackfish	46-70	Pollock	45-60
Bluefish	64-75	Striped Bass	56-77
Bonito, Atlantic	65-76	Swordfish	58-70
Cod, Atlantic	44-58	Tuna, Albacore	61-80
Drum, Black	56-80	Tuna, Bigeye	60-75
Drum, Red	56-84	Tuna, Bluefin	56-84
Flounder, Summer	65-72	Tuna, Yellowfin	64-80
Flounder, Winter	53-60	Weakfish	55-70
Mako	64-70		

water temperature and the LORAN TDs when the temperature was recorded.

While a hull mounted temperature gauge can only read the surface water, it is still helpful in locating fish. Shallow bay waters often have the same temperature from top to bottom. Offshore species like tuna and sharks often move only a few feet from the surface. There are other temperature gauges that can be lowered on a cable to deeper waters, the temperature displayed on a hand held dial. Some downriggers have temperature gauges built into the trolling weight.

Radar

Ever smaller in size, radar is well within range of small boaters. It will clearly show fleets of fishing boats and increase the safety of your boat when cruising to fishing spots at night or in dense fog. Boats that run at night to the canyons use Radar to spot other ships, offshore markers and can even show thundershowers to avoid.

The radar set transmits very high frequency pulses that get reflected back to the receiver from nearby objects and which are then displayed on a small screen. In principle it is very similar to a depth sounder but the pulses are beamed through the air, not the water.

Fishing With LORAN

Fishermen who keep records note that over time, fish demonstrate certain patterns of behavior. Not only will they return to a particular area year after year, but certain portions of a structure will invariably yield more fish than others. Canyon fishermen, for example, will tell you that tuna and marlin do not favor random locations along those long miles of the shelf waters. By keeping careful records of hookups, they're able to troll more efficiently. That saves fuel and time, and pays off with better catches of fish.

Shark drifts are another case in point. Over the years, shark aficionados have developed some fairly conclusive evidence that a pattern exists to the routes that sharks travel as they feed and search for bait. Although there are no guarantees on a trip-to-trip basis, the odds are certainly tilted in the angler's favor if the TDs of previous year's hookup spots are recorded and used to control drifts on subsequent outings.

Blackfish enthusiasts can talk about behavior, too. They know that tog will often hole up on one portion of a wreck, leaving the other end to the bergalls and associated lesser critters. So once you determine the productive end of the hulk you're positioned over, record the appropriate TDs and use them to focus your fishing attention on the prime spots the next time out.

Drifting Tips For Weakfish, Flounder And Bluefish

Aimless drifting for fluke only catches fish when the angler "lucks" into a good fishing spot. For more consistent results, fluke drifters jot the beginning numbers at the start of each drift. Should that drift produce few fish, it's an easy matter to make a short run back to the original starting point and make the identical drift over the identical fish holding bottom.

Offshore bluefishermen diamond jigging for slammer size blues also use LORAN to stay on the best fishing grounds. Typical sea conditions may have a wind that runs crossways to the current flow. If the numbers aren't written down it's impossible to return to the starting position. Running

Drifting for Bluefish

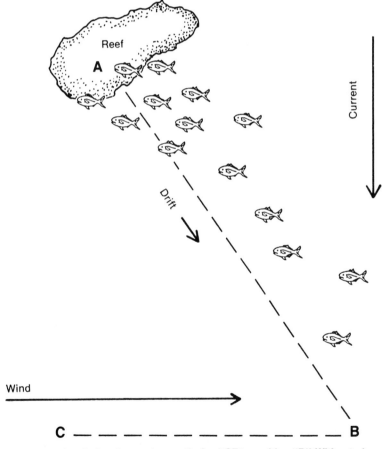

In this example, wind and current move the boat SE to position "B". Without a loran, an angler might run to "C" and miss the school of fish. Loran helps the fisherman get back to "A" and another good drift over schools of blues.

into the wind may not get you back into the right position because there's been no adjustment for the action of the current on the boat. Check the diagram to see what happens to a fisherman without LORAN while drift fishing offshore.

Drifting For Sharks By The Numbers

It doesn't always pay to drift endlessly for sharks. And that old taboo about not breaking the slick has been reappraised - and, at times, found wanting. Short drifts, about one and a half hours in length, can sometimes out-produce traditional methods.

This technique is effectively accomplished by using your LORAN. First, locate appropriate structure on your navigational charts and trace over the pale outlines with a marking pen. Calculate the starting TDs and run to the location. Once there, determine the upwind point at which you'll start the drift and record the TDs. When your recorder indicates you've dropped off the structure, return to the starting TDs and begin again. If you've had a hookup along the way, note the TDs and consider starting the next drift closer to the hookup spot.

The technique works whether you're alone or in tournament fishing

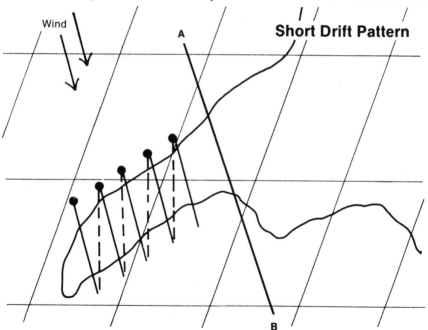

The best shark fishermen like to fish as many structure edges as they can during a day's fishing. Starting at point "A" and making a long drift to "B" would only cover two productive edges. A better strategy would be to make several short drifts to cover the edges several times.

crowded waters. In the latter instance, short drifts may enable you to work structure overlooked by your longer-drifting competitors. By combining this technique with your LORAN readings to control the starting point of each drift, you're assured the most efficient drifting pattern.

Trolling By The Numbers

Aimlessly trolling east, west, north or south will catch few fish. The best trolling patterns use a fish finder and a LORAN in combination. The LORAN helps to navigate directly to an offshore fishing location where fish are likely to be in residence. Once on the spot, the fish finder marks game fish, bait and the changing bottom contours.

It is helpful to use the LORAN to create a grid trolling pattern that takes the boat over all parts of the ridge, lump, slough or bar that you are trolling over. Some structure is quite large and it is likely that the fish may not be located at the exact spot you first begin to troll. The fish may be a few hundred yards away, still in the general area, but far enough away to go unnoticed if the grid pattern with its crisscrossing patterns across the structure is not conscientiously applied. The next section on Locationg Offshore Wrecks will discuss a grid pattern in detail.

When a fish is hooked, write the LORAN TDs down on a pad or scribble them on the console with a pencil. They'll clean up later when you're back at the dock, but while you are fishing, they are a handy reference as to the exact locations where a school of fish is holding. Troll back over the spot you hooked fish number one and number two is probably waiting there ready to take a swipe at a lure.

Locating Offshore Wrecks

The Atlantic Coast is dotted with numerous wrecks and small ridges or lumps that hold many kinds of gamefish from bottom dwellers like cod, ling, sea bass and tautog to pelagic species like bluefish, sharks and tunas.

In the past many of these wrecks were out of reach of the average fishermen who owned a small boat, but today with LORAN and graph recorders any boat with a range of 20 to 50 miles can find some excellent angling opportunities at these offshore hot spots.

The LORAN list in the following pages can be used as the key to open the door to some terrific fishing if you know how to use these electronic marvels to help you pinpoint the wrecks or small lumps and ridges.

The basic equipment you will need includes a LORAN, graph recorder, two or more buoys, a bottle of baby oil, a list of the wrecks and their LORAN numbers and a good chart. The charts are published by the National Oceanic and Atmospheric Administration (NOAA) and are sold in most marine supply stores.

Drop Back

Between A & B 100'   Between B & C 200'

Positioning over a wreck is easily accomplished with the help of two buoys. Drop the first buoy on the wreck (A). Drift about 100 feet away and drop the second buoy (B). Run a straight line course past both buoys to (C), drop the hook and settle back on the line until your recorder indicates you're over the wreck. Once there, secure the anchor and enjoy the fishing.

Wreck search pattern

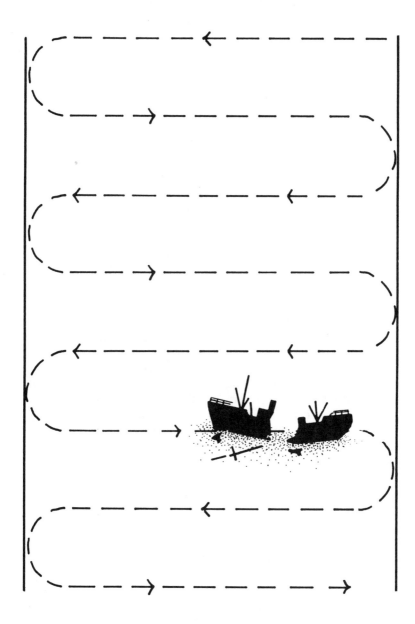

Running an east/west or north/south pattern from the chart position of a wreck will quickly uncover the structure's actual position. Once there, record the TDs shown on your LORAN receiver and use them on subsequent visits to the location.

You can pick out the wrecks by visually finding them on the NOAA chart yourself, or you can take numbers from any of the lists and transpose the numbers to the NOAA charts. You will find that the numbers don't always match the position of the wreck as printed on the chart. The error lies in the chart, since many of the wrecks were identified based on sextant or visual reports at the time of the sinking. The LORAN numbers are accurate to within 50 feet and represent the actual position of the wreck as verified by many boaters and captains. The numbers are real, not the chart positions, although occasionally the two do match up.

Once you have found a wreck, it is easy to find it again by simply running the LORAN numbers until they match up with the numbers you had the last time you fished the wreck. To find a new wreck you must run a search pattern to pinpoint it accurately. There can be minor variations from one LORAN to another, so you MUST verify all the numbers with your own LORAN receiver. Don't trust someone else's numbers until you check them.

Insert the coordinates into the LORAN and run the course to the wreck you have selected. Once you arrive at the position numbers you may not be right on top of the wreck so you have to run a search pattern to actually find the wreck. If you are lucky, you may only be off by 50 feet; you could also be off 500 feet.

The secondary LORAN numbers most commonly used in the North-east to Mid-Atlantic areas are the 25000 to 27000 and 43000 to 39000 numbers. In the extreme northern part of the region, the 15000 secondary may be used in place of the 26000 line. These lines are shown on the NOAA charts as pale lines running approximately north and south for the 26000 lines and east/west for the 43000 lines. I find it easiest to run the "lines" rather than a compass heading when searching for the wreck. For instance, to head east, you would keep the 43000 line number constant with no charge, but watch the receiver show decreasing numbers on the 26000 numbers.

As you run due east the 26000 numbers will get smaller; larger as you head west. The 43000 numbers get larger as you head north, smaller as you head south. Keeping this in mind it is relatively easy to run a grid pattern that takes you north/south or east/west.

When you arrive on the numbers that you took from a chart or list, toss a buoy overboard to mark that spot as a reference of your starting point. Run the north/south or east/west search pattern according to your prefer-ence, keeping your eyes glued to the recorder until it shows the wreck. Toss a second buoy and write the numbers down on the pad or helm so there is no chance you will erase them from the LORAN memory. Contin-ue to make passes over the wreck from several different angles to help show you a clear profile of the wreck from every angle and location of fish.

I've found it interesting and helpful to save the graph paper from each wreck as I first found it and write notes on the paper to indicate the direction of the pass over it. After a few passes you will see which way the wreck lies, which end it is highest, and if it is several pieces or a single hulk. Your recorder should also show you the relative abundance of fish at various parts of the wreck.

Now that you found the wreck, toss a buoy over to mark it visually. Retrieve the marker buoy you tossed over on the original numbers, then get back on the wreck. This exercise forces you to confirm the wreck numbers again. Have the second buoy ready. Take your boat out of gear and drift AWAY from the wreck for about 100 feet or more. Drop the buoy. This buoy will be your reference to show the relative direction of the wind and current. This is important because it is not always what it seems to be.

With your boat back in gear, head in a straight line course along an imaginary line between the buoys and beyond them by about 200 feet. Drop the anchor and settle back on the anchor line until you are positioned over the wreck. Many times on the first try you will not be in the perfect position. Try again. It is common to miss on the first try since the current and wind may not act together and will shift the position of the boat away from the wreck.

After you have found wrecks several times, you can quit using the buoys and instead use a bottle of fish oil or baby oil to splash on the water. The slick it leaves is a clear indication of the position of the wreck and the direction of the drift. The small slicks disappear in a few minutes so you have to be quick while getting into position. The slicks also drift slightly with the wind, but once you are comfortable finding the wrecks you learn to fudge it as you set out the slicks and run into the anchoring position. It becomes second nature.

It is critical to get the best position. Some wrecks have good fishing only at one end, or in the middle.

Most of these blackfish and sea bass wrecks lie in about 40 to 60 feet of water, so you don't need much anchor line. In fact, I use 200 feet of line most of the time. For fishing purposed, three times the water depth is usually sufficient. Too much anchor line allows the boat to swing on the line taking you on and off the wreck. Too little line causes you to slowly drag bottom and drift into the wreck.

Keep your numbers in a book and guard them with your life. Mine are filed in a notebook, along with the graph paper "pictures" of the wreck and a complete set of numbers for the center of the wreck and its boundaries.

Some Good Fishing Locations

The following sets of LORAN numbers pinpoint the exact location of over 1800 major offshore fishing grounds and wrecks along the East Coast from New England to North Carolina. Just "plug 'em in" to your LORAN and you're ready for some good fishing. If you don't have a

LORAN on your boat, plot TDs on a NOAA coastal navigation chart and run a timed compass course to the area you wish to fish. NOAA charts are readily available in marinas and marine supply stores. If you have a tough time locating a particular chart, write Bluewater Books and Charts, 1481 SE 17th Street, Fort Lauderdale, FL 33316.

Some areas like The Butterfish Hole, Manasquan Ridge, Five Fathom Bank, the Stone Beds, 21 Mile Hill and The Rocks are relatively large in size, so the numbers for these locations are rounded to whole numbers. However, wrecks, which are smaller in size and require more accuracy, are given in tenths of a micro-second. It is important to note that many wrecks shown on the NOAA coastal charts are marked with letters "Pa" which stands for "position approximate" so the LORAN numbers listed here do not always match the chart locations.

There is also some variation in reception of the LORAN signals from one receiver to another and in the software of the LORAN's computer program so it is possible for two different LORAN receivers to display numbers that may vary by several tenths of a micro-second between each set.

When navigating to an offshore wreck or hot spot, if you do not get right on the area on the first try, you must run an east/west, north/south search pattern until you do locate the wreck. Once the wreck is located, write down the numbers (TDs) in your own log book so you can return to that spot on future trips. Your TDs may vary slightly from those listed here.

I welcome comments from readers about the accuracy of the LORAN TD's printed in the GUIDE and for information about numbers that have been omitted. It would be impossible, but a delightful project, for me to fish every one of these locations, but I believe the numbers here are accurate. Many of them I've located and fished myself over the last 15 years, others were traded with other fishermen and charter captains whose information I trusted.

To help locate good fishing locations, there are several excellent fishing charts available at bait and tackle shops, marine dealers and by mail that can be of invaluable assistance in locating good fishing areas. For more information, write to the following companies or see your dealer:

ADC of Alexandria
6440 General Green Way
Alexandria, VA 22312

Bluewater Charts
41 Cornhollow Road
Succasunna, NJ 07876

Captain Sea Gull's Nautical Charts
PO Box 323
Rehobeth, MA 02769

Captain Vic's Fishing Chart
Series 8 Iris Court
Milltown, NJ 08850

Home Port Fishing Charts
PO Box 730
Rio Grande, NJ 08242

Nautical Publications
PO Box 11501
Birmingham, AL 35202

Waterproof Charts
International Supply
320 Cross Street
Punta Gorda, FL 33950

Wreck fishing can be fascinating, not only in the good fishing opportunities it affords, but in the mystery of ships themselves. The following books provide more information about coastal wrecks, how they got there and where they are located.

THE FISHERMAN LIBRARY
1620 Beaver Dam Road
Point Pleasant, NJ 08742
　　Atlantic Wrecks
　　by John Raguso
　　Shipwrecks of the Atlantic
　　by Bill Davis

GARY GENTILE PRODUCTIONS
PO Box 57137
Philadelphia, PA 19111
　　Shipwrecks of Delaware and Maryland
　　Shipwrecks of Virginia
　　Shipwrecks of North Carolina, North
　　Shipwrecks of North Carolina, South
　　all by Gary Gentile

MT PUBLICATIONS
Two Avery Street
Mystic, CT 06355
　　Fishable Wrecks & Rockpiles
　　by Tim Coleman & Charley Soares

MASSACHUSETTS TO MONTAUK
(TDs are east of 25900 and north of 43250)

Acid Barge Wreck	14538.7	43820.2
Addie Anderson	14424.0	43989.9
Annapolis Wreck	14534.4	43945.9
Aransas	13837.0	43909.1
Arco #8	13992.8	25839.0
Atlantis Canyon	14325.0	43300.0
Baby Doll	26880.3	43954.8
B-Buoy Hump	13894.3	44267.1
Blackfish Schooner	26116.5	43978.6
Blackpoint Wreck (Black Diamond)	14456.2	43938.5
Block Island East Grounds	14495.0	43873.0
Block Island North End Buoy	14528.5	43932.0
Block Island North Peak (The Hump)	14521.9	43921.9
Block Island North Rip	14522.0	43912.8
Block Island Pinnacle	14547.7	43864.8
Block Island SE Light	14536.5	43867.7
Block Island SW Hooter	14563.3	43878.9
Block Island SW Point	14568.0	43873.2
Block Island Stone Rubble	14585.0	43965.7
Block Island Tuna Grounds	14496.0	43843.0
Block Island Tuna Fleet (North)	14498.0	43824.5
Block Island Tuna Fleet (South)	14519.0	43788.0
Brenton Reef Tower	14421.0	43978.0
Brown's Ledge	14335.0	43912.0
Butterfish Hole	14725.0	43725.0
Cabin Cruiser	26352.2	43995.6
Cape Fear	14394.7	43993.5
Cartwright Shoal	25967.0	13793.0
Cartwright	14655.0	43815.0
Celtic	26798.7	43989.6
Cement Boat	13729.5	25895.1
Catacomb Rocks	14636.0	43967.0
Cerebus Shoals	14685.0	43920.0
Chelsea	13777.6	25797.5
Chester Poling	13840.9	44327.8
CIA Grounds	25909.0	43792.0
City of Salisbury	13974.4	44283.3
Cohasset Dumping Ground	13895.5	44213.8
Cole Ridge	13877.5	44321.0
Cox Ledge	14441.2	43799.4
Cox Ledge SE Corner	14420.0	43790.0
Coyote	13920.8	44266.2
Cultivator Shoals (George's Banks)	13300.0	43800.0
Delaware	13965.5	25714.4

Devil's Bridge (Martha's Vineyard)	14235.0	43900.0
Drop-off (Jefferies Ledge)	13670.1	44332.9
Dump	14375.0	43650.0
Dumping Grounds	14360.0	43715.0
East Ground	14486.0	43855.0
Fishing Ledge	13894.0	44074.0
Fishtails	14650.0	43325.0
Forty Fathom Bank	25825.0	43540.0
G-1	14386.8	44010.7
Gales Ledge	13885.4	25833.0
German Sub Wreck	14472.0	43895.0
Great Eastern Rock	14653.0	43865.0
Grecian Wreck	14546.7	43839.7
Guard	14623.8	43967.3
Gully	14497.8	43813.7
Halfway Rock	13901.6	25821.5
Hatchett's Point Wreck	26231.6	43982.1
Henry Endicott	13967.7	44081.1
Herbert Wreck	13961.2	44297.1
Heroine	14525.7	43946.0
Hilda Garston	14238.8	43953.3
Hills & Ledges	13918.1	25823.2
Horatio Hall	13856.2	43897.0
John Dwight	14238.0	43922.3
June K	13935.4	44127.9
Kershaw	14094.6	43922.1
Kiowa	13991.6	44265.5
L-8	14423.1	43959.1
Lake Crystal	14598.4	43944.9
Lansford	13782.7	43981.6
Larchmont Wreck	14616.4	43949.0
Lightburn Wreck	25836.2	43872.7
Lucas Shoal (Martha's Vineyard)	14192.0	43917.0
Marise	26091.6	43979.6
Mars Wreck	13956.8	44093.5
Mary Arnold	14530.2	43962.0
Moonstone Beach (RI)	14500.9	43968.4
Mud Hole	14450.0	43845.0
Nebraska Shoal	14506.7	43962.1
Newcomb's Ledge	13886.8	25809.0
Nomans SW Shoal	14275.0	43842.0
Nomans Tuna Grounds	14306.0	43777.0
Old Tuna Grounds (BC Buoy)	13714.0	43924.0
Onondaga	14627.7	43966.4
Peaked Hill	13800.0	44118.0
PC 1203	14029.2	43921.8
Pendleton	13867.7	44914.0

Pigeon Rip	26193.5	43960.0
Pinnacle Rock	15326.5	43973.7
Pinthis Wreck	13924.4	44175.3
Plum Gut	14784.0	43939.0
Poling Brothers Number Two	26894.8	43970.6
Port Hunter	14097.7	43930.7
Pottstown Wreck	13997.8	44033.7
Pump Barge	26872.2	43976.5
Ranger Wreck	14719.6	43632.7
Republic Wreck	14073.0	43453.6
Rip Rock	26129.5	43952.0
Romance	13969.4	44290.6
Saturday Night Ledge	13858.6	25796.4
Seneca	14019.6	43891.9
Shagwong Rock	26018.2	43878.0
Shark's Ledge	14530.0	43830.0
Southwest Ledge	25898.3	43867.1
S.S. Coyote	13920.8	44266.2
Stellwagon Bank	13800.0	44175.0
Stellwagon Bank NW Corner	13819.4	25668.0
Stellwagon Bank SE Corner	13790.0	25520.0
Stony Bar	13900.0	44200.0

"Over the rail and into the pail." This bluefish hit a diamond jig fished in deep water.

Storm Petrel	14643.2	43947.3
Suffolk Wreck	14468.7	43726.2
Sulpher Wreck	14538.0	43821.0
Sweet Sue	13979.2	25815.0
Swordfish Wreck	14465.0	43725.0
SW Shoal	14275.0	43842.0
Tanta's Ledge	13360.7	25908.4
Tautog Hill	14203.0	43930.1
Thames	14863.7	43955.6
The Mountain	14365.0	43830.0
The Towboat	14593.5	43953.9
Trojan	14291.4	43921.4
Tuna Banks	25948.8	43743.3
U-853 Wreck	14472.8	43894.8
Uncle John	14200.0	43970.1
Unknown Wreck	13924.0	25553.1
Unknown Wreck	14915.9	43946.5
USS Bass Wreck	14560.4	43817.4
Valiant Rock	26124.5	43955.0
Vineyard Lightship	14289.6	43931.3
Washington Ledge	14417.0	43965.8
Washington Ledge	14419.5	43959.4
Weekpaug Breachway Stones	14585.0	43965.7
Wilkes Ledge	14223.0	43967.0
Wood Barge	15314.1	43978.9
Wreck Rockpile	14283.7	43917.5
Yankee	14205.6	43975.9
47-Foot Hill	13894.6	44288.3
47 Hill	13885.1	25816.5
101 Hill	13927.2	44265.8
101 Hill	13888.1	44287.2
113 Hill	13704.0	44334.6
115 Hill	13885.1	44319.8
115 Hill	13894.6	44288.3
124 Hill	13725.0	44336.0

LONG ISLAND SOUND

Barge	14902.3	43989.1
Barge	26930.5	43945.7
Baraitai	14863.9	43965.9
Bayville Wrecks (Barge)	26847.1	43938.2
Bayville Wrecks (Engine)	15324.0	43941.0
Cities Service Number 4	14806.9	43970.7
Coal Barge	26930.5	43945.7
Condor Wreck	26831.9	43984.7
Flat Barge	26895.7	43961.3

Glen Island	26893.6	43937.6
Gwendoline Steers Wreck	26798.7	43951.3
Lake Hemlock	14902.3	43978.1
Lexington Wreck (bow)	26652.1	43962.8
Lexington Wreck (paddle wheel)	26679.1	43979.9
M-35	26893.0	43960.0
Old Schooner Wreck	15315.1	43978.6
Race Rock	14708.5	43961.0
Rock Shoal	15316.6	43979.4
Sailboat Wreck	26825.2	43993.9
Smithtown Reef #1	15186.0	43915.6
Smithtown Reef #2	26667.5	43916.2
Steel Barge	14806.9	43970.7
Thumper	14666.9	43978.2
Wood Wreck	15326.6	43973.7

LONG ISLAND SOUTH SHORE TO NEW JERSEY AT MANASQUAN INLET

(TDs are west and south of 25900/43800 at Montauk, north of the 43400 line at Manasquan Inlet)

Acara Wreck	26800.5	43750.5
Acid Waters	26840.0	43635.0
Adonis Wreck	26950.2	43598.8
Ajace Wreck	26956.6	43754.0
Alan Martin Wreck	26792.0	43482.4
Ambrose Light	26910.0	43700.0
Ambrose Wreck	26912.5	43703.0
Andrea Doria	25147.7	43480.8
Angler Bank	26788.0	43655.0
Annex	26891.0	43558.0
Arundo Wreck	26796.5	43533.9
Arundo Wreck	26792.4	43515.1
Asfalto Wreck	26831.2	43620.8
Atlantic Beach Reef	26870.0	43735.0
Augies Lump	26890.0	43544.0
Austin W. Wreck	26705.9	43515.9
Ayshire Wreck	26935.0	43420.0
Ayuruocca Wreck (Oil Wreck)	26842.3	43547.7
BA Buoy	26877.0	43632.0
BA Wreck	26874.7	43619.6
Bald Eagle Wreck	26831.2	43640.3
Barge Wreck	26783.5	43717.5
Barge Wreck	26737.0	43728.5
Barge Wreck	26881.5	43728.5
Barge Wreck	26870.4	43734.7

Barge Wreck	26869.5	43738.5
Bendix Wreck	26844.8	43570.8
Benson Wreck	26868.4	43570.8
Black Warrior Wreck	26951.8	43755.3
Blue Boy (1)	26803.4	43492.8
Blue Boy (2)	26814.8	43508.2
Bonanza Wreck	26453.1	43676.9
Brencen Wreck	26859.5	43566.4
Brenton Reef No 2	25777.7	43977.6
Bridge Rubble	26906.2	43509.8
Bridge Rubble	26910.5	43505.1
Bridge Rubble	26910.6	43506.7
Bridge Rubble	26910.4	43495.1
Bridge Rubble	26911.8	43503.6
Bridge Rubble	26910.5	43504.4
Bridge Rubble	26911.3	43504.4
Bridge Rubble	26910.3	43503.7
Bridge Rubble	26909.5	43505.1
Brunette Wreck	26916.4	43476.0
Caddette Wreck	26816.3	43475.5
Broadcast Wreck	26752.2	43600.0
Burnside Wreck	26578.4	43551.5
Butterfish Hole	25944.1	43747.5
Cadet Wreck	26916.4	43475.8
Car Float #52	26911.0	43500.7
Carlson II Wreck	26912.3	43497.6
Choapa Wreck	26832.5	43549.5
Cholera Bank	26773.0	43672.0
Cinderella	26917.2	43497.6
City of Athens Wreck	26920.3	43705.3
CIA Grounds	25909.0	43792.0
Clam Beds	26945.0	43670.0
Clay Head	25847.6	43904.8
Clay Head	25836.0	43898.2
Coffee Wreck	26881.0	43425.3
Coimbra	26204.1	43676.0
Concrete Bridge	26906.2	43509.8
Coney Island Wreck	26792.0	43481.3
Continent Wreck	26884.7	43637.4
Cornelia Wreck	26954.7	43759.1
Coal Wreck	26796.4	43671.7
Coal Wreck West	26798.0	43713.2
Coast Wise Wreck	26645.5	43595.9
Coleman Barge	26941.9	43642.4
Concrete Rubble	26944.0	43649.0
Concrete Rubble	26944.2	43650.2
Concrete Rubble	26944.0	43649.0

Concrete Rubble	26945.0	43653.0
Concrete Rubble	26945.0	43651.0
Concrete Rubble	26945.0	43649.0
Concrete Rubble	26943.0	43649.0
Concrete Rubble	26943.0	43647.0
Concrete Rubble	26944.0	43649.0
Concrete Rubble	26945.5	43650.0
Concrete Rubble	26945.0	43655.0
Concrete Rubble	26945.0	43658.0
Concrete Slabs	26779.5	43714.5
Concrete Slabs	26780.2	43714.9
Cormorant Reef No 1	25718.6	43975.5
Cranford Wreck	26906.8	43503.3
Cruiser San Diego	26543.6	43693.1
Cruiser San Diego	26543.3	43692.8
CWARP	26631.3	43734.1
Dave Moran Wreck	26797.2	43448.2
Delaware Wreck	26928.4	43467.7
Dodger Wreck	26617.9	43673.4
Dorothy	26942.8	43647.5
Drums	26912.1	43497.5
Dry Dock Wreck	26860.5	43559.6
Dry Dock Wreck (Jack Pot's Wreck)	26908.7	43506.7
Drumelizier (Quadrant) Wreck)	26674.0	43754.0
Duke Wreck	26781.5	43737.1

This blue shark has just been tagged and is about to be released to fight again.

Dumping Grounds	26325.0	42915.0
Dunlap Wreck	26929.8	43722.2
Eagle Wreck	26891.0	43531.0
East End Steel	26627.3	43734.3
East Grounds	26932.5	43499.8
East Lump	26867.0	43434.0
Edna Wreck	26705.8	43516.0
Edna's Bottom	26629.1	43514.2
Elisha	25669.8	43963.3
England Bank	26920.0	43570.0
Eureka Wreck	26772.1	43600.0
Ferry Boat Wreck (1)	26908.8	43506.7
Ferry Boat Wreck (2)	26921.6	43547.0
Ferry Boat Wreck (3)	26906.7	43503.4
Fire Island Lightship	26599.0	43644.7
Fire Island Reef	26635.0	43735.0
First Lady	26897.3	43943.3
Florence Wreck	26680.6	43574.7
Foley Wreck	26890.2	43513.7
Fort Victoria Wreck	26940.1	43710.2
Fourteen Foot Hump	26219.6	43899.1
Fran S. Wreck	26874.1	43733.8
Frederick P. Wreck	26678.9	43431.7
Galley Wreck	26788.0	43484.4
Gas Barge	26912.5	43492.4
Gates City Wreck	26420.6	43790.3
G & D Wreck	26671.2	43572.7
Geralda Wreck	26891.2	43508.8
German Wreck	26859.4	43564.1
Gloria & Doris Wreck (1)	26671.2	43572.7
Gloria & Doris Wreck (2)	26671.8	43574.3
Glory Wreck	26907.9	43447.8
Glover Reef No 38	26910.6	43977.0
Gong Grounds	26975.0	43748.0
Goulandris Wreck (1)	26852.5	43575.3
Goulandris Wreck (2)	26862.0	43581.0
Great Eastern Rock	25974.0	43864.4
Gulhia Wreck	26754.1	43491.5
Gun Boat Wreck	26609.4	43610.2
HA Buoy	26645.0	43480.0
Hankins Wreck (1)	26883.8	43470.7
Hankins Wreck (2)	26884.0	43408.3
Happy Days Wreck	26675.4	43602.6
Hempstead Reef	26783.8	43714.1
Hempstead Reef (Barge A)	26786.5	43716.5
Hempstead Reef (Barge B)	26788.5	43716.5
Hempstead Reef (Barge C)	26785.0	43715.0

Hempstead Reef (Barge D)	26785.0	43714.0
Hempstead Reef (Barge E)	26783.5	43714.5
Hempstead Reef (Barge F)	26788.5	43717.5
Hilton Castle Wreck	26569.4	43695.3
Holiday Wreck	26268.7	43434.0
Howard Wreck	26773.7	43753.4
Humpty Dumpty	26795.0	43434.0
Iberia Wreck	26855.3	43736.2
Immaculata Wreck	26801.8	43584.0
Ionnis Goulandris Wreck (1)	26852.5	43575.3
Ionnis Goulandris Wreck (2)	26853.9	43577.0
Irma C. Wreck	26661.2	43570.8
JB's Lump	26775.4	43412.2
Joe Wreck	26799.6	43714.8
Kiley B	26908.9	43494.6
Klondike Banks	26898.0	43517.0
Kranston Wreck	26417.3	43402.8
Lana Carol Trawler Wreck	26860.2	43419.7
Lido Coal Barge	26798.1	43713.2
Lieutenant Wreck	26633.7	43735.3
Lightburne	25836.2	43872.7
Lightship Wreck	26599.0	43644.7
Lightship WAL-505 Wreck	26903.5	43695.9
Lillian Wreck (Main Section)	26697.0	43419.4
Linda Wreck (1)	26507.5	43600.9
Linda Wreck (2)	26508.7	43601.2
Lizzie D. Wreck (1)	26869.0	43693.3
Lizzie D. Wreck (2)	26828.8	43686.4
Logwood Wreck	26856.4	43474.6
Long Branch Rock Pile	26938.0	43615.7
Lucky Strike Wreck	26926.3	43526.5
Mahagoney Wreck	26877.2	43483.6
Maine Schooner Wreck	26890.9	43447.5
Mainship (Mold)	26912.0	43492.6
Mako Hotel	26525.0	43400.0
Manasquan Ridge	26891.0	43444.0
Manasquan Wreck	26945.2	43497.3
Marie	26905.4	43510.7
Marion Barge	26914.5	43502.5
Martinsburg Wreck	26889.7	43506.2
Margret Wreck	26901.1	43756.3
Mildred Wreck	26829.0	43447.5
Millville Barges	26915.0	43472.5
Mistletoe Wreck	26933.3	43747.6
Mohawk	26877.6	43439.7
Monster Ledge	26738.0	43472.0
Mud Buoy	26903.4	43654.3

Call 'em blackfish, tautog or tog, these tasty fish are excellent sport when fishing over wrecks or rocky bottom.

Mud Hole - West	26755.0	43485.0
Mud Hole Wreck	26864.3	43587.5
Navy Barge	26776.5	43714.0
New Steel	26630.9	43736.8
Norness Wreck	26487.6	43506.8
North Reef No 1B1	25864.7	43922.5
Ocean Prince Wreck	26625.4	43731.3
Oil Wreck Reef	26842.3	43547.7
Oil Rig	26841.6	43546.0
Old Schooner Wreck	26116.5	43978.6
Olsen Wreck	26924.5	43476.5
One Twenty Wreck	26873.4	43468.3
Oregon Wreck	26453.2	43676.9
Panther Wreck	26248.7	43802.0
Park City Wreck	26933.0	43461.0

Pencil Wreck	26636.5	43736.9
Pentland Fifth Wreck	26922.5	43682.0
Phoenix Wreck	26729.0	43458.1
Pineapple	26940.2	43600.3
Pinta Wreck	26880.5	43563.5
Pliny Wreck	26949.2	43579.8
Princess Ann Wreck	26968.3	43758.1
Queen Wreck	26927.5	43465.5
Railroad Barge	26910.3	43499.2
Rattlesnake	26925.0	43635.0
Red Church Lump	26943.8	43597.7
Reggi Barges	26906.6	43449.4
Reggie Wreck	26594.3	43659.2
Relief Lightship WAL-505	26903.5	43695.9
Republic	25119.5	43490.0
Rockaway Reef - North	26930.0	43750.0
Rockaway Reef - South	26926.0	43748.0
Rockpiles	26638.6	43734.1
Rock Piles	26440.0	43441.0
Rock Piles	26480.0	43471.0
Rock Piles	26490.0	43500.0
Rockland County Tug Wreck	26905.3	43508.5
Ron Stoll Wreck	26767.7	43484.3
Roda Wreck	26741.3	43756.7
RR Barge Wreck (Squan Barge)	26910.3	43499.2
Rubble Pile	26632.0	43734.3
Rubble Pile	26634.6	43735.2
Rubble Pile	26634.5	43735.1
Rubble Pile	26633.2	43735.7
Rubble Pile	26632.6	43735.3
Rubble Pile	26635.0	43735.8
Rubble Pile	26632.8	43734.8
Rubble Pile	26633.3	43735.0
Rubble Pile	26637.8	43734.8
Rubble Pile	26632.6	43735.2
Rubble Pile	26637.6	43735.5
Rubble Pile	26633.2	43734.7
Rubble Pile	26635.0	43735.0
Rubble Pile	26632.6	43735.0
Rubble Pile	26632.4	43734.0
Rubble Pile	26633.3	43735.3
Rubble Pile	26632.9	43735.1
Rubble Pile	26632.7	43735.2
Rubble Pile	26632.6	43734.6
Rubble Pile	26633.7	43735.6
Rubble Pile	26633.3	43735.9
Rumrunner Wreck	26829.0	43696.3

Sam Berman Wreck	26792.8	43482.9
San Diego Cruiser Wreck	26543.6	43693.1
Sandy Hook Reef (Center)	26945.0	43650.0
Coleman 45' barge	26941.9	43642.4
Dorothy	26942.8	43647.5
V.L. Keegan	26943.0	43647.1
Sandy Hook Wreck	26908.3	43700.4
Scallop Ridge	26930.0	43735.0
Schooner Wreck	26915.3	43499.7
Scotland	26932.0	43690.0
Schooner Wreck	26417.3	43402.8
Sea Girt Wreck	26860.5	43471.6

An offshore wreck gave up this pollock which will make a fine dinner when the boat gets back home.

Sea Girt Reef (Center)	26910.0	43505.0
A Frame Barge	26905.4	43510.7
Car Float	26905.4	43510.7
Car Float #52	26911.0	43500.7
Carlson	26912.2	43497.6
Cinderella	26917.2	43497.6
Concrete Rubble	26910.5	43505.1
Concrete Rubble	26906.2	43509.8
Cranford Ferry	26906.8	43503.3
Dry Dock	26908.7	43506.7
Kiley B	26908.9	43494.6
Mainship mold	26912.0	43492.6
Marie Oil Barge	26905.4	43510.7
Marie Tug	26905.4	43510.7
Morania Barge	26912.5	43492.4
Railroad Barge	26910.3	43499.2
Rockland County	26905.5	43508.2
Schooner Barge	26915.3	43499.7
Spartan	26910.7	43491.1
Subway Cars	26911.1	43496.3
Swenson Barge (I)	26911.1	43502.7
Swenson Barge (II)	26911.8	43493.5
Dupont Drums	26912.1	43497.5
Severign Wreck	26927.0	43417.0
Shark Ledge	26775.0	43435.0
Shark Ledge	26894.7	43515.6
Shinnecock Reef	26288.0	43785.0
Shinnecock Tuna Hole	26194.4	43722.6
Shopping Cart	26900.0	43444.0
Shrewsbury Rocks	26950.0	43635.0
Slough	26780.0	43430.0
Skippy Wreck	26609.9	43609.7
Snow Wreck	26964.3	43759.8
Sommerstad Wreck	26425.2	43456.5
Southeast Grounds	26760.0	43700.0
Spartan Tug Wreck	26910.7	43491.1
S.S. Rusland	26950.2	43598.8
Steamship Wreck	26932.4	43707.0
Steel Drums	26912.2	43497.5
Steel Wreck (1)	26794.6	43687.3
Steel Wreck (2)	26794.5	43697.2
Stefano Wreck	25121.4	43426.0
Stolt Dagali Wreck (1)	26768.0	43410.0
Stolt Dagali Wreck (2)	26787.7	43484.3
Stolt Dagali Wreck (3)	26768.8	43434.1
Stone Barge Wreck	26782.5	43728.2
Subway Cars	26911.1	43496.3

Swenson Barge (1)	26911.1	43502.7
Swenson Barge (2)	26911.8	43493.5
Subchaser Wreck	26935.5	43649.5
Suffolk	25647.8	43729.7
Sunken Dry Dock	26908.8	43506.8
Tarantula	26609.8	43609.8
Tarpon Lump	26923.5	43607.5
Taylor	25788.8	43975.1
Tea Wreck	26801.4	43750.8
The Farms	26887.0	43595.0
The Rump	26918.8	43435.1
Three Fairs Wreck (1)	26652.1	43605.2
Three Fairs Wreck (2)	26651.3	43505.3
Three Sisters Wreck	26791.6	43642.1
Tin Can Grounds	26972.0	43740.0
Tug Wreck	26916.5	43476.2
Tug Wreck	26881.5	43737.3
Turner Wreck	26930.3	43725.6
Unknown Barge Wreck	26913.7	43474.7
Unknown Barge Wreck	26803.9	43492.2
Unknown Wreck	26629.5	43735.5
Unknown Wreck	26638.5	43736.2
Unknown Wreck	26771.1	43557.7
Unknown Wreck	26722.5	43622.5
Unknown Wreck	26913.0	43717.1
Unknown Wreck	26845.4	43421.6
Unknown Wreck	26860.6	43472.2
Unknown Wreck	26904.3	43502.3
Unknown Wreck	26887.8	43507.9
Unknown Wreck	26794.4	43496.5
Unknown Wreck	26903.6	43492.6
Unknown Wreck	26730.7	43483.7
USCG RC Mohawk Wreck	26867.2	43670.8
USS San Diego	26543.3	43692.9
USS Tarantula	26609.8	43609.8
USS Turner	26936.4	43725.5
Valpariso Wreck	26912.0	43475.0
Vessel Fran S	26874.1	43733.8
Vessel Iberia	26855.3	43736.2
Victory Wreck	26812.4	43743.5
Virginia Wreck	26425.0	43456.1
V.L. Keegan	26943.0	43647.1
Winstead/Millville Barge Wrecks	26915.5	43472.5
Wolcott Wreck	26518.7	43712.9
Wood Barge	26630.4	43735.4
Wooden Drydock	26633.7	43735.3
Wooden Drydock	26288.3	43786.1

Yankee Wreck	26609.5	43592.1
Zeeliner Wreck	26622.9	43735.8
17 Fathoms	26889.0	43654.0
41 Fathom Ridge	25968.1	43464.8
59 Pounder Wreck (Schooner)	26632.4	43601.1

MANASQUAN TO BEACH HAVEN

Anastasia Wreck	26857.5	43393.5
Asdic Special	26405.5	43287.8
Barnegat Light Ship Buoy	26785.0	43278.0
Barnegat Ridge - North	26791.0	43240.0
Barnegat Ridge - Middle	26775.0	43230.0
Barnegat Ridge - South	26778.0	43201.0
Bidevend Wreck	26357.6	43280.5
Big Wreck	26801.8	43189.1
Bone Wreck	26923.5	43307.5
Brick Rock	25578.4	43335.4
Brick Wreck	26876.0	43245.0
Caddo Wreck	26891.5	43207.5

Fishing for bluefish is a great way for a father and son to spend the day together.

Carolina Wreck	26453.0	42785.0
Casoon	26895.8	43350.1
Cedars	26922.1	43339.2
Chaparra Wreck	26847.6	43239.9
Charlemagne Tower, Jr. (Cedar Creek)	26912.8	43339.2
Chesapeake Wreck	26807.5	43250.5
Chicken Canyon	26450.0	43270.0
Cornelius Hargraves Wreck	26854.8	43296.9
Cow Wreck	26625.6	43360.9
Duncan Wreck	26874.1	43399.1
Durley Chine (Bacardi Wreck)	26308.1	43310.6
Ess Ridge	26778.9	43263.5
Emerald City	26873.6	43394.8
"EN" Rocks	26925.0	43444.0
F.F. Clain Wreck	25857.0	43306.5
Garden State Reef North (Center)	26875.0	43195.0
A.H.Dumont	26872.1	43197.5
Aqua II	26872.5	43194.7
Choctaw	26873.9	43199.3
Coleman II	26872.1	43192.9
Fatuk	26871.7	43196.1
Mary C	26875.2	43191.6
Molasses Barge	26874.0	43195.1
Shirley Ann Barge	26875.5	43194.1
Garden State Reef South (Center)	26900.0	43155.0
Miller Barge	26900.1	43155.2
The Rhino	26897.5	43155.8
Viking Mold	26900.6	43153.6
Good Times Wreck	26873.1	43192.5
Granite Wreck	26797.1	43448.4
Great Isaac Wreck (1)	26846.5	43213.4
Great Isaac Wreck (2)	26840.9	43195.2
Gulf Trade Wreck (Bow)	26886.9	43260.8
Gulf Trade Wreck (Bow)	26889.2	43263.5
Gulf Trade Wreck (Stern)	26821.3	43318.3
Hankins Wreck	26884.5	43340.6
Harry Rush Wreck	26855.5	43295.5
Harvey Cedars Wreck	26907.0	43223.0
Huntington Wreck	26538.2	43200.2
Insure Tug	26845.9	43213.0
Larson's Wreck	26456.2	43234.2
Ledges	26891.6	43361.6
Ledges	26890.1	43359.0
Lexington Wreck	26380.1	43278.1
Magnus Wreck	26921.5	43245.5
Maurice Tracy (1)	26889.8	43357.1
Maurice Tracy (2)	26891.6	43361.6

Maurice Tracy (3)	26890.1	43359.0
Mediator Wreck	26906.5	43248.5
Northwest Barges	26878.9	43295.3
Off Shore Tug	26831.3	43188.8
Oklahoma Wreck (Bow)	26972.4	42277.2
Oklahoma Wreck (Stern)	26717.9	43079.4
Oley's Lump	26738.0	43275.0
Persephone Wreck (1)	26897.1	43287.6
Persephone Wreck (2)	26895.2	43289.5
Reliance Blimp Wreck	26778.5	43227.5
Republic Wreck	25119.5	43490.0
R.P. Resor Wreck	26638.3	43277.1
San Saba Wreck	26853.2	43240.6
Schooner Irene Wreck	26871.5	43359.5
Schooner Wreck	26889.4	43239.8
Seaside Lump	26864.0	43378.0
Shirley Ann Wreck	26875.5	43194.1
Southeast Lump	26864.0	43378.0
Spanish Wreck	26856.5	43293.5
Special Wreck	26380.4	43278.1
SS Chaparro	26839.6	43229.4
SS Winneconne	26370.8	43068.0
Texas Tower	26313.1	43267.5
The Dusky Hole - North	26675.0	43265.0
The Dusky Hole - Middle	26680.0	43225.0
The Dusky Hole - South	26680.0	43205.0
The Fingers - North	26665.0	43200.0
The Fingers - Middle	26675.0	43150.0
The Fingers - South	26685.0	43110.0
The Glory Hole - West	26615.0	43375.0
The Glory Hole - Middle	26575.0	43365.0
The Glory Hole - East	26530.0	43360.0
Tire Reef	26897.8	43154.9
Tolten Lump	26813.0	43336.0
Tolten Wreck	26815.0	43360.1
Trawler Wreck	26819.5	43295.5
Truro Barge Wreck	26869.5	43359.5
Unknown Barge Wreck	26871.7	43277.6
Unknown Wreck	26538.2	43200.5
Unknown Wreck	26853.3	43359.5
Unknown Wreck	26855.2	43360.1
Vixen Wreck	26646.9	43289.1
Vizcaya Wreck	26854.6	43295.2
Whaler Wreck	26852.5	43286.5
William R. Farrel	26912.2	43240.5
Yellow Flag	26871.5	43230.6
45 Fathom Ridge	25964.4	43351.0

SURF CITY TO ABSECON

AC Airplane	25855.5	43113.5
AC Lobster Pots	26915.0	42937.0
AC Wescoat	26915.0	42962.8
A H Dumont Wreck	26872.1	43197.5
Akron Wreck (Main Section)	26726.7	43076.0
Akron Wreck (Tail Section)	26724.9	43076.7
Almirante Wreck	26918.0	43025.7
American Wreck	26896.5	42944.9
Aqua II	26872.5	43194.7
Astra Wreck (1)	26900.6	43013.6
Astra Wreck (2)	26901.2	43014.5
Atlantic City Buoy	26985.5	43023.1
Atlantic City Reef (Center)	26910.0	42960.0
A.C. Wescoat Barge	26915.0	42962.8
Ada Adella	26909.4	42962.4
First Lady	26897.3	42943.3
Francis S. Bushey	26896.0	42948.7
Morania Abaco	26896.1	42948.1
Nils S	26900.5	42942.4
Pauline Marie	26895.4	42944.0
Point Pub Tug	26911.4	42961.6
Margaret Nancy	26908.6	42958.2
The American	26896.5	42944.9

An inshore weakfish, safe in the large landing net, is swung aboard to be unhooked and readied for the cooler.

Troy Tug	26910.4	42960.3
Spaghetti Pile (Cable)	26902.0	42948.0
Vicky-Pat Dredge	26915.1	42959.7
Auto Wreck	26901.1	42958.6
Avalon Tug	27008.2	42863.4
Azua Wreck	26857.2	43804.9
Barge Wreck	26990.5	42895.8
Blackie Wreck	26881.9	42939.5
Brigantine Shoal (2BS)	26933.0	43048.0
Brigantine Shoal (4BS)	26957.0	43051.0
Caldwell Barge	26900.1	43155.4
Camilla May Page Wreck	26927.5	43063.2
Captain Starns Wreck	26968.0	42991.1
Car Float Wreck	26996.0	42884.7
Carl Scott Wreck	26910.1	42909.2
Carmens	26961.3	42814.7
Carolina Wreck	26456.7	42773.5
Cayru Wreck	26724.5	42963.0
C.F. Pritchard Wreck	26907.0	42934.3
Choctaw	26873.9	43199.3
City of Athens	26920.3	42705.3
Clam Boat Wreck	27020.7	42938.6
Collier Wreck	26928.0	42991.2
Cross Ledge	27260.0	42880.0
Dans Wreck	26937.4	42822.7
Dolphin Wreck	26920.1	42940.5
Dorothy B. Barrett	26963.4	42773.1
Dredge	26956.4	43027.2
Dry Dock Wreck	26971.5	42981.5
Dry Dock Wreck	26923.0	43124.8
Edward B. Cole Wreck	26974.0	42830.0
Edward H. Cole Wreck	26594.6	42876.1
Edward H. Cole (Black Sunday)	26536.2	42853.7
Eugene F. Moran Wreck	26939.0	43022.2
Fall River Wreck	26917.7	43007.2
Fall River Wreck (AC Barge Wreck)	26898.1	43984.2
False Cayrue	26724.3	42962.8
Fatuk	26871.7	43196.1
First Lady	26897.3	43943.3
Florida Wreck	27001.2	43000.7
Flour Wreck (1)	26918.0	43024.8
Flour Wreck (2)	26915.0	43023.7
Forty Two Mile Wreck	26536.2	42853.7
Francis S. Bushey Wreck	26896.2	42950.0
Francis Wreck	26950.5	43110.5
Garden State Reef North	26875.0	43195.0
Garden State Reef South	26900.0	43155.0

GE Bell	27016.2	42974.9
Gloria Wreck	26895.7	43078.4
Good Times Wreck	26873.1	43192.5
Harry Ruse Barge Wreck	26732.5	43144.5
Herb Parker Wreck	26494.5	43188.2
Hornet IV Wreck	26934.3	43071.6
Isabel B. Wiley Wreck	26472.5	42914.9
Jacob M. Haskell Wreck	26458.1	43165.8
J.H. North	26468.0	43185.0
Kahuka Wreck	27034.0	42835.6
Lemuel Burrows Wreck	26928.2	42991.1
Lobster Hole	26900.0	42970.0
Margaret Nancy	26908.6	42958.2
Mary	26875.2	43191.6
Maternity Ward	26780.6	43034.3
Molasses Barge	26874.0	43195.1
Morania Abaco	26896.1	43948.1
Mountain Wreck (Akron)	26781.2	43035.1
Nils S	26900.5	42942.4
Northern Barge Wreck	26877.5	43136.5
Oil Wreck	26964.2	42952.2
Old Mud Digger Wreck	26987.2	42993.0
Patrice McAllister	26930.5	43061.5
Pauline Marie Wreck	26895.4	42944.0
Peanuts Wreck	26901.8	42967.9
Pet Wreck	26944.5	43005.5
Pig Iron Wreck	26942.5	43022.5
Pinnacle	26896.8	43127.3
Plane Wreck	26972.2	43061.5
Plum Bob Wreck	27043.6	42901.5
Point Pub	26911.4	42961.6
Post Marine Reef Wreck	27016.4	42906.2
Queen Mary	26873.3	43193.3
Quicksand Wreck	26502.5	42636.3
Remedios Pascue (Bone Wreck)	26886.7	43289.7
Rio Tercero Wreck	26233.9	42963.7
Salem Wreck	27008.4	42863.3
San Jose Wreck	26877.5	42955.4
Sawanaka Wreck	26878.0	42967.2
Seven Mile Wreck	26906.5	43024.5
Shaw Wreck	26909.8	42933.0
Shirley Ann Wreck	26875.5	43194.1
Shukas Wreck	26717.9	43079.4
South East Wreck	26904.5	42989.5
Sumner Wreck	26916.8	43271.7
Tear Drop	26910.3	42912.5
Teaser Wreck	26913.8	43006.4

Texel Wreck	26501.1	42796.2
The American	26896.5	42944.9
The Fingers	26661.0	43169.0
The Rhino	26897.8	43155.8
Tire Reef	26897.8	43154.9
Tire Units	26874.1	43196.4
Tire Units	26875.7	43194.1
Tire Units	26872.3	43197.5
Tire Units	26871.6	43199.1
Tire Units	26897.8	43154.9
Tire Units	26898.3	43155.9
Tire Units	26903.3	43155.8
Tire Units	26896.0	43156.5
Tire Units	26903.3	43153.9
Tire Units	26894.8	42943.2
Tire Units	26896.5	43153.3
Triangle Towing Wreck	26810.9	42767.7
Troy	26910.4	42960.3
Twenty-Fathom Fingers	26675.0	43175.0
Twenty-One Barge Wreck	26857.5	43094.5
Twenty-Five Dollar Wreck	26939.5	42934.5
Twenty-Seven Fathom Hole	26712.9	42855.8
Unknown Wreck	26270.3	43189.5
Unknown Wreck	26914.5	43188.5
Unknown Wreck	26894.5	43152.5
Unknown Wreck	27805.5	43119.5
USS Nina	27032.3	42350.7
Vicki-Pat	26915.1	42959.7
Viking (Mold)	26900.6	43153.6
Viking (Mold)	26900.5	43153.4
Wellington Wreck	26926.5	43093.5
Wethea Yacht Wreck	27008.5	42919.5
11 Fathom Lump	26777.0	43171.0

ABSECON TO CAPE MAY

AC Ridge	26868.0	42860.0
Adolphus Wreck	27177.0	42681.0
Alex Gibson	27027.3	42750.0
Alligator Bite (Wilmington Canyon)	26577.3	42461.7
Avalon Shoal	27012.0	42849.0
Azua Wreck	26856.5	42798.5
Big Bill	26976.9	43023.5
Big Clam	27050.6	42809.4
Bonito Lump	26970.0	42630.0
Bridge Rubble	27022.7	42709.5
Buck Ridge	27038.0	42745.0

Cape May Reef (Center)	27025.0	42695.0
Becky Lee	27026.5	42708.8
Ben Franklin (Concrete Slabs)	27022.7	42709.5
Captain Henry	27029.7	42686.6
Laita	27032.5	42680.6
Lisa Michelle Barge	27021.8	42713.4
Peggy Diane	27030.1	42682.5
Rt 47 Bridge Rubble	27027.6	42708.7
Steel and Concrete Parts	27025.5	42711.0
Steel and Tires	27019.1	42712.9
Winthrop	27029.2	42682.6
Wyoming	27024.0	42707.2
Cape May Rips - North	27133.7	42727.2
Cape May Rips - South	27107.0	42694.0
Captain Henry	27029.7	42686.6
Car Float	26996.0	42884.7
Carolina Wreck	26456.7	42788.4
Champion	26849.2	42735.9
China Junk Wreck	27062.9	42866.7
China Wreck	27098.0	42658.3
City of Georgetown	26980.3	42461.5
East Lump	26943.0	42655.0
Elephants Truck (Tip)	26780.0	42512.0
Evelyn K	27051.5	42822.5
Evening Star (Pig Iron Wreck)	27032.1	42760.9
Five Fathom Bank Light Buoy	26977.0	42648.0
Five Fathom Bank (FFB)	27010.0	42715.0
Gibson	27022.5	42756.5
Green Blinker (3FB)	26035.0	42765.0
Green Light Bunker	27013.9	43770.9
Hotel Slough	27095.0	42700.0
Inshore Stone Beds	26990.0	42900.0
John L Martino Wreck	26921.5	42879.5
Junk Wreck	27024.7	43894.9
Kahuka Wreck	27034.5	42835.5
King Cobra	27096.1	42675.3
Laita	27032.5	42680.0
Lisa Michelle	27021.8	42713.4
Little Bill	26983.7	43024.1
Little Clam	27056.8	42838.5
Little Piece	27039.0	43749.0
Mary Lou Slough	27035.0	42670.0
Middle Lump	27034.0	42868.0
McCrie Shoal - East	27056.0	42691.0
McCrie Shoal - West	27102.0	42691.0
Mud Wreck	26967.1	42886.9
N.E.End Buoy (2FB)	26982.0	42769.0

Northern Lump	27029.0	42872.0
Northern Pacific Wreck	26896.9	42558.9
Number 6	26974.8	42882.8
Ocean City Reef	27022.0	43900.0
Peggy Diana	27030.1	42682.5
Pope Barge	27084.7	42767.7
Port Marine Reef	27016.4	42906.2
Poseidon	26980.0	42670.4
Post (Mold)	27023.4	42898.1
Post (Mold)	27024.7	42897.0
Riggs	27082.4	42731.0
Salem Wreck	27008.5	42863.5
Sea Isle Shoal	27030.0	42848.0
Sea Isle Lump	27042.0	42868.0
Show Barge	26917.0	42728.9
South Buoy (4FB)	27995.0	42672.0
Southern Lump	27036.0	42865.0
South Paw	26890.0	42180.0
Sprague	27025.8	42758.5

A tournament winning bigeye tuna that will also make for some excellent barbecuing for the next few weeks.

Steel Tower Reef	27016.8	42907.6
Steel Tower/Tires Reef	27018.2	42904.9
Steel Tower/Tires Reef	27020.3	42902.7
Steel Tower/Tires Reef	27021.1	42900.7
Stone Harbor Lumps	27045.0	42820.0
Table Top	27001.0	42890.0
Texel Wreck	26488.0	42714.0
The Fingers	26974.0	42830.0
The Hole	26921.1	42802.3
The Plumb Bob	27043.6	42901.5
The Submarine	26810.5	42580.5
Tire Units	27025.3	42702.7
Tire Units	27030.2	42687.2
Tire Units	27027.4	42687.4
Tire Units	27021.3	42901.8
Tire Units	27024.4	42899.2
Tire Units	27025.0	42896.5
Tire Units	27025.7	42897.0
Tire Units	27017.9	42903.9
Tire Units	27017.0	42905.0
Tire Units	27023.6	42897.9
Tire Units	27028.0	42685.0
Tire Units	27025.1	42688.1
Tire Units	27027.5	42700.8
Tire Units	27027.7	42702.7
Tire Units	27027.4	42705.4
Tire Units	27024.7	42702.5
Tire Units	27025.2	42705.5
Tire Units	27025.2	42707.7
Tire Units	27025.4	42710.3
Tire Units	27024.9	42712.6
Tire Units	27024.8	42715.0
Tire Units	27022.5	42702.4
Tire Units	27022.5	42705.1
Tire Units	27022.4	42707.5
Tire Units	27022.6	42712.6
Tire Units	27027.0	42686.0
Tire Units	27028.0	42692.0
Tire Units	27028.1	42693.1
Tire Units	27027.0	42692.0
Tire Units	27026.9	42693.8
Tire Units	27027.7	42692.3
Tire Units	27026.9	42692.5
Tire Units	27028.1	42692.7
Tire Units	27027.4	42693.8
Tire Units	27027.5	42692.0
Tire Units	27026.0	42694.0

Tire Units	27025.9	42693.6
Tire Units	27029.0	42691.3
Tire Units	27027.4	42694.3
Toms Canyon	26280.0	42875.0
Tower	27016.8	42907.6
Tower	27018.1	42904.9
Tower	27020.3	42902.7
Tower	27020.7	42900.7
Twenty Mile Slough	27080.8	42710.7
Unknown Wreck	27058.7	42719.0
USS Cherokee (Gun Boat)	26982.0	42519.1
USS Jacob Jones (Bow)	26930.4	42564.5
USS Jacob Jones (Bridge)	26929.7	42573.8
USS Jacob Jones (Stern)	26895.1	42544.4
Varanger (28 Mile Wreck)	26825.5	42803.7
Wayne Wreck	27033.9	42842.4
William B. Diggs	27038.9	42746.1
Wilmington Canyon (Tip)	26574.8	42510.1
Wilmington Canyon (East Wall)	26565.4	42438.1
Wilmingtin Canyon (West Wall)	26597.8	42396.5
Wilmington Canyon (Toilet Seat)	26595.3	42461.8
Wilmington Canyon (Deep Tip)	26584.6	42435.0
Winthrop	27029.2	42682.6
19-Fathom Lump	26855.0	42475.0
20-Fathom Lumps	26850.0	42180.0
28-Mile Wreck	26825.5	42803.7
30-Fathom Lump	26645.6	42575.0

DELAWARE BAY

Abandoned Lighthouse	27260.0	42881.3
A Buoy (Anchorage - SE Corner)	27207.4	42744.6
Adolphus	27179.0	42682.0
Artificial Reef E Cluster	27188.8	42733.8
Artificial Reef N Cluster	27190.2	42734.8
Artificial Reef S Cluster	27189.2	42732.1
Artificial Reef W Cluster	27190.6	42733.5
Banana Peel Slough	27207.0	42820.0
B Buoy (Anchorage - Mid East)	27218.0	42762.0
Beach Ball	27218.2	42720.1
Ben Davis Shoal	27297.0	42940.0
Big Stone	27265.0	42800.0
Big Stone (Inshore)	27260.0	42780.1
Big Stone (South Tip)	27240.0	42772.0
Bowers	27290.0	42810.0
Brandywine Light	27189.0	42763.0

Broadkill Slough	27220.0	42720.0
Brown Shoal	27186.8	42733.0
Brown Shoal	27189.6	42741.8
Brown Shoal North	27195.2	42749.8
Bug Light	27165.1	42835.2
C3 "Green Can"	27234.0	42739.0
Cape May Canal - R8	27142.5	42755.0
C Buoy (Anchorage - NE Corner)	27232.5	42785.9
Coral Beds (1)	27220.0	42699.0
Coral Beds (2)	27225.7	42697.4
Cross Ledge	27260.0	42880.0
Cross Ledge Light	27274.7	42894.2
Crossovers	27238.0	42800.0
Crossover Shelf	27239.1	42803.7
Deadman Shoal	27174.9	42840.1
D Buoy (Anchorage - NW Corner)	27239.6	42779.0
E Buoy (Anchorage - Mid West)	27224.0	42753.0
Egg Island Flats	27219.5	42860.1
Egg Island Flats (#1 Buoy)	27211.0	42871.0
F Buoy (Anchorage - SW Corner)	27214.0	42736.0
Fish Trap Area	27180.0	42870.0
Flounder Alley - South	27210.0	42810.0
Flounder Alley - North	27199.0	42745.0

Delaware Bay has excellent fleets of party boats offering top-notch fishing for weakfish, drum, blues and flounder.

Bucktails are a favorite lure for catching trophy-sized weakfish in Delaware Bay, like this 11 pounder coming to the net.

Flounder Hotel	27198.0	42746.0
Fourteen-Foot Light	27222.5	42804.0
Gypsum Prince	27146.2	42641.5
Hawksnest Shoal	27265.0	42258.0
Haystacks (Ice Breakers)	27168.0	42660.0
Horseshoe Slough	27200.0	42817.3
Lewes Outer Wall	27164.0	42658.0
Little Egypt	27211.0	42870.9
Lower Middle	27227.6	42778.5
Lumps North	27220.0	42880.1
Lumps South	27225.0	42819.2
Margheri	27097.8	42657.9
Maurice River	27194.0	42895.0
Maurice River Cove (#2 Buoy)	27194.0	42896.0
Miah Maull Shoal (1)	27243.0	42855.0
Miah Maull Shoal (2)	27238.0	42849.0
Middle Shoal	27133.0	42607.0
Mid Flats	27170.5	42875.5
Mispillion Jetty	27243.2	42724.0
Mohawk Wreck	27223.0	42773.0
NE of Old C Buoy	27232.3	42773.7
New Pluto's	27195.0	42735.0
North Crossovers	27248.9	42806.6
North of Bug Light	27175.0	42862.0
Old A Spar	27207.5	42700.2
Other Big Stone	27240.0	42772.0

Other Crossover Shelf	27242.7	42799.1
Other North Crossovers	27250.6	42806.6
Overfalls Shoals	27128.9	42685.8
Pin Top	27201.5	42786.6
Pluto's Flounder Lower	27199.0	42738.0
Port Mahon	27315.0	42892.0
Punk Grounds	27195.0	42830.0
R2 - Bidwell Creek	27136.0	42865.0
Red Band	27208.0	42751.0
Roosevelt Inlet	27174.0	42630.0
Rope Barge	27083.6	42736.1
Sarah Lawrence	27138.9	42611.7
Shad Stakes	27195.1	42865.0
Ship John Shoal	27336.0	42978.0
Sixty-Foot Slough	27165.9	42777.3
Slaughters Subm Piles	27226.0	42698.0
Somer Shoal	27118.0	42695.0
South of #1 Buoy	27197.1	42842.0
South of Brandywine	27184.6	42759.4
Southwest Line	27250.0	42895.0
Southwest of Dennis Creek	27160.5	42878.5
Stardust	27153.8	42663.9
Sunrise Wreck	27147.0	42686.5
The Anchorage	27219.0	42750.0
Trout Hole (Lower Middle)	27235.3	42801.6
Wreck Buoy	27274.1	42914.0
#2 Fortescue	27254.0	42933.0
2B Buoy	27183.0	42703.0
#9 Buoy	27175.0	42720.0
#10 Buoy	27179.4	42733.1
#12 Buoy	27193.0	42759.0
#19 Buoy	27229.0	42827.1
#32 Buoy	27293.5	42930.0
60-Foot Slough	27172.0	42789.0

DELAWARE AND MARYLAND COAST

Adolphus Wreck	27177.0	42581.0
African Queen Reef	27024.6	42203.8
African Queen Wreck	27024.6	42263.8
Ammo Wreck	26920.5	42706.5
Anna Murray Wreck	27112.0	42496.1
Atlantic Mist	27030.2	42039.8
Baltimore Canyon Bump (West Wall)	26680.0	42280.0
Baltimore Canyon Tip	26680.0	42330.0
Barge 887 Wreck	27074.5	42519.5

Barge Wreck	26575.0	42448.5
Barge Wreck	27016.7	42070.1
Barge Wreck	27074.5	42519.1
Bass Grounds - East	27019.0	42299.4
Bass Grounds - West	27024.4	42305.0
Bass Hole	27091.0	42291.6
Beth Dry Dock	26928.4	42470.9
CB Buoy	27129.0	42239.0
Cherokee	26982.0	42519.1
China Wreck	27097.8	42658.4
City Of Athens	26920.3	42705.3
David Atwater	27047.7	42059.2
Elephants Trunk (North End)	26785.0	42535.0
Elephants Trunk (Tip)	26779.0	42512.0
Elizabeth Palmer	27019.5	42420.1
Ethel C.	26876.8	41754.8
Fenwick Shoal (North)	27057.4	42411.4
Fenwick Shoal (South)	27055.7	42411.7
Fenwick West Quarter	27067.4	42072.3
Fenwick Wreck	27071.0	42414.4
FH Beckwith Wreck	27085.5	42704.5
Fifty-Six Mile Wreck	26696.3	42525.4
Francis F. Powell	27038.0	41766.2
Great Gull Bank	27060.8	42278.1
Gun Boat Wreck (1)	26967.6	42519.2
Gun Boat Wreck (2)	26982.0	42513.1
Great Gull Reef	27060.8	42278.1
H Buoy Wreck	26992.0	42358.3
Harold Weston Sailboat Wreck (1)	26987.3	41974.6
Harold Weston Sailboat Wreck (2)	26987.1	41975.3
Hauslef (aka Hvoslef)	26931.8	42450.0
Hot Dog - North	26810.0	42225.0
Indian Arrow	26694.1	42531.1
Insane Barge	26903.5	42559.3
Irene Muril	27031.8	41977.3
Isle of Wright	27030.2	42340.2
Jack's Spot	26955.0	42177.0
Jack Wreck	26974.8	42172.8
Jacob Jones Wreck (Bridge)	26920.9	42578.3
Jacob Jones Wreck (Midships)	26929.7	42573.7
John R Williams	27090.9	42608.2
JR Williams Tug Wreck	27085.0	42613.0
Kelly's Reef	27076.5	42278.8
Lori Dawn Wreck	26864.4	42578.3
Machipongo Inlet "A"	27141.7	41624.8
Machipongo Inlet "B"	27148.2	41615.5
Manhattan (1)	27014.4	42425.6

Manhatten (2)	27007.4	42419.6
Marie Beasley Barge	26990.5	42502.4
Marine Electric (Bow)	26942.6	42038.4
Marine Electric (Stern)	26943.2	42037.6
Merida	26873.7	41729.8
Middle Grounds	27019.3	42038.1
Misty Blue	26885.9	42641.4
Mona Island Wreck	27096.0	41744.0
Monroe	27049.1	41805.6
Moon Stone Wreck	26927.3	42470.4
Mothers Day Wreck	27061.0	42359.1
Muff Diver	26785.4	42251.1
Mystic Blue Wreck	26885.3	42641.5
New Orleans Wreck	27057.0	42567.5
Nina Wreck	27032.2	42450.7
Norfolk Canyon Tip	26865.0	42530.0
North Beach	27045.5	42225.1
North Pacific Wreck	26899.1	42556.8
Ocean Venture Wreck (1)	26913.8	41495.1
Old Grounds	27025.0	42496.0
Pharoby	27026.8	42307.2
Poor Man's Canyon	26740.0	42080.0
Purnells Reef	27081.1	42331.2
Quantro	27087.0	42364.2
Quicksand Wreck	26502.5	42636.3

A diamond-jigged bluefish. This lip-hooked fish will be released for another day's action.

R Buoy	27059.8	42392.3
Rock Pile	26800.0	41925.0
Rocket Grids	26412.0	42292.0
San Gil	26906.1	42180.7
Sausage Lumps	26835.0	42200.0
Sergeant Wreck	27112.0	42568.0
Schooner Wreck	27058.3	42296.3
Schooner Wreck	27109.0	42580.0
S.G.Wilder	26971.7	42265.4
Southern Sword Wreck	27080.3	42516.3
Star Obstruction	27018.3	42385.4
Sub Wreck	27074.9	42516.0
Submarine Wreck	27024.2	42005.7
Sugar Wreck	26998.4	42401.4
Sunrise Wreck	27142.0	42686.4
Texel Wreck	26488.0	42714.0
The Meat Cleaver	27075.0	41575.0
The Norfolk Canyon Hook	26850.0	41650.0
The Pimple - East	27038.0	42555.0
The Pimple - West	27050.5	42555.5
The Submarine	26810.5	42580.5
Thomas Tracy Wreck	27130.0	42570.0
Three Mast Schooner	27007.5	42418.0
Tiger Wreck Buoy	27107.5	41887.5
T.J. Hooker Barge Wreck	26875.1	42428.1
Tug Boat	27078.4	41969.1
Tuna Lump	26645.6	42580.7
Twin Wrecks (1)	26971.7	42265.2
Twin Wrecks (2)	26973.4	42264.1
Unknown Wreck	27012.0	42448.5
Unknown Wreck	26630.4	42585.7
Unknown Wreck	26719.2	42425.1
Unknown Wreck	26707.3	42546.0
Unknown Wreck	26673.9	42549.8
Unknown Wreck	26577.3	42469.0
Unknown Wreck	26682.3	42551.4
Unknown Wreck	26696.3	42525.4
USS Blenny (sub)	27024.1	42203.4
USS Nina	27032.4	42350.7
Walter H. Page Wreck	27095.5	41746.3
Washington (BB-47)	26843.3	41420.0
Washingtonian Wreck	26998.8	42402.6
Washington Canyon	26830.0	41800.0
Wilmington Canyon	26575.0	42510.0
Winter Quarter Lightship	26994.8	42055.9
Winter Quarter Shoal - East	27061.9	42067.8
Winter Quarter Shoal - West	27068.0	42070.0

Wooden Sailboat (1)	26987.3	41974.6
Wooden Sailboat (2)	26986.9	41975.0
Wooden Sailboat (3)	26987.1	41975.3
150 Wreck	27048.6	42152.3
160 Wreck	27000.5	42162.5
19-Fathom Lump	26855.0	42475.0
20-Fathom Fingers	26915.0	41730.0
20-Fathom Line	26915.0	41730.0
44-Fathom Wreck	26913.7	41494.8
21-Mile Hill	27020.0	41700.0
26-Mile Hill	27000.0	41580.0
60-60	27060.0	42460.0

VIRGINIA COAST

Anglo African	27163.2	41372.6
Arco Powell (1)	27013.5	41269.7
Arco Powell (2)	27014.0	41270.3
Bluefish Alley - North	27025.0	41150.3
Bluefish Alley - South	27025.0	41120.0
Captain Rick	27035.7	41245.2
CBJ Buoy	27164.0	41282.0
Chesapeake Light Tower	27101.0	41288.0
Chango Wreck	26878.0	41100.0
Chesapeake Barge	27102.8	41286.5
Chesapeake Light	27101.5	41288.5
Chilore (Cape Henry Wrecks)	27180.3	41294.2
City of Annapolis	27334.0	41909.5
Clark Wreck	27020.0	41387.4
Coast Guard Boat	27022.4	41369.0
Cuyahoga	27022.4	41369.7
Deep Rock	27303.2	41661.9
Dump Site	27135.0	41200.0
Ed Clark Wreck	27018.8	41386.1
Edgar Clark Liberty Ship	27018.8	41386.2
Electric Barge	27102.8	41285.0
Eureka	26875.3	41243.8
Francis Powell (1)	27013.5	41269.7
Francis Powell (2)	27014.1	41270.4
George P. Harrison Wreck	27020.5	41390.7
Gulf Hustler	27069.7	41272.7
Hanks Wreck	27020.0	41390.7
Haviland Wreck	27020.9	41389.6
Hot Dog	26980.6	41230.4
Jim Haviland Wreck	27020.0	41390.0
John Morgan Wreck (1)	27032.7	41390.7
John Morgan Wreck (2)	27033.7	41391.4

Kingston Ceylonite	27131.2	41218.2
Latimer Shoal (North of CBBT)	27200.0	41420.0
Lillian Luckenback Wreck	27032.0	41372.7
Margaret P. Hanks	27048.3	41188.9
Owl-Kingston Calonite	27121.5	41218.1
River Front Junction	27024.3	41260.3
Rudee Inlet "1"	27155.0	41208.0
Salty Sea II	27087.7	41241.7
Santore	27117.1	41276.9
Southeast Lumps	26995.5	41120.3
Spring Chicken Wreck (1)	26958.5	41320.2
Spring Chicken Wreck (2)	26965.1	41319.8
The Cigar - North	26870.0	41170.0
The Cigar - South	26870.0	41055.0
The Elevens	26963.0	41087.5
The Fingers - North	26965.0	41425.0
The Fingers - South	26905.0	41400.0
The Fish Hook - East	27028.0	41250.0
The Fish Hook - West	27045.0	41240.0
The Lumps - North	26995.0	41210.0
The Lumps - South	27000.0	41065.0
Tiger Tanker	27101.6	41188.6
The Reef	27100.0	41240.0
Tiger Wreck Lumps	27090.0	41170.0
Triangle Wrecks Area	27030.0	41375.0

Cobia thrash madly when gaffed, so a quick lift into an open fish box is called for.

Tower Reef Drydock	27103.0	41286.2
Triangle Wreck	27025.0	41380.0
Tripca Wreck	27032.9	41388.7
Webster Wreck	27020.2	41391.4
Westmoreland Wreck	27165.3	41288.9
Winthrop tug	27145.1	41268.0
60-Foot Lump	26983.0	41125.0

CHESAPEAKE BAY

Abbey Point Grounds	27610.0	42980.0
African Queen	27024.6	42263.8
Airplane Wreck	27497.5	42493.0
American Mariner Wreck	27357.5	42043.5
Barge Reef	27103.0	41286.2
Bass Grounds - East	27019.0	42299.4
Bass Grounds - West	27024.4	42305.0
Belvidere Shoal	27605.0	42797.0
Bluefish Alley	27025.0	41150.3
Bluefish Rock	27247.5	41352.5
Bodkin Island Grounds	27537.0	42648.0
Brick House Bar	27567.0	42680.0
Butler's Hole	27332.0	41715.7
Cabbage Patch Area (1)	27210.0	41440.0
Cabbage Patch Area (2)	27213.0	41443.0
Cape Charles "1"	27221.1	41478.5
Cape Charles "2"	27218.8	41482.8
Cape Charles Reef - East	27228.0	41490.0
Cape Charles Reef - West	27230.0	41490.0
Cape Charles Test Reef	27231.0	41539.4
Cape Henry "1"	27164.4	41267.7
Cape Henry "2"	27180.4	41291.4
Cape Henry Wreck	27180.3	41294.2
Cedarhurst Reef	27567.2	42532.0
Chesapeake Bay "CBJ"	27164.0	41281.5
Chesapeake Bay Channel "CB"	27129.0	41239.0
Chesapeake Bay Channel "CBJ"	27164.0	41281.6
Chesapeake Beach	27566.2	42510.0
Chesapeake Tower Reef	27101.0	41288.8
Cherrystone Reef	27228.0	41541.0
Chilore Wreck	27180.3	41295.0
Chinese Muds	27465.0	42240.0
Clay Banks	27467.0	42570.0
Coast Guard Boat	27022.4	41369.0
Cobb Island "12"	27107.0	41569.0
Concrete Ship	27198.0	41346.0

A just-tagged striped bass is about to be released to return to its Chesapeake Bay spawning grounds.

Concrete Pipes	27230.8	41539.4
Concrete Strcutures	27189.3	42733.3
Concrete Structures	27189.9	42733.5
Concrete Structures	27189.0	42734.2
Concrete Structures	27190.4	42735.7
Coral Reef	27230.5	41488.0
Corn House	27314.7	41678.2
Cove Point Light	27474.5	42278.5
Craig Hill Light	27631.5	42860.5
Davidson Wreck	27297.5	41878.0
Devils Hole	27535.0	42483.0
Diamonds	27500.0	42440.0
Drum Fish Flats Area	27275.0	41400.0
Drydock	27103.0	41286.0
Dumping Grounds	27585.0	42750.0
Edward Clark Wreck	27018.8	41386.1
Fishing Battery Light	27605.5	43094.5
Flag Harbor	27485.0	42298.0

Fourth Island	27202.0	41348.0
Gas Platform	27477.0	42289.0
Gooses	27509.0	42397.0
Ghost Hole	27271.1	42766.9
Gulf Hustler Wreck	27069.5	41272.5
Gum Thickets	27567.0	42640.0
Gwynn Island Reef	27299.4	41637.2
Hackett Point Reef	27592.2	42714.0
Hickory Thicket	27568.0	42790.0
Hodges Bar	27597.0	42856.0
Holland Point	27567.2	42532.0
Hollicut Noose	27547.0	42609.5
Hooper Island Light	27417.0	41192.0
Jane's Island	27278.7	41994.8
Jim Haviland Wreck	27020.0	41390.0
John Morgan Wreck	27033.7	41391.5
Kelley's	27076.5	42278.8
Kent Point Grounds	27548.0	42608.0
Latimer Shoal	27203.1	41423.8
Lighthouse Lump	27571.0	42782.0
Lil Lukenback Wreck	27032.0	41372.5
Little Cove Point	27465.8	42245.9
Little Creek Inlet "LC"	27219.6	41266.2
Little Creek Reef	27225.3	41259.8
Long Point Grounds	27544.0	42616.0
Love Point	27576.2	42778.0
Lynnhaven Inlet "1"	27194.6	41255.2
Mid Channel	27244.8	41597.4
Millers Island	27631.4	42901.7

Chesapeake Bay is light tackle fisherman's heaven for battling bluefish.

Nautilus Shoal "2"	27203.1	41423.8
Nautilus Shoal "4"	27164.0	41333.0
N. Tunnel "10"	27202.6	41343.4
N. Tunnel "9"	27204.5	41341.2
Oceanview Reef	27225.3	41259.8
Old Barge	27405.8	42080.8
Old Dominion Reef	27225.0	41258.0
Owl Wreck	27121.5	41218.2
Pear Tree	27528.0	42633.0
Plantation Light	27213.0	41478.0
Plum Point Grounds	27600.0	42978.0
Punch Island Bar	27456.0	42310.0
Punch Island Grounds	27460.0	42290.0
Purnell's	27081.1	42331.2
River Front Junction	27024.3	41260.3
Rock Pile	26714.2	42427.7
Salty Sea Wreck	27088.0	41241.5
Sand Shoal "A"	27141.8	41556.1
Sand Shoal "12"	27106.6	41568.1
San Marcos Wreck	27292.2	41819.5
Santore Wreck	27117.0	42177.5
Shad Battery Shoal	27599.0	42993.0
Sharps Island Grounds	27512.0	42430.0
Smith Point Jetty	27357.0	41929.5
Snake Reef	27615.0	42786.0
Spike Buoy	27323.5	41700.5
S. Tunnel "8"	27205.0	41291.6
S. Tunnel "7"	27205.0	41289.5
Stone Rock	27523.5	42476.4
Susquehanna Flats	27585.0	43080.0
Swan Point Grounds	27597.0	42816.0
Swan Point Bar	27580.0	42810.0
Tangier Light	27273.0	41878.0
Tangier Island Targets	27291.0	41889.0
Target Ship	27357.5	41041.0
Tea Kettle Shoals	27616.0	42875.0
Texaco Tanker Wreck	27232.0	41488.0
The Cell	27245.0	41598.5
The Hill	27555.0	42564.0
The Hook	27537.0	42520.0
Thimble Shoal Channel "1"	27188.1	41285.4
Thimble Shoal Channel "2"	27188.4	41287.6
Thimble Shoal Channel "20"	27237.5	41300.1
Third Island	27206.0	41340.0
Thomas Point Light	27583.0	42647.0
Tiger Wreck	27101.5	41188.0
Tire Reef	27100.0	41245.0

Tolechester	27606.2	42903.4
Trepico Wreck	27037.0	41388.2
Triangle Wrecks Area	27030.0	41375.0
Turkey Point Grounds	27572.0	42040.0
Wade Point Grounds	27542.0	42588.0
Wild Grounds	27542.0	42580.0
Winter Goose	27530.0	42413.0
York River "1"	27233.6	41387.8
York River "2"	27233.5	41390.5
York Spit Channel "22"	27240.5	41432.0
York Spit Channel "32"	27243.1	41492.0

NORTH CAROLINA
(North and east of 40150 at Hatteras Inlet)

Acme	26888.9	40229.0
Alpha Tower	26934.0	40910.0
Artificial Reef 130	26979.1	40726.0
Artificial Reef 140	26975.0	40690.0
Artificial Reef 145	26941.4	40685.5
Artificial Reef 220	26951.0	40182.0
Artificial Reef 225	26945.0	40175.0
Artificial Reef 250	26987.0	40024.0
Asphalt Barge	26868.5	40458.8
Australia Wreck (1)	26883.2	40250.5
Australia Wreck (2)	26833.2	40172.7
Bad Rock	26891.7	40498.2
Bedloe	26940.8	40687.3
Benson Wreck (1)	26923.4	40864.9
Benson Wreck (2)	26864.3	40923.1
Bravo Tower	26855.0	40856.0
Buarque	26863.4	40932.8
Byron Benson	26923.4	40865.0
Cape Charles Wreck	26811.1	40913.4
Charley Tower	26915.0	40737.0
Chenango	26872.2	41104.8
Ciltaria (aka Ciltvaira)	26897.0	40400.0
City of Atlanta (1)	26900.3	40403.6
City of Atlanta (2)	26894.3	40399.6
Concrete Rubble	26941.4	40685.7
Consols	27042.8	41011.4
Diamond Tower	26875.2	40478.8
Dionysus	26940.8	40575.6
Dixie Arrow Wreck (1)	26951.3	40038.4
Dixie Arrow Wreck (2)	26949.7	40038.3

Empire Gem Wreck	26903.6	40173.1
Empire Thrush	26869.4	40314.2
Equipoise (1)	26844.1	40999.8
Equipoise (2)	26863.8	40932.8
Green Buoy Wreck	26847.8	40450.9
Gulf Tower	26865.0	40660.0
Harrison	26832.9	40300.1
Hesperides	26910.1	40236.5
Joe Doughty	26877.4	40479.4
John D Gill Wreck (Bow)	27199.5	39085.3
Kassandra Louloudis	26886.9	40274.6
Kashena Wreck (1)	26959.3	40085.3
Keshena Wreck (2)	26960.0	40087.1
Lancing (1)	26889.0	40559.0
Lancing (2)	26897.2	40182.4
Liberator	26936.9	40209.5
Liberty Ship Zane Gray	26940.6	49575.2
Liberty Ship	26940.8	40573.5
Marore	26894.6	40502.3
Mirlo	26940.6	40574.2
Monitor Sanctuary	26883.3	40191.4
Nancy F	26946.7	40816.6
Navy LCU-146	26941.4	40685.5
New Jersey (BB-16)	26864.9	40217.4
Norlavore	26878.3	40237.0
Northeastern	26908.9	40234.7
Norvana (York)	26913.2	40816.9
Old Green Line	26810.0	40400.0
Old Green Line	26811.0	40415.0
Ol' Ugly	26901.6	40503.0
Oriental	26949.3	40559.1
Platt Shoals	26925.1	40631.5
Point Shoals Buoy	26890.0	40246.0
Russian Trawler	26849.4	40886.0
San Delfino	26810.0	40622.8
Slickstink	26897.2	40182.4
South East Rock	26861.0	40234.0
Submarine	26917.0	40713.6
Tenas	26885.7	40214.1
The Cigar	26862.0	41125.0
The Lumps	27000.0	41075.0
The Point	26795.0	40590.0
The Point (Drop-Off)	26785.0	40575.0
Tuna Hole	26800.0	40630.0
Train Cars (1)	26979.1	40726.0
Train Cars (2)	26975.0	40690.0
Unis	26940.4	40191.2

U-85	26917.0	40713.6
Venore	26888.8	40219.2
Veturia	26895.6	40246.4
Virginia (BB-13)	26863.4	40212.1
Wimble Shoals	26885.2	40504.9
Zane Grey	26932.0	40556.5
20-Fathom Lumps	26862.0	40980.0
38 Degree Tower	26930.0	40912.1
65 Degree Tower	26914.6	40739.7
70 Degree Tower	26856.1	40858.0
102 Degree Tower	26865.1	40674.4
280 Rock	26845.0	40280.0
530 Hole	26797.0	40530.0
630 Hole	26803.0	40630.0
662 Wreck	26825.0	40726.1
1250 Rocks	26810.0	40410.0

NORTH CAROLINA
(South and west of 40150 at Hatteras Inlet)

Amagansant Wreck	27042.5	39742.3
Ario	27045.0	39747.5

Summer flounder provide good fishing and lots of fun all along the coast.

Artificial Reef	27127.9	39661.2
Artificial Reef 10	27045.0	39747.5
Artificial Reef 255	26995.9	39998.0
Artificial Reef 298	27019.5	40132.7
Artificial Reef 320	27138.5	39636.9
Artificial Reef 330	27139.7	39569.5
Artificial Reef 340	27162.4	39545.3
Artificial Reef 342	27177.0	39549.8
Artificial Reef 345	27160.2	39524.8
Artificial Reef 355	27210.0	39324.4
Artificial Reef 362	27233.1	39224.5
Artificial Reef 364	27267.4	39161.0
Artificial Reef 366	27214.7	39226.0
Artificial Reef 368	27211.7	39195.0
Artificial Reef 372	27261.0	39068.7
Artificial Reef 376	27243.1	39077.2
Artificial Reef 386	27217.7	39082.9
Artificial Reef 420	27300.7	57421.7
Artificial Reef 425	27303.0	57426.8
Artificial Reef 440	27316.4	57390.2
Artificial Reef 445	27312.6	57375.5
Artificial Reef 455	27325.9	57362.0
Artificial Reef 460	27340.7	57350.1
Atlantic Beach	27127.8	39660.9
Atlas Tanker Wreck (1)	27023.6	39721.6
Atlas Tanker Wreck (2)	27025.2	39723.1
Beaufort Inlet Reef	27128.2	39661.5
Beaufort Sea Buoy	27113.2	39688.7
Big Rock	26982.7	39595.5
Big Rock	27085.0	39575.0
Big Ten (1)	27077.4	39554.8
Big Ten (2)	27077.4	39553.6
Big Ten (3)	27079.6	39555.2
Broken Bottom Ledges	27256.7	39217.3
Carolina Beach Reef	27269.4	39513.5
Caribsea (D-Wreck)	27042.5	39741.0
Cateret Company Wreck	27081.0	39490.0
Christmas Rock	27182.3	39393.8
Clifton Moss	27138.5	39636.9
Concrete Pieces	27267.4	39161.0
Concrete Pieces	27303.0	39013.5
Corner	27075.7	39518.8
Corner	27043.6	39700.6
Corner	27031.5	39551.8
Corner	27031.5	39538.8
Drop	27058.2	39634.7
"D" Wreck (1)	27042.5	39740.0

An Outer Banks bigeye is muscled aboard a boat fishing the outer edge of the Continental Shelf.

"D" Wreck (2)	27042.5	39742.8
East Rock	27043.9	39681.5
East Rock	27048.5	39642.5
East Slough Buoy (1)	27025.6	39670.2
East Slough Buoy (2)	27075.0	39670.4
E.M. Clark Wreck	26905.1	40062.2
Far East Tanker (1)	26989.3	39788.9
Far East Tanker (2)	26981.3	39788.9
Fenwick Island	27064.0	39607.9
Fish Haven	27266.2	39164.8
F. W. Abrams Wreck (1)	26967.5	40073.9
F. W. Abrams Wreck (2)	26953.3	40089.6

Hardee's	27039.3	39574.8
Harris Mears	27268.0	39106.5
Howard Chapin	27139.7	39569.5
Hutton	27143.4	39524.5
Inshore Wreck No 4	27214.7	39076.5
Jerry's Reef	27140.2	39518.1
Key Post - East	27177.4	39563.7
Key Post - West	27178.4	39567.4
Knuckle	27061.2	39618.7
Ledge 4'	27257.4	39214.0
Ledge 5'	27248.8	39215.5
Ledge 7'	27246.9	39214.1
Ledge 8'	27248.2	39215.4
Ledge Area	27188.2	39068.9
Ledge Area	27151.8	39444.5
Ledge Area	27112.6	39410.6
Ledge Area	27139.2	39487.0
Ledge Area	27208.2	39047.2
Ledge Area	27243.2	39215.3
Little Ten (1)	27081.8	39560.1
Little Ten (2)	27080.6	39560.6
Manchase Wreck (1)	26950.3	39960.7
Manchase Wreck (2)	26946.0	39959.4
Menhaden Wreck	27138.5	39636.9
Manuela	26941.1	39881.4
Morehead City Sea Buoy	27113.2	39668.7
Naeko Wreck	27065.6	39387.5
Naeko Wreck	27065.6	39386.8
Masonboro Wreck	27199.5	39091.0
NE #14 Buoy Rock	27037.3	39593.0
NE #14 Buoy Rock	27037.7	39601.1
NE #14 Buoy Rock	27037.9	39599.1
NE #14 Buoy Rock	27034.4	39598.8
NE Big Rock	26984.2	39593.5
Nordal	26977.2	39957.1
NW #14 Buoy Rock	27046.1	39573.1
NW Rock	27159.2	39557.5
NW West Rock	27077.4	39521.5
Ocracoke Inlet	27009.6	40048.9
Papoose Wreck (1)	27074.0	39431.1
Parker	26866.1	40067.3
P Buoy	27056.5	39652.0
Peteroff Wreck	27322.9	39076.0
Pocahontas Tug	27240.6	39048.3
Portland	27056.5	39651.8
Proteus Wreck	26977.2	39957.1
Rock Pile	26903.0	40070.0

Rock Pile	26953.5	39775.0
Rock Pile	27057.0	39700.0
Rock Pile	27135.6	39466.9
Rock Pile	27140.2	39518.1
Rock Pile	27069.7	39493.1
Rock South 13	27134.3	39470.0
Russian Freighter	27037.1	39617.6
Russian Wreck	27037.1	39617.6
Russian Wreck	27066.3	39610.3
Sea Buoy	27113.2	39668.7
SE Naeko	27035.0	39391.0
SE #13 Buoy	27128.4	39556.2
SE #14 Buoy	27032.8	39577.1
SE #14 Buoy	27032.9	39577.3
SE #14 Buoy	27023.2	39570.3
SE #14 Buoy	27024.4	39572.9
Semaeco	27035.0	39391.0
Senateur Dubamel	27092.2	39633.6
Shad Boat	27066.3	39610.3
Shad Boat Buoy R6	27078.4	39595.0
Shad Wreck	27025.3	39724.2
South #14 Buoy	27033.8	39542.6
South West Rock	27066.7	39594.8
South West Rock	27070.4	39507.5
South Wreck	27143.4	39524.3
Steeples	45051.0	59287.2
SS Stone Tug	27241.6	39046.0
Submarine	27063.5	39491.5
Suloide	27146.6	39551.6
Swansboro Sea Buoy BW B1	27189.7	39546.1
SW #14 Buoy	27046.6	39523.5
Tarpon	26946.0	39959.4
Trawler	27092.3	39633.3
Unknown Wreck	27192.8	39069.2
Unknown Wreck	27180.5	39100.0
U.S.S. Schurz	27067.6	39463.4
U-352	27063.5	39491.8
W Big Rock	26987.2	39577.6
W.E. Hutton	27143.4	39524.5
WW1 Wreck	27067.7	39463.2
West Rock (1)	27070.0	39520.0
West Rock (2)	27072.1	39515.7
West Slough Buoy	27083.3	39654.9
WR 2	27129.0	39250.0
WR 2	27128.5	39249.5
WR 13	27146.2	39550.1
1st NW Place	27088.9	39574.0

All along the East Coast, the summer flounder offers great fishing fun in the bays and sounds, and along the ocean front. And, they are great at the dinner table.

2nd NW Place	27085.4	39569.4
3rd NW Place	27089.1	39570.0
7 Train Cars	27316.4	39027.2
10 Train Cars	27312.6	39023.0
10 Train Cars	27261.0	39068.7
10 Train Cars	27243.1	39077.2
10 Train Cars	27177.0	39549.8
#13 Buoy	27146.1	39550.1
#14 Buoy	27040.2	39572.7
15 Train Cars	27139.7	39569.5
30 Minute Rock	27054.6	39686.0
45 Minute Rock	27176.0	39511.2
85 Degree Ledges	27146.0	39415.4
90 Foot Drop	27006.0	39576.0
100 Degree Rock	27064.2	39601.2
120 Degree Rock	27055.4	39621.8

195 Rock	27105.4	39553.2
210 Rock	27069.3	39488.0
210 Rock	27069.3	39493.1
210 Rock	27070.1	39491.4
210 Rock	27069.7	39493.1
240 Rock	27079.0	39495.3
240 Rock	27080.0	39488.8
1400 Line	27936.0	39890.5
1700 Rock	27043.0	39705.8
1700 Rock	27043.4	39709.8
1700 Rock	27043.7	39710.8

SOUTH CAROLINA

Betsy Ross Reef (1)	45504.1	61062.5
Betsy Ross Reef (2)	45504.6	61061.4
BP-25 Wreck (180' ship)	45306.0	59551.4
Cape Romain Reef		
Barge	45363.2	59996.2
Landing Craft	45363.2	59995.7
Capers Reef		
90' Ship	45437.4	60368.4
Drydock	45437.6	60371.0
Landing Craft	45438.3	60370.5
Landing Craft	45438.1	60369.7
Landing Craft	45438.2	60369.9
Lark Wreck	45437.7	60369.5
Barge	45440.0	60367.3
Barge	45439.3	60366.9
Rubble Material	45438.6	60363.5
City Of Richmond	45343.0	59925.2
Edisto Offshore Reef		
100' Ship	45382.7	60692.2
Tug	45380.2	60699.0
Wreckage	45380.3	60699.2
Deck House	45381.6	60690.9
Fish America Reef		
Rubble Material	45616.7	61185.2
Rubble Material	45617.8	61179.8
Fredrick W. Day Wreck	45427.6	60472.6
Fripp Island Drydock Wreck	45566.6	60981.3
Fripp Island Reef		
Structures	45546.1	60969.0
Structures	45546.1	60969.0
Structures	45546.7	60970.2
Barge	45561.1	60969.0

Gaskin Banks Wreck	45609.8	61200.9
General Gordon Wreck	45580.6	61097.2
General Sherman Wreck	45413.4	59455.5
Georgetown Reef		
Structures	45410.4	59882.3
Structures	45411.1	59882.7
Structures	45410.5	59882.0
Structures	45411.4	59882.9
Barge	45411.4	59881.5
Barge	45411.8	59881.1
100' Ship	45410.3	59882.1
Hebe Wreck	45237.1	59612.7
Hector Reef		
200' Ship	45379.6	60026.8
Barges	45379.8	60027.3
Hilton Head Reef		
Tires	45548.1	61178.4
Landing Craft	45548.4	61180.7
Landing Craft	45551.0	61179.7
Barge	45547.5	61178.1
Barge	45545.6	61176.5
Boat	45549.6	61177.8
Tug	45545.6	61174.3
Hunting Island Reef		
Structures	45525.4	60964.8
Structures	45525.8	60964.7
Structures	45525.7	60964.9
Structures	45522.9	60964.0
Structures	45525.5	60965.1
Barge	45523.9	60964.7
Kiwash Reef		
Drydock	45493.2	60693.4
Landing Craft	45493.6	60693.9
Life Boats	45491.1	60693.8
Tug Wreck	45491.1	60693.8
Tug Wreck	45492.7	60692.5
Barge	45491.2	60691.4
Barge	45494.9	60688.2
Tug Wreck	45492.6	60693.7
Barge	45492.7	60693.1
Barge	45495.4	60688.1
Little River Reef		
Rubble Material	45424.0	59409.0
Barges	45423.7	59408.5
Little River Offshore Reef		
Landing Craft	45386.5	59418.5
Landing Craft	45386.9	59417.4

Navy Tower R7	45388.0	61069.1
Navy Tower R8	45220.4	60955.5
Paradise Reef		
Landing Craft	45464.1	59763.2
Barge	45463.7	59761.1
Barge	45463.0	59763.0
Barge	45464.8	59762.1
Pawley's Island Reef		
Landing Craft	45456.9	59814.7
Landing Craft	45457.0	59814.0
Savannah Light Tower	45562.5	61240.0
Ten Mile Reef		
200' Ship	45427.1	59741.3
Landing Craft	45426.4	59742.3
Rubble Material	45426.8	59741.3
Vermilion Reef		
460' Ship	45266.2	59834.8
White Water Reef	45613.8	61241.0
Y-73 Reef		
160' Ship	45317.4	60316.1
Tug Wreck	45319.1	60317.3

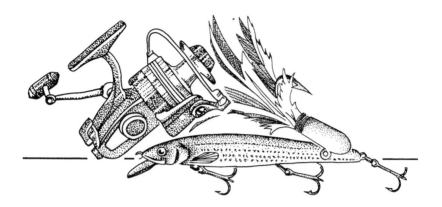

Appendix

PREDICTING THE WEATHER

When it came to predicting the weather for fishing, my grandfather relied on an old rhyme that relied on wind direction, "Wind from the east, fishing the least. Wind from the west, fishing's the best." He was basically right but there are many weather conditions that affect fishing.

West winds usually bring stable weather, sunny skies and a pleasant day for fishing, but west winds don't always mean that catching will be good. East winds generally indicate stormy weather with rough waters that may make fishing very unpleasant, yet a mild northeast wind can trigger a blitz of fish activity that makes catching fish easy.

Most people think of weather in the sense of sunny skies, hot and humid days, rain, a windy day, a chilly day or a cloudy day. They focus on how weather affects them personally, not how weather affects fish. Fishing in weather that is right for fish but not "right" for fishermen can sometimes be vital to making a good catch of fish. Fishermen need to focus on how weather brings changing light conditions to the day's environment and that's what is really important about weather - how it changes the light.

Unlike higher forms of animals, most fish have no pupils to alter the amount of light entering their eyes. On a bright sunny day they can't squint like humans do, or wear sunglasses like the fish on the Blues Brothers T-shirts, so they head for deeper water where the light is less intense. On a cloudy day the light levels are less bright so the fish may tend to feed more aggresively all through the day in shallow water.

Fish migrate on a daily basis from the deeper waters offshore to the shallow waters inshore as the sun sets at dusk, then reverse the direction, heading back to deeper waters offshore as the sun rises. Weather, and the changing light levels it brings, also affects the daily migration of bait and game fish.

Depending on the species, the daily migration may be only a hundred yards as in the case of summer flounder, or it could be several miles in the case of bluefish as they move from the surf at dawn to a ridge several miles offshore by high noon. Cloudy days mean fish don't have to move so far to get away from excessive light.

HOW TO TELL THE WEATHER

Wind Direction	Barometer Reading	Weather
S to SW	30.00 or below & rising slowly	Clearing & fair for several days
S to E	29.80 or below & falling rapidly	Severe storm - clear & colder in 24 hours
E to N	29.80 or below & falling rapidly	Severe NE gale & rain. Winter - snow & cold wave
Going to W	29.80 or below & rising rapidly	Clearing & colder
SW to NW	30.10 to 30.20 & steady	Fair, little change for 1-2 days
SW to NW	30.10 to 30.20 & rising rapidly	Fair, warmer - rain in 2 days
SW to NW	30.20 & above & stationary	Continued fair, little temperature change
SW to NW	30.20 & above & falling slowly	Fair with rising temperatures for 2 days
S to SE	30.10 to 30.20 & falling slowly	Rain within 24 hours
S to SE	30.10 to 3.20 & falling rapidly	Increased wind, rain within 12-24 hours
SE to NE	30.10 to 30.20 & falling slowly	Rain in 12-18 hours
SE to NE	30.10 to 30.20 & falling rapidly	Increased wind, rain within 12 hours
SE to NE	30.00 or below & falling slowly	Summer - no rain. Winter - rain in 24 hours
SE to NE	30.00 or below & falling rapidly	Summer - rain in 24 hours. Winter - rain or snow
E to NE	30.10 & above & falling slowly	Rain will continue for 1-2 days
E to NE	30.10 & above & falling rapidly	Rain, wind - clear & colder within 36 hours

Fishermen who keep accurate log books know that most of the best fishing days occur at dawn, dusk or on cloudy days. Whenever the fishing is good on a sunny day, the best spot is usually in deeper water. This is true for inshore striped bass and offshore tuna, flounder and seatrout in the bays, and bluefish along the surf. Weather, and the changing brightness of the light, influences surfcasters and small boat boat fishermen alike. The theory works whether you fish the canyons for tuna and billfish or work channel edges in a sound or bay for blues, sea trout or fluke.

One day while fluke fishing in a New York bay, I was dissappointed with the lack of fish. My partner, however, noted the approaching clouds and in another hour the sky clouded up and the fluke began to hit aggressively. We caught five fish up to 4 pounds before the rain hit us. Weather has helped me at the offshore canyons and I can recall one particular trip to the Baltimore Canyon where we found a good temperature edge but no fish on that bright clear dawn. A mild cool front approached by mid morning, bringing clouds, drizzling rain and fabulous tuna fishing. Seven bigeye felt the sting of the lures and we had our hands full.

My old beach buggy is history now, but my log is filled with examples of good fishing at dawn that evaporated as the sun rose in the sky moving the fish several hundred yards off the beach. At Nags Head one fall the bluefish blitz hit fast and furious at first light, then quit with the bright sun. The only day that week the blitz lasted through the day was the cloudy morning on a Wednesday when the fish stayed right in the wash.

It's worthwhile for fishermen to be aware of the weather and especially the changing winds which can help us predict the next weather pattern as it approaches. The best fishing occurs at the approach of a weather front, usually as a cold front bumps into a warm front which causes increased cloudiness. The accompanying chart will help predict the weather so the best fishing days can be planned around the changing weather.

ABOUT THE AUTHOR

Pete Barrett has been writing about his fishing experiences along the East Coast for the past 30 years. A licensed charter captain, his "Linda B" is frequently found fishing from North Carolina to New Jersey for offshore billfish, tuna and mako sharks, and inshore for summer flounder, bluefish, striped bass, blackfish, seatrout and school tuna.

Since 1973 he has worked for *The Fisherman*, a weekly magazine with editions in New England, Long Island, New Jersey, Mid Atlantic region and Florida. He is currently associate publisher of the magazine and of The Fisherman Library books.

An advocate of tagging and releasing game fish, he has received several awards, including the AFTCO 1990 Angler of the Year, and awards in 1989 and 1990 for tagging Yellowfin Tuna and in 1992 for tagging Longfin Albacore.

His wife, Linda, is a full-time partner in their writing and publishing activities. His son, Rich, is also a licensed charter captain and full-time member of *The Fisherman* publishing team.